The United States History Abstract

Major Crises in American History

The United States History Abstract

Major Crises in American History

Second Edition

Joseph A. Bagnall

Kendall Hunt
publishing company

Kendall Hunt
p u b l i s h i n g   c o m p a n y

Contents

Acknowledgments ix
Prologue xi

SECTION ONE—An Abstract of the History of the United States to 1875

Chapter One: Exploration and Settlement 3
    Questions for Research and Discussion 6
    Suggested Reading...6

Chapter Two: Pathway to a New Nation...9
    Questions for Research and Discussion 16
    Suggested Reading...16

Chapter Three: Trouble with France and War with England 17
    Questions for Research and Discussion 22
    Suggested Reading...22

Chapter Four: The Age of Jackson...23
    Questions for Research and Discussion 26
    Suggested Reading...26

Chapter Five: Polk and Manifest Destiny 27
    Questions for Research and Discussion 29
    Suggested Reading...29

Chapter Six: The Coming of the Civil War..31
    Questions for Research and Discussion 34
    Suggested Reading...34

Chapter Seven: The Civil War and Reconstruction................................35
    Questions for Research and Discussion 42
    Suggested Reading...42

SECTION TWO—An Abstract of the History of the United States Since 1875

Chapter Eight: Protest, Imperialism, and Progressivism 45
    Questions for Research and Discussion 55
    Suggested Reading...55

Chapter Nine: Normalcy, Depression, and the Age of Roosevelt 57
  Questions for Research and Discussion 67
  Suggested Reading...68

Chapter Ten: The Second World War and Postwar United States 69
  Questions for Research and Discussion 77
  Suggested Reading...77

Chapter Eleven: The Reagan Revolution and Beyond...79
  Questions for Research and Discussion 84
  Suggested Reading...85

**SECTION THREE—Crisis Dialogues: Four Historical Debates with Lessons
                 for Today**

Debate One. The Nullification Crisis: Two Views of the Federal Union............89
  Excerpts from **Daniel Webster:** The Union Is "One and Inseparable" 90
  Questions for Research and Discussion 92
  Excerpts from **Robert Hayne:** The Union Is a Compact Made
  by Sovereign States 93
  Questions for Research and Discussion 94

**Debate Two. The Crisis of Economic Collapse: Advocates of a New Deal
                 vs. The Defenders of the Status Quo** 95
  Franklin D. Roosevelt: American Business Is Moving Ahead 96
  Questions for Research and Discussion 101
  Marriner S. Eccles: Government Spending Is Sound: Balancing
  the Budget Is Not Essential..102
  Questions for Research and Discussion 107
  Herbert Hoover: A Holy Crusade for Liberty...108
  Questions for Research and Discussion 112
  Robert A. Taft: A Declaration of Republican Principles 113
  Questions for Research and Discussion...119

**Debate Three. The Crisis of McCarthyism: Three Views on Defeating
                 Communism.** 121
  Joseph R. McCarthy: Communists in the State Department Must
  Be Rooted Out..122
  Questions for Research and Discussion 125
  Franklin D. Roosevelt: Facing Communism: The True Conservative
  Is Liberal 126
  Questions for Research and Discussion 130
  Margaret Chase Smith: A Declaration of Conscience..131
  Questions for Research and Discussion 134

Debate Four. The Crisis of Thermonuclear and Environmental Threats:
    Five Survival Perspectives 135
The Democratic Platform of 1960...136
John F. Kennedy: One World, One Human Race, with One Common Destiny.....137
Questions for Research and Discussion..................................143
Barry M. Goldwater: The National Interest Must Be Our First Priority..........144
Questions for Research and Discussion..................................147
George H.W. Bush: Excerpt from "The Possibility of a New World Order:
Unlocking the Possibility of Freedom."......................................148
Questions for Research and Discussion..................................151
George W. Bush: Remarks on the War on Terror 152
Questions for Research and Discussion..................................157

SECTION FOUR—The Significance of United States History: An Abstract
The Significance of United States History: An Abstract...............................161
    Questions for Research and Discussion..................................166
    Suggested Reading 167
APPENDICES
    Part One: The Freedom Documents....................................173
    The American Bill of Rights 173
    The Universal Declaration of Human Rights............................175
    The American Declaration of Independence............................181
    Part Two:
    The Constitution of the United States of America.......................185
    Charter of the United Nations and Statute of the International
    Court of Justice..202

About the Author..271
Index 273

Acknowledgments

I am deeply grateful to Naomi Bagnall, Ashley Davis, and Julie Knowles for assistance in preparing the manuscript.

Prologue

The United States History Abstract: Major Crises in American History is a useful *summary* of United States history with emphasis on the major crises in the American experience–The Civil War, The Great Depression, and World War II.

This brief text should help the reader to understand and appreciate how the structure of American federalism has helped promote the American creed, as it is expressed in our Declaration of Independence.

In our struggle to realize our ideals of freedom, equality, and government based on the consent of the governed, we have amended and improved the American Constitution and enforced our Bill of Rights. We have even propelled the sacred contents of the first ten Amendments outward, where they reside in the *Universal Declaration of Human Rights*, for the benefit of the world.

Section Three of this book is titled Crisis Dialogues: Four Historical Debates with Lessons for Today. This section contains vital student readings featuring the words of Presidents, Senators, and government officials during the Major Crises in American History. Section Four features an interpretive essay titled "The Significance of United States History: An Abstract." The author maintains that American federalism is a model for a world security system. The case for American federalism is examined in the context of our major international crises. Questions are directly or indirectly posed about the efficacy of the American system. Has the American system performed well? Is American federalism the model for an ultimate social contract? Or is this idea naïve and impractical? Would the creation of an American-inspired world security system render hope against enormous thermonuclear and environmental threats? Are our present thermonuclear strategies and environmental programs adequate? Realistic? Practical? Hopeful? But more importantly, what are our options on this dangerously conflicted and environmentally battered planet?

Advocates of a world security system, capable of enforcing world law, are cited in Section Four Among them are Dwight D. Eisenhower, John F. Kennedy, Chief Justice Earl Warren, Arnold J. Toynbee, Albert Einstein, Edward Teller, Walter Cronkite, and others. But the proposal to develop world federalism patterned after the American federal system is the author's own.

Part One of the Appendices is titled "The Freedom Documents." It contains the Declaration of Independence, the American Bill of Rights, and the Universal Declaration of Human Rights. *Part Two* features a copy of the United States Constitution and the United Nations Charter and the Statute of the International Court of Justice. The last two documents are seldom consulted and rarely understood. They are offered as vital points of reference in a serious work for serious times.

There is much at stake in the new century. As we commit to our national goals, it seems imperative that we develop a survival perspective. Survival lies within the realm of human possibilities, but it is by no means certain.

Joseph A. Bagnall
Oceanside, California
October, 2010

To

THE FEDERAL UNION

Past, Present, and Future

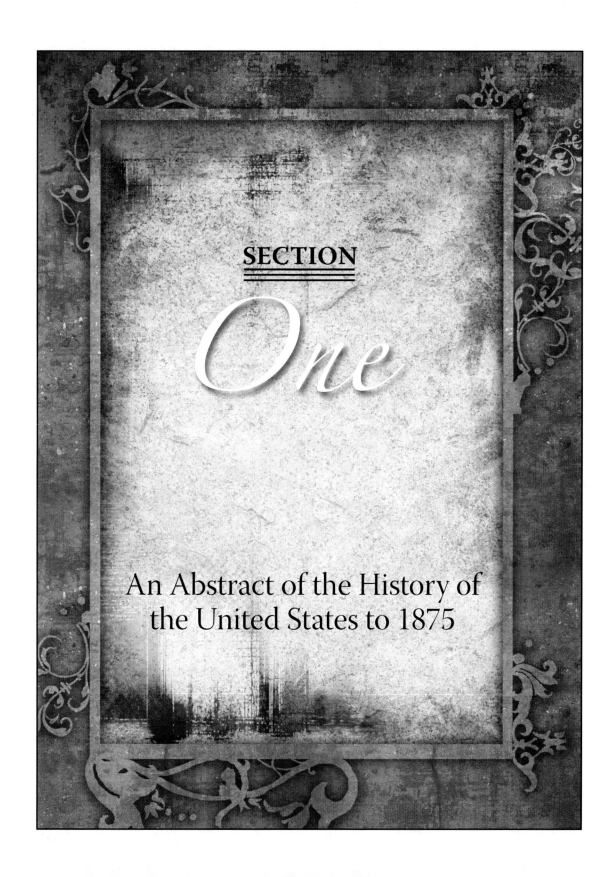

SECTION

One

An Abstract of the History of
the United States to 1875

Chapter 1

Exploration and Settlement

Spain in the New World

In 1492 Christopher Columbus, a Spanish explorer, landed on an island in the Bahamas, which he named San Salvador. Believing he had arrived near the Asian subcontinent of India, he dubbed the inhabitants Indians. In his next three voyages to the New World, Columbus never set foot on the North American continent, but he landed in South America once and claimed vast areas for the Spanish Crown.

As a follow-up to the voyages of Columbus, Imperial Spain arrived in the New World first. The Spanish colonized Florida, the present southwest United States, Central America, and most of South America.

Parts of the Spanish empire eventually become an integral part of the United States. Florida was acquired in the Adams-Onis treaty of 1819, and the acquisition of the portion of New Spain in the American Southwest was by military conquest, after Spanish subjects had established a Mexican nation.

Acquiring the American Southwest

In the period 1811–1821 Spanish revolutionaries struggled against the Crown, eventually wresting a vast area known as Mexico from Spanish rule. Northern Mexico included what is now known as California, Nevada, Utah, Arizona, New Mexico, Texas, and small portions of Wyoming and Colorado.

In the first quarter of the 19th Century, the Mexican government allowed United States citizens to settle in present day Texas. By 1836 Americans had ripped this part of the Mexican anatomy away and established an independent Texas Republic. This new nation lasted from 1836 to 1845, when it was annexed as a state in the American federal union.

Near mid 19th Century, President James K. Polk sent John Slidell to Mexico to purchase California and the New Mexico territory, which included present day Nevada, Utah, Arizona, and New Mexico. When the Mexican government refused to sell, President Polk engaged with Mexico in a border dispute, claiming that the southwest boundary of the new state of Texas was the Rio Grande River. Mexico held that the border was the Nueces River. This dispute led to the Mexican War, a quick American victory, the Treaty of Guadalupe-Hidalgo, and the Mexican cession granting the United States its present southwest region.

The Spanish legacy in the modern American Southwest includes Spanish place names and a rich architectural style, but the Native American Pueblo tradition is pervasive as well. The racial mixture of Spanish and native peoples has furnished an important Mexican element to the American tradition.

The French Arrive

Imperial France established Quebec as a commercial base for fur trade in 1608. Frenchmen settled along the waterways to facilitate their trading ventures. They built fur trading posts and forts along the St Lawrence River, the Hudson Bay in Canada, the Great Lakes region, the Ohio Valley, and down the Mississippi River. This chain of posts and forts served not only the fur traders, but also Jesuit missionaries and the military.

In 1682 Robert Cavelier de La Salle descended the Mississippi River to its mouth and claimed the interior of the continent for France. In addition the Indian nations east of the Mississippi were drawn into a commercial and military alliance.

The French legacy in America includes some colonial architecture in New Orleans and Creole cuisine, which is a rich blend of French and African culinary traditions.

England and the Great War for Empire

The French claim to the American continent in 1628 was trumped by John Cabot, the English explorer, who in 1497 claimed title to all the land in North America. This gave rise to English colonization of the Atlantic seaboard with 13 vibrant colonies. But the French pattern of settlement in the Ohio Valley and down the Mississippi River curbed and contained British designs on the interior. If the British intended to expand westward and claim the continent, they had to remove not only the French, but also their Indian allies.

In three worldwide wars between the French and the British, there were American phases; but the English–French conflict in the New World was not resolved conclusively until the fourth worldwide war. In Europe this war was referred to as the Seven Years War and later aptly renamed, by the British historian Lawrence Henry Gipson, *The Great War for Empire.* In America the war lasted longer than seven years (1754–63) and it was called by British colonists, The French and Indian War. It was in this war that the British conquered the French and the Indians and planted the Union Jack all the way to the Mississippi. This epic war established English as the basic language for North America and gave United States history a British foundation.

It is ironic that George Washington, Benjamin Franklin, and others were loyal British subjects in 1763. They had been proud contributors to British domination of the interior. In slightly more than a decade, however, these men and other American patriots had begun a revolution which would culminate in the founding of a new American nation.

The British Foundation for an American Nation

An assessment of the thirteen original British colonies can provide insights for understanding early American history. It is appropriate, therefore, to provide, at the very least, a colonial snapshot in time.

The first permanent English settlement in the New World was Jamestown, Virginia, established in 1607. This was a company colony, organized in England for profit. The second was Plymouth, settled by religious radicals who sought a complete break with the state sponsored Anglican Church. They were the Pilgrims who sailed on the *Mayflower* in 1620. Their colony was absorbed into Massachusetts Bay. The third was Massachusetts Bay, founded in 1630. This was a company colony that accommodated religious dissenters called Puritans. Puritans were religious reformers; that is, they sought to "purify" the Anglican Church and remain within it.

The New England Colonies were New Hampshire, Rhode Island, Connecticut, and Massachusetts Bay. In New England the economy was based on fishing, manufacturing and ship building. Manufacturing and ship building were financial ventures that were controlled by British companies.

Given the fact that New England soil was unsuitable for agricultural purposes, land development in this region contrasted sharply with the large manors of the middle colonies or the plantations of the South. In New England there were small freeholds organized into townships. The citizenry lived in tight knit villages where an institution known as the town meeting evolved. This region became a hotbed of protest and direct action in the period that led to the American Revolution.

The Middle Colonies were New York, Pennsylvania, Maryland, New Jersey, and Delaware. The economy of the middle colonies was primarily farming, fur trading, and manufacturing. In earliest times New York developed large manors with a labor system fueled by indentured servants. This semi-feudal scene seemed, in some measure, akin to the land development and labor system of the South, but the middle colonies soon became more diversified economically and more urban in style.

The Southern Colonies were Virginia, North Carolina, South Carolina, and Georgia. In the early South, agriculture drove the economy, which was based on production of tobacco, rice, indigo and naval stores. Cotton was not yet a significant product, and slavery was in its initial developmental phase. Much later, particularly after the invention of the cotton gin, the South became primarily a producer of cotton with a firm reliance on plantation agriculture and a slave labor system.

Most of the original thirteen English colonies fell into three basic types. First was the **company colony** that was organized for profit. Examples of company colonies were Virginia and Massachusetts Bay. Second was the **proprietary colony.** These began as land grants by the crown to "royal favorites" or men to whom the king was indebted. Examples of proprietary colonies were Maryland, a haven for Roman Catholics, with Lord Baltimore as the proprietor. Pennsylvania, a haven for Quakers, with William Penn as the proprietor, Georgia, a haven for incarcerated debtors, with James Oglethorpe as the proprietor, and New Hampshire, with Captain John Mason as the proprietor. The colony of Carolina was established when a group of distinguished men became proprietors at the behest of Charles II. This same monarch awarded his brother territory previously ruled by the Dutch when it became a part of New York. The Third type of colony was a **corporate or charter colony.** Examples of these were Rhode Island and Connecticut. Each was founded by religious dissenters who were banished by the Puritans of Massachusetts Bay.

Questions for Research and Discussion

1. Why are the English colonies important in the study of United States history?

2. What was the significance of The Great War for Empire?

3. Describe the differences in the economies of the New England, middle and southern colonies.

4. What were the three basic types of English colonies?

5. What portion of New Spain did the United States eventually acquire? How was it done?

Suggested Reading

Fredi Chiapeli, ed. *First Images of America: The Impact of the New World on the Old* (2 vols. 1976); Richard and Mary Dunn, (eds.) *The World of William Penn* (1986); J. H. Eliott, *Imperial Spain, 1479–1716* (1963); *The Old World and the New: 1492–1650* (1970); Gary Nash, *Red, White and Black: The Peoples of Early America* (1974); Karen Ordahl Kupperman, *Roanoke: The Abandoned Colony* (1984); Edmund S. Morgan,

American Freedom, American Slavery: The Ordeal of Colonial Virginia (1975); David Price, *Love and Hate in Jamestown* (2005); Marcel Trudel, *The Beginnings of New France* (1973); Peter Wood, *Black Majority* (1974); J. Leitch Wright, Jr., *The Only Land They Knew: The Tragic Story of the American Indians in the Old South* (1981).

Chapter 2

Pathway to a New Nation

British Mercantilism Before 1763

In the British imperial-colonial framework, colonies were sought after as sources of raw products, cheap labor, and markets for finished manufactured goods. Under this mercantilist system, the British sought a favorable balance of trade, an abundance of gold and silver, a large merchant fleet, and a powerful army and navy. As an integral part of the British system, American colonies were exploited for the benefit of the mother country.

To implement strict economic control over the colonies, Parliament passed the Navigation Acts. The Navigation Act of 1651 set the regulation that goods coming from the colonies would be transported on British ships manned by British crews. The Navigation Act of 1660 specified that a long list of "enumerated goods" could be shipped to England only. The Navigation Act of 1663 required that ships of other countries that wished to trade in the colonies had to pass through an English port first.

This is the essence of a protected system that guaranteed English prosperity at the expense of colonial subjects. Any thorough analysis of the causes of the American Revolution would necessarily include close scrutiny of economic grievances.

Events that Led to the American Revolution, 1763–1775

The Great War for Empire ended in 1763. The British now controlled the vast area from the Atlantic seaboard to the Mississippi (with the exception of Spanish Florida), but the British were simultaneously experiencing a financial crisis. It became necessary, therefore, to ask American colonists to share the burden of financing the administration of the newly conquered territory. The resultant programs of the Grenville and Townshend governments alienated the colonists and paved the way to the American Revolution.

The following were the divisive and inflammatory measures of the Grenville government:

The Royal Proclamation of 1763 was issued by George III. It was conceived to avoid costly skirmishes with the Indians in the interior. It forbade the colonists to move beyond the boundary of the Appalachian Mountains even though the British flag flew all the way to the Mississippi. This Proclamation displeased colonial agriculturists, speculators, and others who were interested in western land.

The Sugar Act of 1764 replaced the Molasses Act of 1733. The act lowered import duties, but their collection was more strictly enforced. This provided more revenue for the British treasury, but it hampered colonial trade with the West Indies. The colonists dispatched memorials of protest.

The Currency Act of 1764 forbade the colonists to issue paper money as legal tender. Imperial England was interested in acquiring hard specie.

The Quartering Act of 1765 required the citizenry in some colonies to provide barracks and supplies for His Majesty's troops. In practical terms this translated to the practice of housing troops in private homes. Strong colonial reaction to this grievance persisted. In the 1790s, our Founding Fathers created the Third Amendment to the United States Constitution prohibiting the housing of troops in private residences.

The Stamp Act of 1765 placed revenue stamps on about forty commercial items, including newspapers, legal documents, marriage licenses, and playing cards. This highly visible method of taxation alienated the colonists. Patrick Henry of Virginia and other colonial agitators made strong public protests. Sam Adams organized the Sons of Liberty, a mob that engaged in violence against the hated stamp officials. The Stamp Act Congress was called in defiance of Parliament. Twenty-seven delegates were sent from nine colonies, and this illegal legislature passed non-importation agreements against British companies.

The chaos in America brought British merchants to their knees. The merchants quickly pressured the Parliament to repeal the Stamp Act. At this juncture the Grenville administration collapsed.

As the new Townshend government formed up, the colonists challenged the authority of Parliament with the battle cry of "no taxation without representation." The British replied that colonists were "virtually" represented.

The Townshend Duties of 1767 were less visible and seemingly less vexing. Duties were assessed on British imports such as lead, painter's colors, paper and tea, but it was the colonial consumers who paid the duty and ultimately furnished the revenue for the treasury. A dramatic confrontation over the Townshend Duties was about to take place near the Customs House in Boston.

The Boston Massacre resulted when a crowd of about 60 colonists taunted British soldiers at the Customs House in Boston on March 15, 1770. British soldiers fired into the crowd, killing or wounding eleven people. Colonial resistance to the Townshend duties now rose to a crescendo. Parliament repealed virtually all of the hated Townshend Duties, in April of 1770, except for a tax on tea.

A period of quiet resulted from 1770–1773, but radical agitators kept the idea of protest and revolution alive by organizing **Committees of Correspondence.** These "revolutionary cells" were an underground network operated by Sam Adams of Massachusetts, Patrick Henry and Thomas Jefferson of Virginia, and others. The moment for these radicals would soon arrive. The British East India Company was practically bankrupt. It had 17,000,000 pounds of tea to sell, so the British gave the company a monopoly on the sale of tea in America and taxed the tea at a nominal rate.

The Boston Tea Party of 1773 occurred when British East India ships docked in the Boston Harbor. Sam Adams' rowdy mob dressed like Indians; went to Boston Harbor, boarded the tea ship *Dartmouth,* and tossed 342 chests of tea overboard.

The British Parliament responded to the tea party with the **Coercive Acts of 1774,** which included 1) the closing of the Port of Boston, 2) the cancellation of town meetings, and 3) a new requirement that royal officials be tried in England only. **The Quebec Act of 1774** was passed simultaneously. It was a punitive attempt by the British government to give the Ohio Valley back to the French. These desperation measures were symptomatic of a complete breakdown in the imperial-colonial system. The colonists labeled the Coercive and Quebec Acts together as the **Intolerable Acts.**

All of the foregoing events combined to lead to the opening shots of the American Revolution at Lexington and Concord, Massachusetts in the spring of 1775.

The Movement for Independence

On September 5, 1774, the First Continental Congress was convened. This revolutionary act was a denial of the authority of the British Parliament, and this illegal body quickly created the Associations to boycott British trade. And yet, at this same time, George Washington asserted that independence was not desired by any thinking man in North America.

The Second Continental Congress met in the spring of 1775. It was called one month after the hostilities at Lexington and Concord. Delegates emphasized that colonial resistance should not be characterized as a war for independence. The goal, at that time, was to secure the rights of British subjects. In spite of this limited objective, the Second Congress would soon choose General Washington as the Commander of the Continental Army, pass a Resolution of Independence, appoint a committee to draft a Declaration of Independence, issue the Declaration, conduct diplomacy, obtain a treaty with France, and manage a War for Independence. Without executive or judicial help, the Second Continental Congress was the solitary source of American governmental structure until the adoption of the Articles of Confederation in 1781.

It was Thomas Paine who inspired American patriots in their movement toward independence. In January of 1776, he published **Common Sense,** a pamphlet that ridiculed the absurdity of a continent being governed by an island, and he described King George as a "Royal Brute."

Thomas Jefferson followed Paine's lead. In the **Declaration of Independence,** he also indicted the King and Parliament, but the Declaration contained much more. Employing the social contract theory of John Locke and others, Jefferson, in essence, penned America's creed. His opening assumption was that all men are created equal, and that they have God-given natural rights. He then asserted that governments are established to protect fundamental rights, including life, liberty, and an environment conducive to the pursuit of happiness. His next point was that legitimate government is based on the consent of the governed and that when "government becomes destructive of these ends, it is the right of the people to alter or abolish it." This was a powerful rationale for revolution and independence, and a historic proclamation of human rights.

It would be difficult if not impossible to find courage to match the signers of the Declaration of Independence. *In the midst of a war* against one of the great imperial powers of the world, the signers affixed their names to a historic document that ended with this pledge: "And for the support of this Declaration, with a firm reliance on the protection of Divine Providence, we mutually pledge to each other our Lives, our Fortunes, and our sacred Honor." After the signing, Benjamin Franklin is said to have exhorted his fellow patriots to hang together or they would certainly hang separately.

The Winning of Independence

As of July 4, 1776, brave patriots had declared independence from Great Britain, but they would not actually win independence until 1781. In the interim General Washington faced daunting odds. At the height of the military struggle against the Crown, John Adams estimated that only one third of the colonists were committed to the revolutionary cause. One third were Loyalists, committed to British rule, and one third didn't identify with either side. Many Loyalists took up arms with His Majesty's troops, and to make matters worse, the Indians generally lined up with the British against the Americans.

Washington won few battles and suffered grave hardships, but he displayed enormous courage and would never consider surrender as an option. His eventual triumph was achieved, not only because of his own sterling character, but also as a result of aid from overseas.

In the Great War for Empire, the English had eliminated the French in North America. Anxious for revenge, Imperial France decided to assist the American Revolution. Aid at first was secret. Gun powder and artillery were sent through the agency of Pierre de Beaumarchais, a French playwright. When the colonists were successful in the Battle of Saratoga, the French recognized American independence, made a treaty of alliance (1778), and entered the war.

When Lord Charles Cornwallis moved British troops to Yorktown, Virginia in August of 1781, he was caught between a French fleet commanded by Admiral de Grasse, and Washington's land forces, which were strengthened by a French army commanded by Count de Rochambeau. Cornwallis surrendered at Yorktown, Virginia on October 19, 1781.

The New Nation

In 1777, during the throes of the American Revolution, the Second Continental Congress created the semblance of a national government called the **Articles of Confederation**. In the same year that Cornwallis surrendered at Yorktown, the Articles were adopted.

This so-called first American Constitution reflected the spirit of The Declaration of Independence and embodied the freedom that the most dedicated revolutionaries, men like Sam Adams, Patrick Henry, and Thomas Jefferson, had insisted upon. But grave deficiencies in the Articles soon surfaced.

In making their first constitution, Americans had overreacted to the tyranny of George III and the British parliament. They failed to create an appropriate amount of authority in a national capstone over the states. As a result we had no president; a committee of Congress served as the executive. We had no Supreme Court, so when serious disputes between states could not be adjudicated, armed clashes occurred. In addition, Congress could not levy and collect taxes, making it virtually impossible to provide for national defense.

Foreign nations cast a suspicious eye on our failure to create an effective national executive. When a committee of Congress attempted to conduct diplomacy, British diplomats asked if we were seeking one treaty or thirteen. They were also concerned about our lack of a uniform currency and our inability to conduct foreign trade. It was impossible to convince foreign governments that we could make treaties or pay foreign debts, because in reality we had no national government and no discernible national purpose. Congressmen thought in terms of the interests of their states, and rarely considered collective responsibilities and needs.

Under the Articles of Confederation, large states, small states, free states and slave states were loosely combined. They were thirteen in number, economically, politically, and culturally diverse, and fragmented to the point that the prospect of an enduring United States seemed dim.

In this crisis, 55 American patriots sought commonality in "a more perfect union." They met from May through September of 1787, in Philadelphia, where they fashioned a new federal union, created the world's first President, established a national judiciary, and designed an effective new Congress.

In future days, the new federal structure would check tyranny through a system of checks and balances, harbor ideological differences, pursue justice through enforceable federal law, provide for the common defense, promote the general welfare, and secure liberty for the founders and their posterity. The new American Republic would survive the transition from an agricultural to an industrial country, a bloody civil war, a great depression, and two world wars. After the Second World War the American Republic won the competition with international Communism and emerged as the superpower of the world.

Launching the Republic

The success of the American Revolution was attributable, in large measure, to the splendid leadership of General George Washington, and it seems plausible to contend that the success of the Constitutional Convention, in some measure, can be attributed to the fact that Washington presided. George Washington was also the obvious choice to become the first American President. His countrymen awarded him the post with the only unanimous Electoral College vote in history. They knew that the success of the new nation was dependent on choosing a tried and trusted leader.

The success of the new American Republic was immediate and dramatic. In the Washington administration, the country became politically viable and economically solvent. It gained rapid respect at home and abroad, negotiated treaties with England and Spain, and added a sacred Bill of Rights to the greatest political document ever struck by the hand of man.

Jefferson served adequately as Washington's Secretary of State, but it was Alexander

George Washington

Figure 2.1 *The success of the American Revolution, the Constitutional Convention, and the new American republic were in no small measure due to Washington's superb leadership.*

Portrait by Gilbert Stuart, engraved by H.S. Sadd, NY. Courtesy of the Library of Congress Prints & Photographs Division, LC-USZ62-7585.

Hamilton who became powerful and influential as his Secretary of the Treasury. **Hamilton's financial plan** brought economic solvency and political unity to a country that was desperately searching for a national identity. His Bank of the United States and his assumption program shifted economic power from sovereign states to the national government. From this point on it would be easier to finance roads and canals, a navy, and other national projects. Hamilton prophetically emphasized the need to build an industrial base, provide military security, and facilitate commerce.

Hamilton believed that a national debt was a national blessing, but a national debt required revenue commensurate with national spending. For revenue Hamilton secured a tariff on foreign imports, not only to build up the national treasury, but also to protect America's infant industries. He also obtained an excise tax on whiskey. While the latter provided additional revenue, it fell heavily upon the shoulders of subsistence farmers who were desperately trying to convert a portion of their crops to an unfettered, profitable venture.

A strong nationalist tradition emerged from the work of Alexander Hamilton. Hamiltonians were originally called **Federalists,** then **National Republicans,** soon thereafter, **Whigs,** and by 1854, **Republicans.** President John Adams, President John Quincy Adams, Supreme Court Justice John Marshall, Senators Daniel Webster and Henry Clay, and President Abraham Lincoln were advocates of Hamilton's financial program and keepers of the Hamiltonian flame.

A Jeffersonian political movement grew from opposition to Hamilton's call for a "government by the rich and well born," a Bank of the United States that was considered an institution of aristocratic privilege, and a strong central government that favored the industrial and manufacturing interests of the northeast over the agricultural interests of the South and West.

Actually the Jeffersonians first coalesced in an **Antifederalist** movement to oppose ratification of the Constitution of the

Alexander Hamilton

Figure 2.2 *Alexander Hamilton was the guiding spirit behind the calling of the Constitutional Convention. He also made enormous political and economic contributions to the building of the American nation.*

From mural by Constantino Brumidi, part of the Detroit Publishing Company Photograph Collection, Library of Congress Prints & Photographs Division, LC-D416-9860.

United States. They were afraid that the new Constitution would create new central authority, reminiscent of British rule. Later, in the successive presidencies of Jefferson, Madison, and Monroe, they were called **Democratic-Republicans;** but when Andrew Jackson became president, he referred to himself not only as a follower of Jefferson and a champion of the people, but also as a **Democrat.** He left no doubt on either claim when he vetoed the Charter of the Bank of the United States.

Prominent **states' rights Democrats** who could be called Jeffersonians were John Tyler, John C. Calhoun, Stephen A. Douglas, and others who focused their states' rights attacks on Hamiltonian nationalism throughout the first half of the 19th Century.

Questions for Research and Discussion

1. Explain the major facets of British mercantilism before 1763. How was mercantilism implemented?

2. What were the main events, from 1763 to 1765 that led to the American Revolution?

3. Who was the key player in the movement for independence? Explain fully.

4. The Declaration of Independence has been called America's creed. What are the key parts of the document?

5. What were the weaknesses of the Articles of Confederation?

6. What were some of the early achievements of Alexander Hamilton and Thomas Jefferson?

Suggested Reading

Bernard Bailyn, *Ideological Origins of the American Revolution* (1967); Carl Becker, *The Declaration of Independence* (1922); George A. Billius, ed. *George Washington's Opponents: British Generals and Admirals in the American Revolution* (1969); Daniel J. Boorstin, *A Sacred Union of Citizens . . .* (1996); Don Cook, *The Long Fuse: How England Lost the American Colonies* (1995); John Fiske, *The Critical Period of American History* (1888); James T. Flexner, George Washington and the New Nation, 1783–1793 (1969); Sylvia R. Frey, *Water from the Rock: Black Resistance in a Revolutionary Age* (1991); Richard Hofstadter, *The Idea of a Party System,* (1969); Merrill Jensen, *The New Nation* (1950); Linda K. Kerber, *Women of the Republic: Intellect and Ideology in Revolutionary America* (1980); Stephen G. Kurtz, *The Presidency of John Adams* (1957); Edmund S. Morgan, *The Birth of the Republic, 1763–1789* (1959); Richard B. Morris, *The Forging of the Union, 1781–1787* (1987); Arthur Schlesinger, Sr., *Prelude and Independence: The Newspaper War on Britain, 1764–1776* (1958); Gordon S. Wood, *The Radicalism of the American Revolution* (1991).

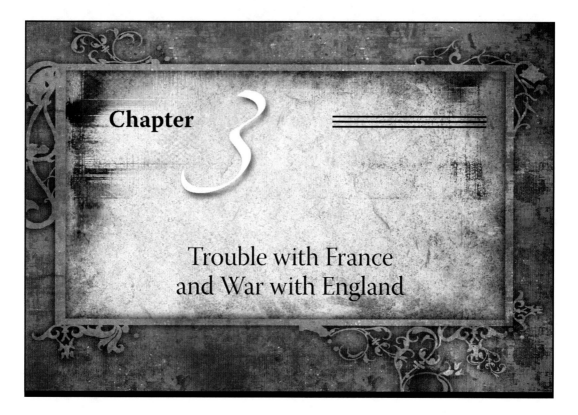

Chapter *3*

Trouble with France
and War with England

Federalist Rule

John Adams defeated Thomas Jefferson in 1796 and became the second President of the Republic. He favored monarchial England in foreign affairs and was constantly at odds with revolutionary France.

As American and French relationships deteriorated, President Adams sent three commissioners to Paris to avoid war. The Directory of France treated the three with contempt. Through three intermediaries, identified by Adams as X, Y, and Z, the French foreign minister demanded a large bribe to initiate talks and a loan of $12 million. This mammoth insult resulted in skirmishes with the French in the Caribbean. Adams wisely chose not to pursue a full scale declared war.

Hamiltonians vs. Jeffersonians

New immigrants of the day passed through the well established Atlantic seaboard to settle the American West. They cut trees, built cabins and barns, planted a few row crops, and raised a few animals. Many of them also converted part of their crops into whiskey. These subsistence farmers had rallied around Jefferson, especially after the so-called Whiskey Rebellion. When the farmers resisted Federalist attempts to place an excise tax on their whiskey, Alexander Hamilton took 13,000 federal troops into the hinterlands and forcefully collected the tax.

Adams and the Federalists brought more trouble for these new immigrants in the West. They passed a **Naturalization Act** increasing the wait period to become a U.S. citizen from four to fourteen years. But this was just a beginning. More important measures to suppress the Jeffersonians came in the form of four acts, known collectively as the **Alien and Sedition Acts.** One of these gave President Adams the power to deport dangerous aliens, but the most fearsome of the lot was the Sedition Act that made it a federal crime to print anything "false, scandalous, and malicious" against the government. Many thought that this act nullified the First Amendment. Nonetheless 25 people, mostly Jeffersonian editors, were indicted under the act. Ten were convicted.

At this juncture the Federalists controlled the Congress and the Supreme Court, so Jefferson and Madison turned to two state legislatures to produce the first significant articulation of the southern stand on states' rights. They fashioned the **Virginia and Kentucky Resolutions** of 1798, interposing the authority of two states against the hated Alien and Sedition Acts. Simultaneously they asserted that sovereign states had created the Union, and since the Union was a **compact** made by sovereign states, it followed logically that sovereign states could nullify tyrannical federal laws and, in extreme circumstances, secede from the Union. In future days this **compact theory of union** was used in numerous debates with Northerners, who countered with the argument that the Union was a union of people, and that it was legally impossible for any state to nullify federal laws or to secede.

The Election of 1800

In the election of 1800 Thomas Jefferson defeated John Adams in a contest that was decided in the House of Representatives. The matter was referred to the House when Thomas Jefferson and Aaron Burr each received 73 electoral votes. A Federalist dominated House gave Jefferson the Presidency. The Twelfth Amendment to the Constitution, ratified in 1804, prevented a future impasse of this kind by requiring electors to cast separate ballots for President and Vice President.

Avoiding pomp and pretense, a plainly dressed Thomas Jefferson walked from a boarding house to his inauguration. While the election had been characterized as "The Revolution of 1800," the President was conciliatory to the opposition in his address.

It was predictable that Jefferson would reduce the period for naturalization, repeal the whiskey tax, and otherwise do the bidding of the small farmers of the West. He also presided over the repeal of a judiciary act that created more judgeships for Federalist appointees and refused to deliver commissions to Adams' "Midnight Appointees."

The Jefferson administration economized in federal spending and reduced the national debt from $83 million in 1800 to $57 million by 1809. Federal revenue was reduced by the repeal of the Whiskey Tax, and funding for the army and navy was cut.

Thomas Jefferson

Figure 3.1 *Thomas Jefferson penned the American creed in the Declaration of Independence, served as Governor of Virginia, Secretary of State under President Washington, Vice President under President John Adams, and finally third President of the United States.*

Portrait by Gilbert Stuart, courtesy of the Library of Congress Prints & Photographs Division, LC-USZ62-117117.

With the purchase of Louisiana in 1803, President Jefferson betrayed his lifelong commitments to strict constructionism in the interpretation of the Constitution, weak central government, and economy in federal expenditures. And yet, the purchase of Louisiana was easily his best work.

Napoleon Bonaparte sold Louisiana to the United States for $15 million, or about 3½ cents an acre. Despite the lack of authorization in the Constitution, Jefferson was willing to take bold executive action and abandon almost every other principle that he had traditionally espoused in order to make the purchase. And so on April 30, 1803, with the stroke of a pen, he doubled the size of the United States.

On June 20, 1803, Meriwether Lewis and William Clark were given instructions by President Jefferson for an extensive exploration of the newly acquired territory. The Lewis and Clark expedition crossed unknown country from the head of the Missouri to the Columbia River. The journey lasted from 1803 to 1806. Much scientific data was obtained and the journey helped establish an American claim to the Oregon country.

War with England

On June 22, 1807, the *Leopard,* a British frigate, ordered an American man-of-war, the *Chesapeake,* to surrender four sailors who were supposed British deserters. The *Leopard's* subsequent attack on the *Chesapeake* inflamed American opinion and brought on talk of war. To avoid hostilities, Jefferson asked Congress to declare an embargo. Under the resulting Embargo Acts, which were passed from 1807 to 1809, ships were denied permission to leave American ports. This ill-conceived strategy was designed to avoid incidents that might lead to war. The Embargo Acts hurt the shipping interests, and they were bitterly denounced in New England.

Tensions mounted when the American 44-gun frigate named *President* crippled the British 20-gun corvette named the *Little Belt.* Things got worse when the British passed weapons to Tecumseh and the Indian confederacy, and those weapons were used against Americans in the West. But tensions peaked in 1810 with the election of the "War Hawks."

War Hawks were young Jeffersonians from the South and the West. John C. Calhoun, Henry Clay, and Felix Grundy were among them. War Hawks were motivated by the desire to strike at British Canada, the source of Indian weapons. They were convinced that the United States should not only annex Canada, but that they should also take Florida from Britain's ally, Spain. So when President Madison asked Congress to declare war against England on June 18, 1812, it was basically because War Hawks of the frontier demanded it. And it is accurate to say that the War of 1812 was fought basically for Southern and Western reasons.

The War of 1812 was ill-conceived. It is never wise to conduct war with a divided country. The vote for war was 79–49 in the House and 19–13 in the Senate. In the last phase of the conflict, the Hartford Convention was called and New Englanders passed resolutions against the war and even spoke of secession from the Union. They were critical of War Hawks who seemed to feel that the doubling of national territory with the Louisiana Purchase meant that we had doubled our national power. As a matter of fact, under President Jefferson, important revenue for the national treasury was eliminated with the repeal of the Whiskey Tax, and the army and navy were cut back as well. As a result we attacked British Canada with a small army and an inadequate navy. At this juncture America had about 20 ships compared to Britain's 600.

What began as an invasion of Canada turned into an invasion of the United States. The British captured Detroit and dominated the Great Lakes. Fortunately, William Henry Harrison led an assault that recaptured Detroit, and a timely victory by Oliver Hazard Perry brought the Great Lakes back under American control.

In 1814 the British invaded the United States at three points. In August British troops captured Washington, D.C., burning the White House and the Capitol. In the second invasion they began to push

James Madison

Figure 3.2 *President Madison served as our fourth president during the War of 1812. He had been the central figure in the Constitutional Convention and in the making of the Bill of Rights. He is often referred to as The Father of the Constitution and the Bill of Rights.*

Portrait by Gilbert Stuart, courtesy of the Library of Congress Prints & Photographs Division, LC-USZ62-13004.

toward the important city of Baltimore. The words of The Star Spangled Banner were written by Francis Scott Key during the bombardment of Fort McHenry. The third invasion landed in Louisiana in December of 1814. On January 8, 1815, General Andrew Jackson's rag-tag army met and defeated the British under General Edward Packenham. This so-called Battle of New Orleans was the most decisive American victory in the War of 1812. Casualties were reported as 8 killed and 13 wounded on the American side, while the British suffered with approximately 700 killed and 1,400 wounded. Neither side was aware that the Treaty of Ghent had been signed on Christmas Eve in 1814, and that this bloody affair was conducted two weeks after the War of 1812 had officially closed.

The Treaty of Ghent, in effect, gave no advantage to either side, but for the United States, there were some important results. Andrew Jackson, the hero of New Orleans became the seventh President of the United States. William Henry Harrison, the man who recaptured Detroit, became the ninth. Americans eliminated Creek Indian power in the South and destroyed Tecumseh's confederacy in the Northwest. These victories opened up portions of the West for settlement. The Rush–Bagot agreement of 1817 demilitarized the Great Lakes and pointed the way to permanent peace between Canada and the United States. The Hartford Convention, called by New Englanders to oppose the war, brought disdain upon a fading Federalist party and caused its demise.

With the demise of the Federalist party, the Democratic-Republicans wisely adopted Hamilton's financial plan. Perhaps the Jeffersonians received a colossal scare in the war. Perhaps they finally understood that a great military effort required sources of revenue and central economic planning. At any rate, in the last days of the Madison administration, a Second Bank of the United States was chartered. It was capitalized at twice the rate of the original, and for a source of revenue, the nation got its first protective tariff. This new wave of Hamiltonian nationalism, conducted by Jeffersonians, spawned a brief span without political conflict. It was known as The Era of Good Feelings. Under one party rule, when James Monroe stood for re-election, he obtained every electoral vote but one. The one elector explained that Washington alone deserved a unanimous election.

New Fragmentation

Post war nationalism soon played out. In the election of 1824, the discredited Federalists were rallying under the new banner of the National Republicans. The Jeffersonians were still called Democratic-Republicans, but often just Republicans, and soon thereafter, just plain Democrats.

Four prominent candidates vied for the Presidency in 1824. They were Andrew Jackson (D), John Quincy Adams (NR), Henry Clay (NR), and William Crawford (D). When the ballots were counted Jackson won 99 electoral votes, Adams 84, Crawford 41, and Clay 37.

Since Jackson won a plurality, and no candidate met the Constitutional requirement to secure a majority of electoral votes cast, the election had to be decided in the House of Representatives. Adams got a majority in the House, but only after Henry Clay gave him his support. When Adams reciprocated by making Clay Secretary of State, furious Jackson supporters cried "corrupt bargain." They kept this battle cry going through one stormy, largely uneventful term for John Quincy Adams.

John Quincy was the son of the second President of the United States, John Adams. Like his father, he was a Hamiltonian nationalist. He advocated federal aid for education, a national university, a program for a stronger navy and federally funded internal improvements. This was all stymied by the Jacksonians, and in the election of 1828, Jackson easily defeated Adams with an electoral count of 178 to 83.

Questions for Research and Discussion

1. How did Federalists in John Adams' administration attempt to thwart the Jeffersonian political movement?

2. How did Jefferson respond to the Federalists before he was President?

3. Was Jefferson an effective President? Why or why not?

4. Why did the country experience a wave of nationalism that culminated in an "Era of Good Feelings"?

5. Why did the election of 1824 have to be decided in the House of Representatives?

6. Was the Adams-Clay deal in 1824 a corrupt bargain?

Suggested Reading

Stephen E. Ambrose, *Undaunted Courage* (Meriwether Lewis) (1996); David Edmunds, *Tecumseh and the Quest for Indian Leadership* (1984); Donald R. Hickey, *The War of 1812: A Forgotten Conflict* (1989); John C. Miller, *The Wolf by the Ears: Thomas Jefferson and Slavery* (1977); Glover Moore, *The Missouri Controversy, 1819–1821* (1953); R Kent Newmyer, *The Supreme Court under Marshall and Taney* (1986); Merrill D. Peterson, *Thomas Jefferson and the New Nation* (1970); Dexter Perkins, *A History of the Monroe Doctrine* (1955); Jack N. Rakove, *James Madison and the Creation of the American Republic* (1990); J.C.A. Stagg, *Mr. Madison's War . . .* (1983); Charles S. Sydnor, *The Development of Southern Sectionalism, 1819–1848* (1953).

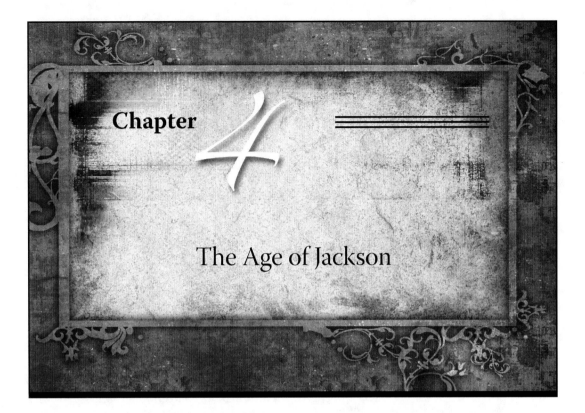

Chapter 4

The Age of Jackson

Andrew Jackson was a spokesman for Northern laborers, immigrants, and subsistence farmers of the South and West. This Democratic coalition stood in defiance of a Whig coalition of northeastern businessmen, Southern planters and merchants.

Who were these Whigs? They had descended from Hamiltonian Federalists and passed through a brief period where they were known as National Republicans. Whigs in England were an anti-king party, and American Whigs were "anti-King Andrew." They caricatured Jackson as a tyrannical figure, complete with royal robes, a scepter, and a crown.

Jackson was indeed a strong leader. He was a man of courage and conviction, but not all facets of Jacksonian Democracy were admirable, nor were they destined to endure. Andrew Jackson believed that loyal supporters and friends should be rewarded with civil service positions, because rotation in office was a democratic practice, and in the words of William L. Marcy, "to the victor belongs the spoils." Over time Jackson's spoils system evolved into corrupt machine politics, which democratic reformers would replace with a modern merit system. For the most part, objective testing now determines who will be granted civil service jobs.

Jacksonian Democracy has also been tainted by the President's actions in regard to Native Americans. When Chief Justice Marshall handed down a decision in *Worcester* v. *Georgia* (1832), that protected the Cherokees against encroachment by the State of Georgia, President Jackson refused to enforce it.

The failure to enforce a decision of the Supreme Court seems to be a violation of the Presidential oath, but this is not the only blight on the President's record. Jackson considered one of the most important measures of his first term to be the **Indian Removal Act of 1830.** Under this federal act he allowed state officials to override federal protection of Native Americans. Ultimately Jackson deployed the U.S. Army to assist in removal of three civilized Indian tribes to a desolate area now known as Oklahoma. Perhaps as many as one-fourth of them died on the 1200-mile trek, which stretched from their homeland in the East to the newly designated Indian territory. This tragic death march has been called the *Trail of Tears.*

Andrew Jackson

Figure 4.1 *Jackson's decisive victory in the Battle of New Orleans made him a national hero. He was elected the seventh President of the United States in 1828.*

Engraved by James Barton Longacre, courtesy of the Library of Congress Prints & Photographs Division, LC-USZ62-117120.

In the **Nullification Crisis of 1832,** Jackson quarreled with his Vice President, John C. Calhoun, over the tariff. In 1828 Calhoun had written *The South Carolina Exposition and Protest* arguing that sovereign states had the power to declare acts of the national government null and inoperative, and under certain conditions they could secede from the Union. Calhoun believed that tariffs should and could be nullified because they protected Northern manufacturing at the expense of the economy of the South.

When a South Carolina convention nullified the tariffs of 1828 and 1832, Andrew Jackson received Congressional authorization, in the **Force Act** of 1833, to stop nullification through military force. Fortunately, military force was unnecessary when Henry Clay and John C. Calhoun engineered the passage of the Compromise Tariff of 1833, which lowered duties each year up to 1842.

Vice President Calhoun and his wife caused many problems for President Jackson. While the vice President was creating a national crisis with his support for nullification of the federal tariff, Mrs. Calhoun was creating a crisis in Jackson's cabinet. Leading a movement to ostracize twice-married Peggy Eaton, wife of Secretary of War, John Eaton, she divided the cabinet into warring factions. Amidst the furor Vice President Calhoun resigned and returned to South Carolina to serve in the U.S. Senate, where he led the South to eventual withdrawal from the Union.

The Bank War

Andrew Jackson correctly identified the Bank of the United States as an institution of privilege—a haven for aristocrats who enriched themselves at the expense of the working class. But like Jefferson, he failed to recognize that the Bank was also a unifying and stabilizing factor in the growth of the nation, promoting the development of roads, canals, and national defense.

As President Jackson planned for re-election, Henry Clay and the National Republicans planned two traps. In 1832 they pushed through Congress a new tariff, designed to alienate the South, and a bill to re-charter the Bank of the United States, which they assumed Jackson would veto. Jackson defended the tariff, thereby creating the nullification crisis, and vetoed the re-charter of the Bank.

Assuming he had a perfect election issue, Clay ran against Jackson, emphasizing the foolish veto of the charter for the Bank. But Jackson was far more popular than the Bank, and he won handily over the hapless Clay.

The veto of the Bank brought new problems for the country. Since the Bank housed the national treasury, Jackson had to withdraw federal funds and deposit the money in what his enemies dubbed "Pet Banks." This economic fragmentation was compounded with the rise of wildcat banks, new paper currency, and chaotic economic practices. Jackson tried to allay some of the confusion with his issuance of the Specie Circular, making gold and silver the medium of exchange for the sale of land, but this stop gap measure had little effect on the developing economic crisis.

Fortunately Jackson was out of office when the Panic of 1837 hit. The ever popular President was in large measure responsible for it, but it was his successor, Martin Van Buren, who took the blame. Plagued by depression and harassed by the Whigs, Van Buren served one miserable term from 1837 to 1841. Perhaps his most notable achievement was the creation of an independent treasury system.

In the election of 1840, the Whigs staged a Jacksonian campaign. Touting General William Henry Harrison as the hero of the War of 1812, they fabricated a story that he was born in a log cabin and drank hard cider. In reality this "man of the people" was born and reared in plantation luxury. And at age 68, he was the oldest man to run for the Presidency up to that time.

On March 4, 1841, on a cold inauguration day, William Henry Harrison took the Presidential oath and delivered an address that lasted an hour and a half. This became his "Swan Song" as he contracted pneumonia and went home in a casket in one month.

As President, Harrison had chosen a powerful Whig cabinet, including Daniel Webster and Henry Clay, but his effort to reinstate Hamiltonian nationalism came to naught. John Tyler, a states' rights Democrat, was called a Whig and chosen as the Vice Presidential candidate, chiefly to attract Southern votes; so when Tyler was elevated to the Presidency, he exercised his states right prerogatives and vetoed a series of nationalistic Whig measures.

Tyler served one stormy term, in which the cabinet spoke seriously of impeachment. It is ironic that after serving as Vice President and President of the United States, Tyler opted to join the Confederacy in the twin crises of secession and Civil War.

Questions for Research and Discussion

1.   Who were the Whigs? Explain fully.

2.   What were the main facets of Jacksonian Democracy?

3.   What were the parts of Jacksonian Democracy that seem controversial today?

4.   Was John Tyler a good choice as a running mate for William Henry Harrison?

Suggested Reading

Thomas Brown, *Politics and Statesmanship: Essays on the American Whig Party* (1985); William H. Freehling, *Prelude to Civil War: The Nullification Controversy in South Carolina* (1966); Michael D. Green, *The Politics of Indian Removal* (1982); John Niven, *Martin Van Buren: The Romantic Age of American Politics* (1983); Merrill D. Petrerson, *The Great Triumvirate: Webster, Clay, and Calhoun* (1987); Robert V. Remini, *Andrew Jackson and the Course of American Freedom, 1822–1832* (1981); Arthur M. Schlesinger, Jr., *The Age of Jackson* (1945); Glyndon G. Van Deusen, *The Jacksonian Era* (1959); Anthony Wallace, *The Long Bitter Trail: Andrew Jackson and the Indians* (1993).

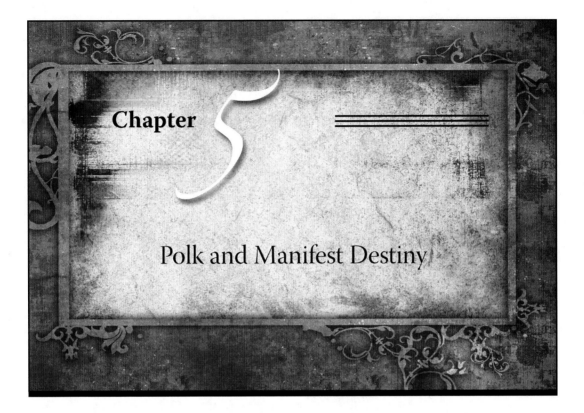

Chapter 5

Polk and Manifest Destiny

James K. Polk has been called our most successful President. In one term **he delivered** on his campaign promises to annex the Texas Republic, add California and the New Mexico Territory to the Union, achieve the exclusive occupation of the Oregon Territory, lower the tariff, and reinstate the independent treasury system. But most of these enormous achievements can be understood only in the context of **Manifest Destiny.**

In 1845 John L. O'Sullivan coined the phrase Manifest Destiny in an essay titled "Annexation" in the *Democratic Review*. Manifest Destiny became the belief that the United States was destined to expand from the Atlantic Seaboard to the Pacific Ocean, and Democratic advocates of Manifest Destiny believed that American expansion was good, obvious, and certain.

The Roots of American Expansion

When President Polk took office in 1845, present day California, Nevada, Utah, Arizona, New Mexico, and small parts of Wyoming and Colorado were the northern portion of the Mexican nation, and the Oregon Territory was jointly occupied by the United States and Great Britain. In the campaign of 1844, Polk had promised to acquire all of this vast territory, and he began by obtaining exclusive occupation of the Oregon Territory in a treaty with Great Britain in 1846.

James K. Polk

Figure 5.1 *In terms of campaign promises made and kept, President Polk is often regarded as our most successful president. He was a highly effective expansionist in the era of Manifest Destiny.*

Courtesy of the Library of Congress Prints & Photographs Division, LC-USZ62-13011.

Texas had already been ripped away from Mexico when American settlers declared an independent Texas Republic in 1836. In the campaign of 1844 Polk had promised to annex the Republic as a state, but he was upstaged by President Tyler who obtained a joint resolution of Congress, annexing Texas, shortly before President-Elect Polk took the Presidential oath.

With Texas firmly in the Union, President Polk sent John Slidell to Mexico to purchase California and the vast area between California and Texas known as the New Mexico Territory. Slidell offered $25 million for California and the New Mexico Territory, and $5 million for New Mexico alone, but Mexico refused to sell.

President Polk then began to quarrel with Mexico over the location of the southwest border of the new state of Texas. The President insisted that the Rio Grande River marked the southwest border. The Mexicans claimed that the border was the Nueces River. Polk quickly sent troops across the Nueces into the disputed area. On May 9, 1846, with the approval of his cabinet, Polk was ready to ask Congress for a declaration of war. Fortunately for Polk, news came that night that General Zachary Taylor's troops had been fired upon.

In his request for a declaration of war, Polk claimed that we should go to war because "Mexico has . . . shed American blood upon the American soil." A young Whig Congressman from Illinois named Abraham Lincoln took issue with that statement. Lincoln challenged Polk to name the spot where American blood was shed on American soil, and he introduced the Spot Resolutions in the House of Representatives.

But neither Abraham Lincoln nor the Whigs could deter President Polk. Using diplomacy, he gained exclusive occupation of the Oregon Territory, settling for the 49th parallel in place of a more expansive northern border. The portion of Mexico he could not purchase, he took by force, receiving it in the Treaty of Guadalupe-Hidalgo in 1848. He also obtained a lower tariff and an independent treasury system, retired after one term, and soon thereafter passed away.

Questions for Research and Discussion

1. What did Americans mean by Manifest Destiny?

2. Why was expansion so identified with the Democratic party?

3. Who deserves the most credit for the annexation of Texas as a state, President Polk or President Tyler?

4. Who was responsible for the outbreak of the Mexican War?

5. President Polk is widely regarded as a successful President. Should he be ranked with the Great?

Suggested Reading

K Jack Bauer, *The Mexican American War, 1846–1848* (1974); Ray A. Billington, *The Far Western Frontier, 1840–1860* (1956); Roy Jeffrey, *Frontier Women* (1979); Frederick Merk, *Manifest Destiny and Mission In American History* (1963); Milo Milton Quaife, *Diary of James K. Polk* (1910); John H. Schroeder, *Mr. Polk's War: American Opposition and Dissent, 1846–1848* (1973); David J. Weber, *The Mexican Frontier, 1821–1846* (1982); Albert K. Weinberg, *Manifest Destiny* (1935).

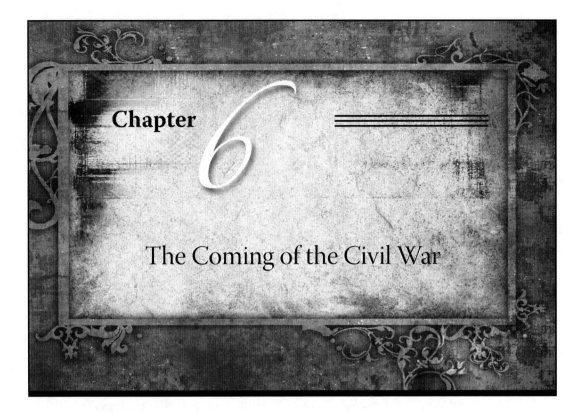

Chapter 6

The Coming of the Civil War

Four Confrontations: North v. South, 1787–1850

There were four major confrontations between North and South before secession, the formation of the Confederate States of America, and the Civil War. Each of them furnishes some insight into the causes of the Civil War.

It is interesting to note that as early as 1787, while making the United States Constitution, delegates to the Philadelphia convention strongly identified themselves as Northerners or Southerners with special regional needs. The conflicts between Southern plantation agriculture and the industrial interests of the North were beginning to take shape, but more importantly, there was a clash between the slave and free labor systems. The conflict centered on the problem of representation in the House of Representatives. Southerners argued that the industrial North was more populous and would therefore have an unfair advantage in representation in the House. They therefore insisted that slaves be counted in determining the number of Representatives allotted to the South. Northerners argued that slaves were considered property, and since they were not citizens they should not be counted in determining representation for the South. This serious dispute was resolved with the **Three-Fifths Compromise,** a measure which allowed Southerners to count each slave as 3/5 of a person.

By 1820 differences between North and South over the tariff, the labor system, and the needs of an agricultural vs. an industrial society had sharpened. Conflict was inevitable when the Union was composed of 11 free and 11 slave states and Missouri had applied for admission to the Union as a slave state. Northerners were alarmed that Missouri was located above 36° 30´, and that the parity in the number of slave vs. free states could be ruptured. The heated debate startled the nation. It came, said Thomas Jefferson, "like a fire bell in the night." The conflict was resolved when the State of Maine was created out of a portion of Massachusetts and simultaneously admitted as a free state. A major feature of this so-called **Missouri Compromise** was the agreement that thereafter all states asking for admission above 36° 30´ would be free. All below it would have slaves.

Disputes over the tariffs of 1828 and 1832 led to serious confrontation between North and South in this so-called Nullification Crisis. John C. Calhoun of South Carolina had written and spoken of the need for southerners to nullify the federal tariff. He had advocated secession as a possibility in this crisis as well. The Nullification Crisis was resolved when Henry Clay, chief architect of the Missouri Compromise, introduced the **Compromise Tariff of 1833.** This tariff was to be gradually reduced over the next decade.

The fourth major confrontation between North and South occurred in the debate over admission of the Mexican cession. After the Mexican War the United States gained the vast territory of present day California, Nevada, Utah, Arizona, and New Mexico. The debate over the admission of the new territory as slave or free threatened to tear the Union apart. Henry Clay was the key person in shaping the **Compromise of 1850.** The Civil war was no doubt postponed when the Compromise was enacted. California was admitted as a free state, a strong fugitive slave act was in place, the slave question would be decided at a later time by the people in the New Mexico Territory, and the slave trade was abolished in Washington, D.C.

Events that Led to the Civil War, 1850–1861

The Compromise of 1850 gave both North and South something of substance. The major concession to the North was the admission of California as a free state. The South, in turn, received the full support of the federal government in the capture and return of runaway slaves. The year 1850, therefore seemed hopeful. Perhaps sectional strife could be minimized. Perhaps violence and war could be averted. But that was not to be.

In the 1850s there were many events that helped precipitate the Civil War. Among them was the **publication of two important books.** The first was *Uncle Tom's Cabin*, an anti-slavery novel by Harriet Beecher Stowe. Published in 1852, it was the best-selling novel of the 19th Century and most certainly intensified the sectional conflict that led to the Civil War. The Second was Hinton R. Helper's *Impending Crisis of the South*, published in 1857. Helper drew extensively from the Census of 1850, arguing that slavery prevented the South from becoming a modern industrial state and that it also prevented whites without slaves from rising to acceptable social and economic positions. His book fueled the inflammatory debate between North and South, and, as a Southern abolitionist, his work became a divisive phenomenon among his Southern friends as well.

A small-scale civil war erupted in 1854 called **"Bleeding Kansas."** This inflammatory event was caused when a debate over slavery escalated into a gruesome prelude to the war between the states.

If "Bleeding Kansas" could be considered small scale, it had large consequences, giving impetus to the **formation of the Republican party.** This new party was decidedly Northern, nationalist, and vigorous in its opposition to states' rights and popular sovereignty, both of which were blamed for North-South hostilities in Kansas. Built upon the ashes of the Free Soil, Liberty, and Whig parties, the new Republican party was composed of dissident elements. The cement that held them all together, but decidedly alienated the South, was an incendiary plank calling for "no further extension of slavery."

On May 19, 1856, Charles Sumner, a Republican Senator, fanned the flames of secession and Civil War when he delivered a speech titled **"The Crime Against Kansas."** He hurled personal insults against several Southerners and ridiculed Senator Andrew P. Butler of South Carolina for his devotion to "the harlot, slavery." On May 22, a distant cousin of Senator Butler, Congressman Preston Brooks, found Sumner at his desk working on a speech. Brooks beat Sumner over the head with an 11 ounce walking cane until he fell to the floor, bloody and unconscious. Sumner recovered, but he had to leave his Senate seat for three and a half years. Part of that period was spent receiving costly medical treatment in Europe. Meanwhile Congressman Brooks was showered with walking canes from his Southern friends and he was handily re-elected by his South Carolinian constituency.

The next divisive event was a crucial case before the Supreme Court in 1856. **Dred Scott,** a slave who resided in the North, had sued for his freedom. The majority decision of the Taney Court contained the assertion that Scott was not a citizen; he was property, and would remain a white man's property regardless of his residence in free territory. This decision inflamed passions in both North and South.

In 1858, Abraham Lincoln, a lanky 6'4" Republican, challenged Stephen A. Douglas, a 4'6" Democrat, for a United States Senate seat from the State of Illinois. In the ensuing **Lincoln–Douglas debates,** national attention was focused on Lincoln's call for no further extension of slavery and Douglas' insistence that slavery could exist in any state where it had majority support. Tensions were heightened as these Northern and Southern differences were dramatized on a national stage.

War sentiment grew with **John Brown's raid** on Harper's Ferry, Virginia in 1859. The raid was an abortive attempt to capture weapons from a federal arsenal in order to arm the slaves. The failed attempt and the hanging of John Brown failed to put a damper on the fact that an effort had been made to incite a massive insurrection of slaves. Southerners reacted in emotional protests.

Finally, in **the election of 1860** Lincoln represented a new Republican party dedicated to enactment of a protective tariff, the vestiges of Hamiltonian economics, and an end to the expansion of slavery. Lincoln and the Republicans were anathema in the South. They were not even on the ballot in several Southern states.

Secession began one month after the election of Lincoln. When the new President took the oath of office, March 4, 1861, seven states had already seceded and a Confederate government was in place with Jefferson Davis as Provisional President and Alexander H. Stephens as Vice President. Now there were two nations where there had been one.

Questions for Research and Discussion

1. What were the four major confrontations between North and South from 1787 to 1850?

2. What were the most divisive events that led to Civil War from 1850 to 1861?

Suggested Reading

David Donald, *Charles Sumner and the Coming of the Civil War* (1960); Don E. Fehrenbacher, *The Dred Scott Case* (1978); Eric Foner, *Free Soil, Free Labor, Free Men* (1970); William H. Freehling, *Road to Disunion: Secessionist at Bay, 1776–1854* (1990); Eugene Genovese, *The World the Slaveholders Made* (1969); Bruce Levine, *Half Slave and Half Free: The Roots of the Civil War* (1992); Stephen B. Oates, (John Brown) *To Purge this Land with Blood* (1970); David M. Potter, *The Impending Crisis, 1848–1861* (1976) and *Lincoln and His Party in the Secession Crisis* (1942); Richard H Sewell, *A House Divided: Sectionalism and Civil War, 1848–1860* (1988); Kenneth Stampp, ed., *The Imperiled Union: Essays on the Background of the Civil War* (1980) and *America in 1857: A nation on the Brink* (1990).

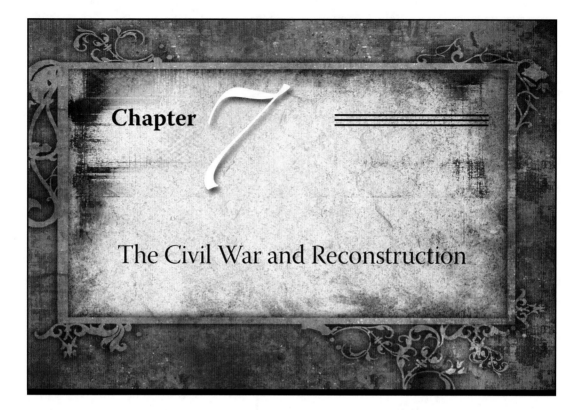

Chapter 7

The Civil War and Reconstruction

In the election of 1860 there were four major candidates. Abraham Lincoln was the candidate of the new Republican Party, pledged to a higher tariff, free land through a Homestead Act, and no further extension of slavery. This clever approach united Western farmers, Eastern businessmen, and Eastern laborers, but it isolated and alienated the South. The Democratic party was split three ways. Stephen A. Douglas, Democrat, and John Bell, Constitutional Unionist, offered Northern and Southern voters conciliatory approaches, but John C. Breckenridge, Democrat, represented the uncompromised sentiments of the South. Sixty percent of the voters cast their ballots against Lincoln, yet the Lincoln vote was so concentrated in the North, that it translated into a lopsided electoral count of 180 for Lincoln, 12 for Douglas, 72 for Breckenridge, and 39 for Bell. Ironically, even if Douglas had carried the entire South, Lincoln would still have been elected.

In his inaugural address, Lincoln asserted that "the Union of these states is perpetual . . . confirmed by the history of the Union itself. The Union is much older than the Constitution." He then denounced the notion that the Union was a compact of states, and that sovereign states could nullify federal laws or secede. On the contrary, he said "no State, upon its mere motion, can lawfully get out of the Union—that resolves and ordinances to that effect are legally nothing, and that acts of violence, within any State or States are insurrectionary or treasonable . . . I therefore consider that the Union is unbroken; and to the extent of my ability, I shall take care that the laws of the Union be faithfully executed in all of the States."

In the last portion of his address, Lincoln said, "In your hands, my dissatisfied fellow countrymen, and not in mine, is the momentous issue of civil war. The government will not assail you. You can have no conflict, without being yourselves the aggressors. You have no oath registered in Heaven to destroy the government, while I shall have the most solemn one to 'preserve, protect and defend' it."

Since Lincoln believed that the Union was unbroken, it followed logically that it was his responsibility to order provisions for Ft. Sumter, a fort that was located on an island off the coast of South Carolina. Lincoln sent ships with supplies, and on April 12, 1861, Confederate guns opened fire. Two days later the Confederate flag was hoisted over the Fort and the Civil War had begun.

On April 15, President Lincoln issued a proclamation in which he called forth the militias of the States of the Union to the "aggregate number of seventy-five thousand." At this juncture four more states seceded from the Union, giving the Confederacy its final count of eleven.

Abraham Lincoln and Tad

Figure 7.1 *The Lincoln family lost two small sons. Tad was a great source of comfort for the President as he faced the enormous challenges of the Civil war.*

Lithograph by L. Prang & Co., courtesy of the Library of Congress Prints & Photographs Division, LC-USZC4-2777.

In the course of the Civil War a nation of about 31 million people lost approximately 620 thousand men. Since Union forces were about three times the size of the Confederates, Northern fatalities were roughly 50 percent greater than those of the South.

Nine million Southerners, including slaves, were pitted against approximately 22 million Northerners who had a greater industrial base and superior resources. But some of the advantages of the North were evened out when considerable Confederate aid came from England in the form of loans, munitions, and ships. In addition, British commerce raiders harassed the Union merchant fleet.

In the first two years of the war the South was winning. Furthermore, almost to the end of the war, General Lee protected the Confederate capitol, holding a succession of Union Generals at bay.

The North staged three main offensive moves. The first was for control of the Mississippi River. It began with the capture of New Orleans and Memphis, and was completed when General Ulysses S. Grant captured Vicksburg in the summer of 1863. The second was connected to General William T. Sherman's march from Tennessee to the sea at Savannah and his thrust northward to the Carolinas, and the third was Grant's drive to the southern border of Virginia, where he overpowered Lee's army.

The Emancipation Proclamation

Throughout the early stages of the war, abolitionists had been pressuring President Lincoln to emancipate the slaves. They kept reminding him that not only were Union soldiers fighting to preserve the Union, but they were also fighting to eliminate slavery. In addition they argued that freeing the slaves would create a new pool of recruits that could be drafted into Northern ranks.

For three years Lincoln had ignored their clamor, fearing that a policy of emancipation would drive the loyal slave states of Delaware, Maryland, Missouri, and Kentucky, out of the Union. However, on September 22, 1862, under extreme pressure from Republican Senators to declare his position on slavery, President Lincoln issued the preliminary Emancipation Proclamation. This clever document declared that persons held as slaves *in areas of rebellion* would be free on and after January 1, 1863. It made no mention of slaves within the aforementioned loyal slave states.

Lincoln had previously affirmed that his primary purpose was to save the Union, with or without slavery. After January 1, 1863, his secondary mission was to free the slaves. At this juncture, slaves in the South and runaway slaves in Canada responded to the Proclamation. By the war's end, African-American soldiers comprised over 10% of Union ranks. Many were "free Negroes" residing in the North, but a goodly portion of them were runaway slaves. In the aggregate, sixteen African-American soldiers were awarded the Congressional Medal of Honor.

The Emancipation Proclamation was, of course, a war measure, a military strategy employed by the Commander in Chief. It had the practical effect of breaking the backbone of the economy of the South. It also became the first step in permanent emancipation of all slaves in the United States, which was achieved by the 13th Amendment to the Constitution, a measure that President Lincoln helped marshal through the Congress before his tragic assassination.

Lincoln as Commander in Chief

In the crisis of Civil War, Abraham Lincoln drew upon emergency powers, and as he appropriated to himself, many traditional Constitutional powers held by Congress, he was called a tyrant and a dictator. He blockaded southern ports, increased the size of the army and navy, instituted an income tax, purchased weapons, declared martial law, conducted war, and suspended the Writ of Habeas Corpus, all without Congressional approval.

His suspension of the writ of Habeas Corpus gave him the power to arbitrarily incarcerate war protesters, and they could not obtain release, even if the detainment did not conform to law. When the suspension of this right was combined with the declaration of martial law, traditional American freedom was severely impaired, if not snuffed out.

Lincoln not only declared martial law, but he also authorized traveling military tribunals to adjudicate in place of the normal justice system. During the Civil War the Union army conducted over 4,000 military trials.

Were Lincoln's critics correct in characterizing him as a dictator? The answer must be framed in the context of the enormous challenges the President faced. From his special vantage point, it was important to stifle resistance and create a unified Northern effort to save the Union. It therefore seems abundantly clear that Lincoln was not engaged in a cynical grab for power. His gentle disposition and his powerful words identify him as a lover of democracy and an advocate, in his own words, of "government of the people, by the people, and for the people." In the crisis of Civil War, he met the grim challenges of the day, ruling in a manner that provided the best chance that our Federal Union would "not perish from the earth."

Lincoln served as President for one term and one month. In that brief period he managed to distinguish himself above all who have served. His speeches live in the annals of mankind and his reputation has been enhanced by being ranked as our greatest President in every major poll of historians and political scientists since 1948.

Presidential vs. Congressional Reconstruction

On March 4, 1865, President Lincoln delivered his Second Inaugural Address. He had defeated George B. McClellan, a Union general he had fired for failing to prosecute the war. If the nation had chosen McClellan, a negotiated peace might have left the Confederacy permanently in place. Instead, President Lincoln addressed his countrymen with the prospect of Northern victory in sight and the Union intact.

His inaugural address was a masterpiece in content and style, and it set a conciliatory tone for reconstruction of the defeated South. In his closing paragraph he said:

> "With malice toward none; with charity for all; with firmness in the right as God gives us to see the right, let us strive on to finish the work we are in; to bind up the nation's wounds; to care for him who shall have borne the battle, and for his widow, and his orphan—to do all that would achieve and cherish a just and lasting peace, among ourselves and with all nations."

Lincoln implemented these brotherly sentiments toward the South with a plan to readmit Southern states when 10% of the men eligible to vote in 1860 had sworn allegiance to the Union. Virginia, Louisiana, Arkansas, and Tennessee responded to Lincoln's magnanimous invitation, but Congress refused to seat them.

Radical Republicans who dominated the Congress were outraged with Lincoln's leniency. Led by Thadeus Stevens, Charles Sumner, and Benjamin Wade, the radicals responded to the 10% plan with passage of the **Wade-Davis Bill,** a measure that required states to obtain a majority of 1860 voters to swear allegiance to the Union before they were allowed to return.

Lincoln responded to this more stringent Congressional measure with a pocket veto. In the interim he attended Ford's Theater, was assassinated, and never had to face-off with a hostile Congress on the issue of reconstruction. Vice President Andrew Johnson inherited that task.

Andrew Johnson, a southern Democrat, had been chosen as Lincoln's running mate, not only to attract northern Democratic voters, but also to reward him for the courageous act of remaining in his Senate seat when his native Tennessee left the Union to join Confederate ranks.

Johnson followed Lincoln's policy, offering a reconstruction plan which gave general amnesty to all except ex-Confederates and rebels whose wealth exceeded $20,000. This general pardon also included the requirement that Southerners swear an oath of allegiance to the Union and ratify the 13th Amendment, abolishing slavery.

Since Johnson's plan made no mention of voting rights or civil rights for former slaves, once again Radical Republicans rallied in strong opposition. They insisted that harsh terms be imposed on the conquered South, and that all semblance of the Confederacy be destroyed. They maintained that African-Americans had the right to vote and to assume political positions in reconstruction governments. They argued against the Lincoln-Johnson notion that it was legally impossible for a state to secede. They vehemently denied the concept that rebellious people had risen up against the nation and it was the President's prerogative to issue a pardon. Finally they insisted that Sovereign states had seceded from the Union and that Congress clearly had the Constitutional authority to set the terms for re-admittance.

Support for the radical agenda grew enormously in the election of 1866. Thereafter Radicals could easily summon two-thirds majorities for their vengeful programs. This meant that they could override President Johnson's veto and that radical reconstruction would prevail.

From 1866 to 1877, southerners experienced a period of **radical reconstruction** in which the last vestiges of the Confederate States of America were destroyed. It commenced with passage of the bill creating the **Freedmen's Bureau,** a federal agency that protected the civil rights of the freedmen in the Southern states. Operating under the War Department, this new agency assisted in the transition from slavery to freedom. It furnished food and clothing to needy African-Americans and aided them in finding jobs. It granted homesteads on public lands and supervised labor contracts to insure justice for the illiterate. It established schools and hospitals for freedmen as well.

Mustering two-thirds majorities, Radicals not only overrode President Johnson's veto of the Freedmen's bureau, but also the second important feature of the radical program, the **Civil Rights Acts of 1866.** This legislation granted citizenship to African-Americans and prevented states from abridging their rights.

The Reconstruction Act of 1867 was also veto proof. It divided the southern states into five military districts. The governors of the states were replaced by five military leaders, who presided over the systematic disenfranchisement of ex-Confederates and the granting of suffrage to African-Americans. This act of 1867 has sometimes been called the **Command of the Army Act** because it had the practical effect of making Secretary of War Edwin Stanton the virtual Commander in Chief. Stanton sat in President Johnson's cabinet, undermining every attempt the President made to thwart radical reconstruction. Stanton was in close cooperation with General Grant, the Commanders in the five military districts, and the members of the Radical Republican Congress, engineering the Congressional juggernaut that rapidly diminished the President.

When the Radical Congress produced the **Tenure of Office Act,** it was assuredly setting a Presidential trap. Passed March 2, 1867, over Johnson's veto, the act prohibited the President from removing civil officers without Senate consent. Violation of the act was deemed a high misdemeanor, so when President Johnson fired Secretary of War Stanton, without Senate consent, the Radical Congress proceeded with its long laid plans to impeach the President.

The House of Representatives issued eleven articles of impeachment, nine of which were based on violation of the Tenure of Office Act. These indictments were passed onto the Senate, where the trial of President Johnson began in March of 1868. Late in May of 1868, the Republican dominated Senate voted to remove President Johnson by a vote of 35 to 19. It is ironic that after repeatedly mustering two-thirds majorities to enact veto proof reconstruction measures, Radical Republicans failed, by one vote, to deliver the two thirds majority that was required to convict and remove the President.

Northern armies continued to occupy the South until 1877, when the last of the troops were withdrawn. Radical reconstruction had spawned the 14th and 15th Amendments to the Constitution, guaranteeing African-American citizenship, and ensuring African-Americans the right to vote. But these rights were soon denied.

Once the last of the federal troops were withdrawn, Southern whites rallied to redress the excesses of Radical Republican rule. Vengeance had already been returned when in 1866, Confederate veterans organized the Ku Klux Klan, making terrorism against African-Americans commonplace. As southern legislatures passed back into the hands of whites, Democrats protected their majorities with oppressive "Jim Crow" laws. These laws fell into three general categories. The first was "grandfather clauses" that prevented African-Americans from voting if their progenitors had not voted. The second was poll taxes that discriminated against former slaves, and the third was literacy tests that were administered in a discriminatory manner against African-Americans. In addition there were new state laws legalizing segregation on public conveyances, in schools, and other public places.

For almost one hundred years the South defied the Amendments to the Constitution guaranteeing African-American rights, but the Civil Rights crusade of the 1960s helped reinstate the authority of the Constitution throughout the land.

The Civil Rights Crusade

In a victory for NAACP attorney Thurgood Marshall, on May 17, 1954, the United States Supreme Court ruled on the landmark case of *Brown v. Board of Education of Topeka, Kansas*, unanimously agreeing that segregation in public schools was unconstitutional.

On December 1, 1955, NAACP member Rosa Parks refused to conform to southern customs in regard to segregated seating on a Montgomery, Alabama bus. In response to her arrest, Reverend Martin Luther King, Jr. led a Montgomery bus boycott that lasted until buses were desegregated on December 21, 1956.

In September of 1957, Governor Orval Faubus of Arkansas used the National Guard to block nine black children from entering the all white Central High School of Little Rock. President Dwight D. Eisenhower sent federal troops and the National Guard to escort the "Little Rock Nine" into their rightful place at the school.

Organized by the Congress of Racial Equality (Core) and the Student Non-violent Coordinating Committee (SNCC), black and white volunteers began taking integrated "freedom rides" on buses in the South. These brave volunteers met with violence, but they persevered over the spring and summer of 1960.

The most prominent leader of the civil rights movement was Martin Luther King, Jr. King was jostled, spat upon, stabbed, jailed, and finally killed for his brave stand for African-American rights. He won the Nobel Peace Prize and was honored posthumously with a national holiday to commemorate the day of his birth. His non-violent strategies brought massive changes in the field of human rights, and he was admired throughout the world.

Martin Luther King, Jr.

Figure 7.2 *Dr. Martin Luther King delivering his "I have a dream" speech in Washington, D.C., 1963.*

U.S. Information Agency. Press and Publications Service. Image courtesy of the National Archives and Records Administration.

The genuine heroes of the civil rights movement are too numerous to mention. Many lost their lives in beatings, shootings, and bombings. After King's death, new leaders emerged who advocated direct action, black power, and black pride.

In the mid 1960s, for the first time since Radical Reconstruction, the power of the federal government was used to further African-American rights. President Lyndon B. Johnson led the way in obtaining voting rights legislation, an affirmative action program, the outlawing of literacy tests, and an Anti Poll Tax Amendment to the Constitution.

Questions for Research and Discussion

1. Evaluate Lincoln as Commander in chief and as President. Do you think he should be ranked as a Great President?

2. Evaluate the following in the elevation of African-Americans: A) the Emancipation Proclamation, and B) the 13th, 14th, and 15th Amendments. Why was the civil rights movement of the 1960s necessary?

3. Discuss the nature of the dispute between President Lincoln and Congress over reconstruction of the defeated South. Compare the Presidential reconstruction policies of Lincoln and Johnson with those of the Radical Republicans. Which approach was the most enlightened?

4. Did President Johnson deserve impeachment?

5. What were some of the tangible achievements of the Civil Rights Crusade of the 1960s?

Suggested Reading

Richard H. Abbot, *The Republican Party and the South, 1855–1877* (1986); W. E. Dubois, *Black Reconstruction in America, 1860–1880* (1935); Eric Foner, *Reconstruction: America's Unfinished Revolution, 1863–1877* (1988); John Hope Franklin, *Reconstruction After the Civil War* (1961); William Gillette, *Retreat from Reconstruction, 1869–1879* (1979); Kenneth M. Stampp, *The Era of Reconstruction, 1865–1877* (1965); Allen W. Trelease, *White Terror: The Ku Klux Klan Conspiracy and Southern Reconstruction* (1971); C. Vann Woodward, *The Strange Career of Jim Crow* (3rd ed.—1966).

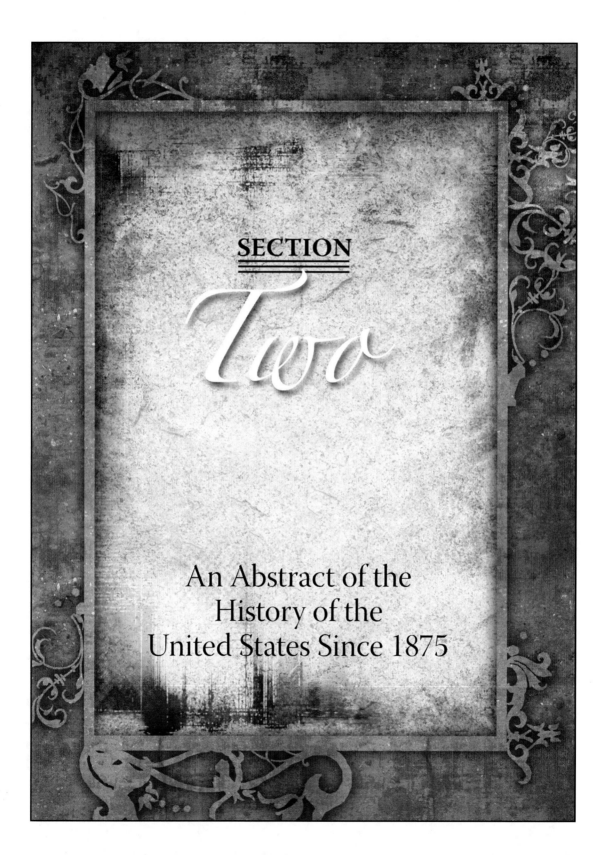

SECTION

Two

An Abstract of the
History of the
United States Since 1875

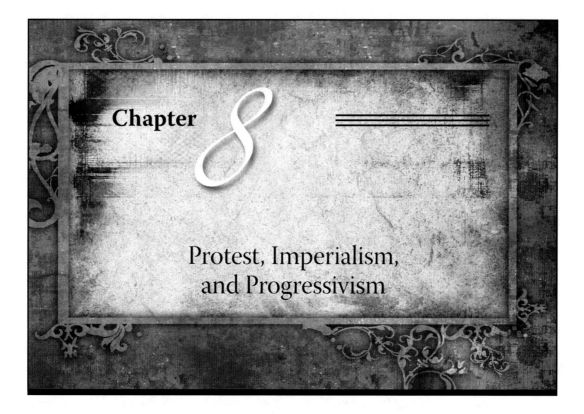

Chapter 8

Protest, Imperialism, and Progressivism

The decade following the period of 1877 was the most ruthless period in the history of the development of American business. In their quest for power and position, business combinations took many forms. There were pools which divided markets, set prices, and controlled output; trusts which brought many companies together and turned their stock over to a board of trustees who conducted all business; and holding companies which were incorporated specifically to own stock in other corporations.

While these new business monopolies assuredly increased efficiency, they also promoted the economic aims of large industrialists at the expense of the industrial workers and the farmers. Attempts to rectify workers' grievances through trenchant unionism were easily thwarted. Industrialists simply planted spies and detectives in the mills to compile black lists which stigmatized union members throughout entire industries. Businessmen also issued "yellow dog" contracts, which made a non-union pledge a requirement of employment. If these devices failed to curb union activities, they also used court injunctions to stop strikes, boycotting, and picketing.

Many workers began to feel that they had put down a slave power only to fall into the clutches of a more rapacious money power, and many industrial workers responded to the grim world of long hours and low pay with a series of thunderous strikes.

Nearly 7,000,000 workers participated in about 30,000 strikes between 1881 and 1905. Violence was associated with many of them. The railroad strike of 1877 was perhaps typical. It began in response to wage cuts on the Baltimore and Ohio Railway, spread to many other railroads, and resulted in the deaths of nearly 100 people. The violence was quelled only when President Hayes called out federal troops.

Many labor disorders occurred in the 1880s, and these years of "great upheaval" culminated in the Haymarket Riot in Chicago, May 4, 1886, where seven fatalities resulted from a bomb thrown at a strike meeting.

In the Homestead Strike of 1892, which took place at the Carnegie Steel Plant in Pennsylvania, workers fired on Pinkerton detectives who had been imported to break the strike. Three detectives and ten strikers were killed, and the "pitched battle" which ensued destroyed the iron and steel workers union.

The Pullman Strike of 1894 resulted in the refusal of American Railway Union members to handle trains carrying Pullman cars. This strike was broken when President Cleveland ordered mail cars attached to Pullman trains and sent federal troops to Chicago to quell the resultant disorders.

The Knights of Labor was perhaps the most effective labor union of the period, but its downfall came with the infamous Haymarket Riot, and by the 1890s its membership was largely absorbed in the Populist revolt.

The Populist Revolt

Populism took root from the farmers' numerous grievances. Railroads discriminated against farmers in fixing carrying charges for farm goods and in setting prices for storage of their crops. Banks, loan companies, and insurance companies charged high interest rates for farmers, and finally, farmers sold their crops for low prices in a competitive market, but bought manufactured goods in a domestic market protected by tariffs and dominated by trusts and corporations.

These grievances led farmers to join agricultural organizations such as the Northern Alliance, the Agricultural Wheel, and the National Farmers Alliance. Representatives from these and other farm groups combined and formed the Populist Party of 1892.

Nominating James B. Weaver as a candidate for President of the United States, Populists armed him with the following planks in the so-called Omaha Platform: (1) abolition of national banks, (2) a postal savings bank system, (3) a sub treasury plan of loans to farmers, (4) an increase in the circulating medium to not less than $500 per capita, (5) free and unlimited coinage of silver at a rate of 16 to 1, (6) a graduated income tax, (7) government ownership of railroads, telephone, and telegraph lines, (8) popular election of senators, (9) an eight-hour day for labor, and (10) immigration restriction.

Weaver garnered over one million popular votes and 22 electoral votes. In the same year Populists elected five senators, ten representatives, and three governors.

What fun the Eastern press had made of the Populist platform, and Populist leaders "Sockless Jerry Simpson" and Mary Ellen Lease. The latter had advised the farmers to "raise less corn and more hell!" But the levity soon turned to apprehension with the results of the election of 1892, and by 1896 Populism was absorbed into the Democratic party. By integrating themselves into the structure of a major party, the Populists took the only practical course to secure the eventual acceptance of their program.

William Jennings Bryan was the Democratic candidate in 1896. His acceptance of many Populist tenets signified that the country was dividing along class and sectional lines. His panacea for the economic problems of the times was the Populist-initiated free and unlimited coinage of silver at a rate of 16 to 1. Under this proposed form of inflation, the United States Treasury would coin into dollars a cheaper form of money which theoretically would move the crops faster, help pay off farm mortgages, and restore rural prosperity. Mr. Bryan and his party also endorsed an income tax, a low tariff, and other popular causes of the day.

The campaign of 1896 was full of intense excitement. Free silver was the chief issue in a frantic contest, but the *New York Tribune* solemnly assured its readers that Bryan was planning to destroy the Ten Commandments.

"Uncle" Mark Hanna organized a lavish propaganda machine for the Republican candidate, William McKinley. Hanna was so successful in raising money for the campaign that the contribution of one firm, Standard Oil, was only slightly smaller than the entire Democratic campaign chest.

Eastern money was more powerful than Western and Southern votes as the country was plastered over with posters and pelted with pamphlets detailing the fallacies of free silver. Men were paid $25 a day merely to wear McKinley buttons; businessmen told their workers not to report for work if Bryan won, and the banks made farmers understand that credit would be denied to their section if it voted for Bryan.

In the closing days of the campaign the Republicans had 18,000 speakers "on the stump," but Hanna shrewdly kept William McKinley limited to a "front porch" campaign. He was no match for Bryan in the political fray.

McKinley won the election, polling 271 electoral votes to Bryan's 176; and the victor's popular vote was a majority of approximately 600,000. Businessmen were relieved at the defeat of Bryan, for as one editor of the time explained, no man in public life ever wrought so much terror as this "boy orator of the Platte."

Soon after the election, Republicans raised the protective tariff to a new high level. Now that Bryan's dire threats to the gold standard and capitalism were averted, businessmen could savor a new period of protection and prosperity. Events immediately after the election of 1896 seemed to confirm business principles and confound the prophets of doom.

Bryan would challenge McKinley for the Presidency again in 1900, but silver would no longer be the issue. In the interim, however, the problem of the regulation of trusts was beginning to cause some concern even for conservative William McKinley. It was at this juncture that Spain provided a diversion.

War with Spain

United States interest in Spanish-owned Cuba went back to the early days of our history, and it was whetted by the Ten Years' War (1869–78) between Spain and Cuba. An arms-running expedition from the United States to Cuban insurgents could have brought the U.S. into the Ten Years' War as a full-scale participant against Spain, but the time for confrontation had not yet arrived.

Encouraged by the adverse effects on Spanish prosperity by our Wilson-Gorman tariff, the Spanish insurgents commenced the Cuban War of Independence in 1895. Spanish General Valeriano ("Butcher") Weyler set up concentration camps throughout Cuba in an attempt to isolate and confine the "insurrectos." American public opinion was soon inflamed over Spanish atrocities in the island—real and imagined. At this juncture, the Spanish minister insulted President McKinley in the de Lome letter, and the sentiment for the liberation of Cuba grew.

When the battleship U.S.S. Maine mysteriously blew up in Havana harbor, it was readily assumed that the Spaniards had done it, and the "yellow press" in the United States whipped a long-cultivated war sentiment to fever pitch with the slogan "Remember the Maine."

Even though he had important Spanish concessions in hand, President McKinley sent Congress a war message on April 20, 1898. A declaration followed which included the Teller Amendment, promising that the U.S. would withdraw from Cuba as soon as her independence was achieved. It seems that President McKinley and his administration were pushed inexorably toward war, even though Spain was prepared to grant Cuba autonomy or even independence.

Four months after the war was declared, Spain sued for peace. Relinquishing Cuba and ceding Puerto Rico, Guam, and the Philippine Islands, she also gave up a chain of minor Pacific Islands to the United States.

The Platt Amendment replaced the Teller Amendment, thwarting the promise of Cuban independence. Instead Cuba was made a U.S. satellite. Under the Platt Amendment the U.S. gained a naval base in Cuba, the right to control land transfers by Cuba, the right to control Cuba's foreign commerce and her diplomatic actions, and the right to intervene whenever the United States deemed it necessary. Marines were occasionally landed to keep order, up to 1934, when the Platt amendment was abrogated.

President McKinley decided it was our Christian duty to civilize the Filipinos, but an insurrection led by Emilio Aguinaldo indicated that the natives were more immediately interested in independence from the United States. The Jones Act of 1916 increased Filipino participation in the government, and the Tydings-McDuffie Act of 1934 set 1946 as the year of Philippine independence, which was granted on July 4, of that year.

Emergence as a World Power

The Spanish-American War produced a curious departure from traditional American foreign policy. With newly won dominance in the Caribbean, the acquisition of numerous Pacific Island "stepping stones," the simultaneous annexation of Hawaii as a territory, and the acquisition of the Philippines, America was impelled into adventures outside its traditionally accepted geographical sphere of interest. Dominance in the Caribbean brought a pathway to the isthmus, and the pathway to the isthmus was soon extended in the form of a Panama Canal. The Canal, of course, was the great connecting link between the major oceans, and it facilitated the trade and commerce of the United States as well as the development of a powerful two-ocean navy.

When the United States took over the Philippines, it also became involved heavily in the Oriental trade. This was at a time when China was being threatened with partition by rival European imperialistic powers and Japan. Now a great power with Pacific and Far Eastern territory, the United States effected a temporary balance of power within China on the basis of the Open Door policy. It was January 13, 1905, when Secretary of State John Hay proclaimed that it was the policy of the United States "to maintain the integrity of China and the Open Door in the Orient."

Convinced of the absence of aggressive tendencies on the part of the United States, the Chinese government had granted to the United States expansive trading privileges and guarantees. Without enmity the United States had thus gained rights within China which had been granted to European powers on the basis of military conquest. To the United States it was desirable that the territory and sovereignty of China be kept intact lest these equal trading rights and the so-called Open Door be closed.

President Theodore Roosevelt's role in helping negotiate an end to the Russo-Japanese war won him a Nobel Peace Prize, but more importantly, his actions retained the power balance between Russia and Japan on the Asiatic mainland and preserved the Open Door.

The Spanish–American War brought the United States a colonial empire and a new military system. The latter included an expanded regular army, federal supervision of the National Guard, the creation of a system of officer training schools and the Army War College at Washington. In 1903 a General Staff was modeled on the example of European staffs with a Chief of Staff at the helm. Thus, the United States entered the 20th Century as a significant world power with an emerging modern military system.

The Quest for Social Justice

If a new era in foreign policy opened in the new century, it is equally certain that drastic changes in domestic politics occurred as well. A new crusade in foreign and domestic affairs opened when young Theodore Roosevelt succeeded to the Presidency upon the assassination of President McKinley. Admirably prepared by inheritance, training, and temperament, Roosevelt understood the profound changes which had occurred in our country over the past 30 years. Furthermore, he had the commitment and the boundless vitality needed for a crusade against custom and privilege. His inauguration of what is called the Progressive Era (1901–1917) made the "standpat" Republican party into an instrument of reform. Roosevelt expressed his hope for a "Square Deal" for all segments of American Society, and then dramatized and implemented his slogan by refusing to take sides in the Anthracite Coal Strike of 1902. His leadership brought a settlement of the dispute by arbitration; and management, labor, and consumers at large were the beneficiaries. Roosevelt's "Square Deal" approach to this problem contrasts sharply with President Cleveland's handling of the Pullman Strike of 1894. In the latter, President Cleveland threw the full weight of the Presidential office behind management.

Roosevelt's reputation as a "trust-buster" was garnered at a time when trade in tobacco, steel, oil, meat, and many other necessities of life was controlled by super corporations. These combinations of great wealth strangled competition, placed labor at the mercy of capital, and in many instances, increased interest rates and prices in order to pay dividends on swollen capitalization.

Three Presidents before Roosevelt had the Sherman Anti-Trust Act, but none of them used it to prosecute business "conspiracies in restraint of trade." Roosevelt and his Attorney General, Philander Knox, used the Anti-Trust Act for the first time in 1903 against the Northern Securities Company, a gigantic railroad combine. This holding company was successfully "busted," but it was only a short period of time until the Hill-Harriman-Morgan interests had recombined in a new legal structure which differed only slightly from the holding arrangement the courts had disallowed. Undaunted, however, the Roosevelt administration brought legal proceedings against the Beef Trust, Standard Oil Company of New Jersey, the American Tobacco Company, and others.

A number of laws relating to corrupt practices on the railroads were passed in Theodore Roosevelt's administration. Among them were the Elkins Act, which strengthened the law against rebates, and

Theodore Roosevelt

Figure 8.1 *"Teddy" Roosevelt was a significant leader in the Progressive Era of 1901 to 1916, His many achievements as president included development of a Panama Canal and the creation of millions of acres of national parks and national forest reserve.*

Photograph by Pach Brothers, courtesy of the Library of Congress Prints & Photographs Division, LC-USZ62-13026.

the Hepburn Act, which increased the size and authority of the Interstate Commerce Commission.

Roosevelt slightingly dubbed the journalists who were writing in behalf of reform "muck-rakers." They included Ida M. Tarbell, Frank Norris, Jacob Riis, Ray Stannard Baker, Lincoln Steffens, Upton Sinclair, David Graham Phillips, and others. Engaging in a torrid literature of exposure, they published their disclosures of the corruption of that day in such magazines as *Munsey's, Colliers, McClure's,* and *Cosmopolitan.* Upton Sinclair's novel, *The Jungle,* was in large measure responsible for the Pure Food and Drug Act and the Meat Inspection Act. Much impetus for other reforms came directly from the published articles and books of the "muckrakers."

If the journalists gave impetus to reform, it must be quickly added that Theodore Roosevelt expedited it. From the vantage point of the Presidency (his "bully pulpit") he extended the classified civil service lists, cleaned up waste and corruption, curbed the looting of the public domain, and created vast forest reserves and national parks. Preaching civic responsibility and practicing public virtue, Theodore Roosevelt set his country on its 20th Century pathway in domestic and foreign affairs.

His vision in the realm of conservation of natural resources was prophetic. He appointed Gifford Pinchot National Conservation Chairman and supported his expansion of a staff which grew from 123 to 1,500. Over 200 million acres were withdrawn from public use and transformed into forest reserve and national parks, and finally Roosevelt called a National Conference of Governors to make certain that conservation commissions were organized in each state. President Theodore Roosevelt's achievements in conservation, by themselves, qualify him for his place on the side of Mount Rushmore.

Roosevelt and Imperialism

In foreign affairs, the achievements of the Roosevelt administration are identified with the emergence of the United States as a world power. After the Spanish–American War, Europeans expected America to take a leading role in world politics, and Roosevelt fulfilled their expectations. Roosevelt's policy was "Speak softly and carry a big stick," and the "big stick" soon bludgeoned Panama, the weakest portion of the Colombian nation.

Through intrigue and blatant imperialism, Roosevelt wrested an isthmian canal from Colombia and opened a water pathway which gave the United States quick access to both coastlines, and a link between the two great oceans.

His action facilitated our commerce, improved our defense, and gave momentum to the development of a two-ocean navy. New American ships now had quick access to the newly won island possessions in the Pacific, and a brisk trade with the Orient developed.

In the Far East, it was Roosevelt and Secretary of State John Hay who worked to preserve the territorial integrity of China; and Roosevelt's secret diplomacy helped end the

Russo-Japanese War. The impasse that was negotiated kept a balance of power in China, furthered American interests, and brought President Roosevelt the Nobel Peace Prize.

In the Americas, the Monroe Doctrine developed into something more powerful than a U.S. warning against intervention; the addition of the "Roosevelt Corollary" made it instead an assumption of responsibility for weak Caribbean republics.

Republican Demise

Roosevelt declined a third term in 1908 and practically "hand-picked" his friend, William Howard Taft, as his successor. Lacking in temperament and the ability to capture the imagination of the public, Taft nonetheless was able to point to many progressive legislative accomplishments. The civil service classified lists were expanded; the national forest reserves were extended; postal saving banks and parcel post began; labor gained cabinet status; corporation taxes were instigated; and Taft himself initiated the income tax amendment.

While much useful progressive legislation was passed during his term, Taft was never hailed as a progressive. Even though Taft "broke" more trusts than TR, no one referred to him as a "trust buster." In spite of these solid accomplishments, he managed to alienate progressives, split his party, and give Theodore Roosevelt credible reasons to seek a non-consecutive third term. Taft's firing of Gifford Pinchot, the National Conservation Chairman; his approval of a Canadian Reciprocity Treaty, which threatened to destroy farm prosperity; and his acceptance of the inordinately high Payne-Aldrich tariff convinced progressives that he had sold out to the "interests." All of these actions lent credence to Theodore Roosevelt's 1912 battle cry that under Taft, progressivism was betrayed.

Roosevelt sought to regain the Republican nomination but was "steamrollered" out of the convention. Chagrined and deeply hurt, Roosevelt formed the "Bull Moose" party and sought to unite the progressive forces of the nation under his banner of the New Nationalism. This strategy was thwarted, however, when Governor Woodrow Wilson of New Jersey, one of the nation's rising young progressives, was nominated to head the Democratic ticket.

In the hard-fought campaign of 1912, Wilson won only 41 percent of the popular vote; yet he scored a victory over Roosevelt and Taft in an election that gave Eugene Debs 6 percent of the votes cast, the all-time high for a Socialist presidential candidate.

Wilson and "The New Freedom"

Wilson had campaigned under the banner of the "New Freedom," a slogan which suggested that he would lead his party toward a negative states' rights tradition. Once elected, however, the former professor demonstrated that progressive democracy could be developed more effectively with an enlightened and constructive nationalism.

After Wilson routed lobbyists from the Congress, the Democratic party was able to redeem its pledge of tariff reduction. The resulting Underwood-Simmons tariff of 1913 has been called the first scientific tariff, and it was the first significantly reduced tariff since the Civil War.

Wilson's domestic accomplishments included the Underwood-Simmons Tariff; the Clayton Anti-Trust Act, which was designed to limit the use of court injunctions and anti-trust legislation against labor unions; the Federal Reserve Banking System, which stabilized bank reserves and created mobile credit and an elastic currency; the Federal Trade Commission, which was designed to investigate unfair business practices and impose higher standards of conduct on business; the Adamson Act, which gave railroad workers an eight-hour day with the same pay they had received for a ten-hour day; the Smith-Lever and Smith-Hughes Acts, which provided federal funds for education; and dollar-matching, which provided federal money to states for the development of federal highways. In addition, the Sixteenth, Seventeenth, Eighteenth, and Nineteenth Amendments were adopted during the Wilson administration. They provided for the income tax, direct election of Senators, prohibition, and women's suffrage, respectively.

Spartan idealism gave impetus to this plethora of reform, but it was short-lived. For after one term the attention of President Wilson and his progressive backers was focused on U.S. involvement in a great world war.

World War I and Its Aftermath

While Wilson's New Freedom was unfolding, a great war involving the major powers of Europe was raging. From 1914 to 1916, President Wilson maintained an official stance of neutrality, even in the face of a significant loss of U.S. shipping to German submarines.

When Germany, contrary to pledges previously made, announced unrestricted submarine warfare in waters surrounding Great Britain, and further sinking of U.S. ships occurred, the United States declared war on Germany, April 6, 1917.

Wilson had proposed an idealistic peace settlement between warring European powers before U.S. entry into World War I. "Peace without victory" was his alternative to a terrible war of attrition, for he believed

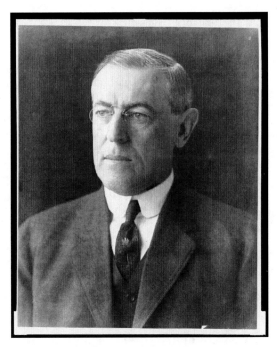

Woodrow Wilson

Figure 8.2 *After World War I, Wilson's call for a League of Nations was rejected by the United States Senate, but after World War II, with the dawn of the atomic age, the Senate accepted the United Nations with a smashing vote of 89 to 2.*

Photograph by Pach Brothers, courtesy of the Library of Congress Prints & Photographs Division, LC-USZ62-13028.

that future war could be averted only if nations would seek just and lasting settlements based upon historical claims and good conscience.

He also believe that boundaries imposed by force and settlements made under duress were destined to breed new resentments and new conflicts. Accordingly, after U.S. entry into World War I, Wilson further stated his desire for a magnanimous peace. His official war aims were embodied in his idealistic "Fourteen Points" for a just and lasting peace. Phrases such as "no territorial aggrandizement" and "no war debts or indemnities" were issued and uttered while American lives and treasure were spent in a great "war to end wars" and to "make the world safe for democracy."

The fourteenth point in Wilson's peace plan called for the "establishment of a general association of nations" to secure and maintain world peace, and the President personally participated in the postwar peace conference, hoping to implement his ideas in the treaty. He was the first American President to leave the country while in office, but his dream of a just peace was thwarted in spite of his heroic efforts. Forced to compromise most of his Fourteen Points, Wilson salvaged his demand for a "League of Nations," and a "Covenant of the League of Nations" was made the first section of the Treaty of Versailles.

Wilson left the peace conference diminished in reputation, but with a genuine sense of achievement. He had predicted a new world conflict if the nations of the world failed to seek equitable settlements or if they failed to implement the concepts of "peace without victory" and "peace among equals." And even though these ideals had been shuttled aside in the settlements, Wilson believed that it might be possible to achieve them in part through the League of Nations, without recourse to war.

Wilson was awarded the Nobel Peace Prize for 1919, but in the United States he encountered a strong Senate opposition to ratification of a treaty which had as an integral part a League of Nations. Refusing to compromise even on non-essential terms of the Covenant, President Wilson set upon a country-wide speaking tour to put the great issue before the people. The strain of the speaking tour broke President Wilson's health. Suffering a stroke on October 1, 1919, President Wilson became an invalid for the rest of his second term in office. Beset by relentless political foes, the President could not garner the necessary two-thirds vote in the United States Senate to ratify the Treaty of Versailles and the League of Nations.

The League became a reality for virtually every nation, however, and even in its limited success, it pointed to the dangers Wilson had foreseen and foretold. A generation after Versailles, with smoke rising from three continents, the elements of hope were reassembled again. A United Nations took form, and this time the U.S. Senate gave Wilson's basic plan a ringing 82-to-2 endorsement.

It was Senator Henry Cabot Lodge, Sr., Chairman of the Senate Foreign Relations Committee, who led the fight to defeat ratification of the Treaty and the League. Ironically, the first time Republicans won the Presidency after World War II, President Eisenhower chose Henry Cabot Lodge, Jr. to be U.S. Ambassador to the United Nations.

Questions for Research and Discussion

1. Is it possible to defend U.S. imperialism on both moral and economic grounds? Explain.

2. Identify some of the major elements in the rise of Progressivism.

3. Was Woodrow Wilson's foreign policy a failure? Explain fully.

Suggested Reading

Jane Addams, *Twenty Years at Hull House* (1910); Sean Dennis Cashman, *America in the Gilded Age* (1984); John M. Blum, *Woodrow Wilson and the Politics of Morality* (1956); Allan F. Davis, *American Heroine: The Life and Legend of Jane Addams* (1973); Robert H. Ferrell, *Woodrow Wilson and World War I, 1917–1921* (1985); Philip Foner, *Women and the American Labor Movement* (1979); John Arthur Garrary, *Woodrow Wilson: A Great Life in Brief* (1956); Ray Ginger, *Age of Excess* (1965); Lawrence Goodwyn, *The Populist Movement: A Short History of the Agrarian Revolt in America* (1978); Richard Hofstadter, *Social Darwinism in American Thought* (1955); Herbert Hoover, *The Ordeal of Woodrow Wilson* (1958); Morton Keller, *Theodore Roosevelt: A Profile* (1967); Charles F. Kellogg, *The NAACP: The History of the National Association for the Advancement of Colored People* (1967); Aileen Kraditor, *Ideas of the Women Suffrage Movement* (1965); Gerald F. Linderman, *The Mirror of War: American Society and the Spanish-American War* (1974); Arthur S. Link, *Woodrow Wilson: A Brief Biography* (1963), and *Woodrow Wilson and the Progressive Era* (1963), and with Richard L. McCormick, *Progressivism* (1983); Harold C. Livesay, *Andrew Carnegie and the Rise of Big Business* (1975), and *American Made: Men Who Shaped the American Economy* (1979); Rayford W. Logan, *The Negro in American Life and Thought: The Nadir, 1877–1901* (1954); Nathan Miller, *Theodore Roosevelt: A Life* (1992); Edmund Morris, *The Rise of Theodore Roosevelt* (1979); Alan H. Spear, *Black Chicago: The Making of a Negro Ghetto, 1890–1920* (1967); John L. Thomas, *Alternative America* (George, Bellamy, Lloyd) (1967); Alan Trachtenberg, *The Incorporation of America* (1982); David R. Trask, *The War with Spain in 1898* (1981); Norman J. Ware, *The Labor Movement in the United States, 1860–1895* (1929).

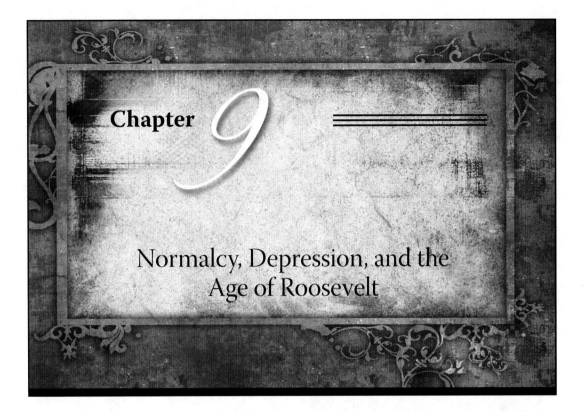

Chapter 9

Normalcy, Depression, and the Age of Roosevelt

By 1920 the nerves of the country had been rubbed raw by the long era of muckraking, altruism, and self sacrifice. "Meatless, wheatless and heatless days" were part of the bitter memories connected with the Great War, but these experiences paled when compared with the "shell shock" of casualty lists, the bitter debate over the League of Nations, and the disillusionment with a peace settlement which fell far short of President Wilson's idealistic Fourteen Points.

Cynicism, provincialism, and intolerance marked the decade of the 1920s as the Democratic party disintegrated into snarling factions which rendered it incapable of providing responsible opposition to the era of Republican ascendancy.

Xenophobic legislation virtually closed the gates of immigration, and unfair quotas discriminated against people of Southeast Europe as fears of Bolshevism and labor violence gripped the land.

The Ku Klux Klan was revived in Georgia in 1915 and spread with astonishing rapidity through the "Bible Belt" and the Middle West. The Klan bore a close relationship to the anti-foreign "nativist" movement of the 1850s, and it was anti-Negro, anti-Catholic, anti-Jewish, anti-pacifist, anti-Communist, anti-evolutionist, anti-intellectual, anti-internationalist, anti-birth control, and anti-bootlegger. It was also pro-Protestant, pro-Anglo Saxon and by its own definition, "one hundred percent American."

Scandalous grafting by Klan leaders brought a Congressional investigation and a collapse of the reign of hooded horror in the late 1920s, but not before 5,000,000 Klanners had exercised important influence on U.S. Politics and contributed to shameful lynchings and terrorism.

In the last days of the Wilson administration, Attorney General A. Mitchell Palmer had conducted wholesale denunciations of liberals and pacifists and indiscriminate raids, arrests, and deportations of aliens. This so-called "Red Scare" was an integral part of a pattern of intolerant provincialism which characterized the 1920s. Other parts of the pattern included immigration restriction, the antics of the Klan, a fundamentalist Christian crusade against science, and the sordid fiasco of prohibition.

The politics of complacency, the climate of isolationism, and the atmosphere of materialism and comfort contributed to the discontent, alienation, and in many cases, expatriation of intellectuals. But to most Americans, Detroit was Mecca and Henry Ford was the Prophet. When a group of college students voted Henry Ford the third greatest figure in the stream of world history, they were only confirming the widespread commitment to business ethics which ran rampant throughout the "New Era" of the 1920s.

Bruce Barton, an ad writer, captured the imagination of the general public in 1925 and 1926 with his bestselling book titled *The Man Nobody Knows*. This businessman's life of Christ characterized the parables as advertisements, and Jesus as "an A-1 Salesman." In this gospel according to Barton, Christ was also "the most popular dinner guest in Jerusalem" and "the founder of modern business." The widespread acceptance of this theme illustrated, perhaps better than any other phenomenon, that in the 1920s business had become the national religion.

Warren G. Harding

Figure 9.1 *President Harding looked as if he should be president. Unfortunately he possessed few other qualifications for the office.*

Courtesy of the Library of Congress Prints & Photographs Division, LC-USZ62-13029.

"Normalcy"

Typifying the mediocrity of the times was President Warren G. Harding, the Ohio Republican who was President from 1921 to 1923. His brief administration was dedicated to "normalcy" and marked by colossal scandal.

Thomas W. Miller was given the post of Alien Property Custodian. He accepted graft for supporting false claims to the property of the American Metal Company and was sentenced to eighteen months in prison.

Colonel Charles R. Forbes was entrusted with the administration of the Veterans' Bureau. He and his accomplices stole approximately 250 million dollars, chiefly in connection with the building of Veterans' Hospitals. Forbes was sent to Leavenworth Penitentiary, and his attorney committed suicide.

Jess Smith, a member of Harding's poker-playing "Ohio Gang," committed suicide in Attorney General Daugherty's apartment, giving rise to the scandal of further official corruption. That Jess Smith was distributing graft taken from "bootleggers" was well known, but attempts to convict Attorney General Daugherty for sharing graft with Smith failed.

The infamous Teapot Dome scandal occurred when Harding's Secretary of Interior, Albert Fall, secretly leased naval oil reserves at Elk Hills, California, and Teapot Dome, Wyoming, to private oil men Edward Doheny and Harry Sinclair. Fall was convicted of accepting a bribe for this favor and sentenced to federal penitentiary in New Mexico, but the two oil men escaped through clever lawyers.

Other scandals erupted around Harding, but death spared this naïve man from facing the full revelation of one of the most corrupt administrations in American history.

In diplomacy, the Washington Naval Conference (1921–1922) was called by Harding's Secretary of State, Charles Evans Hughes. This "Republican Versailles" brought major naval powers together in a five-power pact to limit the production of capital ships, a four-power pact to respect each other's possessions in the Pacific, and a nine-power pact to guarantee the territorial integrity of China.

A Disarmament conference was also held in Geneva during the Coolidge administration, and in 1928 the famous Kellogg-Briand Pact outlawing war was signed. Ultimately this pact was ratified by 62 nations, including all the major powers of the world, but its practical effect was tragically clear in the next decade when signatory nations of Europe and Asia violated their pledge not to use war as an instrument of foreign policy. As a result, World War II began.

Laissez Faire and Status Quo

Business planning was extensive in the 1920s. By controlling prices, wages, and production, business monopolies partially nullified the self-adjusting mechanisms of the free competitive market. In fact, the "New Era" of the 1920s (popularly referred to in the folklore of capitalism as a model period of free enterprise) was a period when large corporations carefully planned their own economic position in relation to other important segments of the American economy.

"The business of America is business," President Calvin Coolidge asserted in the mid 1920s, and his national political leadership helped make it so. Regulatory agencies such as

Figure 9.2 *President Coolidge was an inactive president who took long afternoon naps. On occasion he posed in cowboy attire, Indian head dress, and in casual settings. He is pictured here shaking hands with Walter Johnson, baseball pitcher for the Washington Senators.*

From the National Photo Company Collection, Library of Congress Prints & Photographs Division, LC-USZ62-32732.

the Interstate Commerce Commission and the Federal Trade Commission were staffed with men who believed in little or no business regulation. The Tariff Commission was staffed with high protectionists; the anti-trust laws were ignored, and the essential work of the Progressive Era was thereby nullified, leaving huge business corporations an open field in which to impose a trenchant business policy.

Andrew Mellon was Secretary of the Treasury during the entire "New Era" of the 1920s. Widely hailed as the greatest Secretary of the Treasury since Alexander Hamilton, his tax policies unduly favored the rich and provided huge capital surpluses for business expansion, investments and speculation.

From Confidence to Collapse

President Herbert Hoover rode the wave of Coolidge prosperity to the White House in 1929. He had noted that we were near the "final triumph over poverty" in America, but after one term in office, the statistics of the Hoover administration told a far different story. The gross national product declined from $104 billion in 1929 to $59 billion in 1932. Farm prices fell by nearly 60 percent. Home and farm foreclosures reached all-time highs. One third of the mileage on the nation's railroad tracks fell into bankruptcy. Between 1930 and early 1933, over 5,500 banks failed with the resultant wipeout of all the depositors' savings. As the depression deepened, one fourth of the labor force was idle and one third of American families had no income at all.

How did this tragic economic collapse occur? **The basic causes of the Great Depression included:**

1. **Unrestrained Stock Market Speculation.** Too many investors had purchased stocks on margin. They had not invested enough in their stocks to cover the range of fluctuation. They had little chance to cover significant losses. Excessive speculation caused inflated prices, and when confidence broke, marginal speculators were in the vanguard of a huge wave of panic selling. The resultant stock market crash of 1929 became the fuse on the Great Depression.

2. **Capital Surpluses and Industrial Overexpansion.** Business profits were too high. There had been too much emphasis on reinvestment, expansion of plants, and increased production. Laborers and farmers had not made enough money to

consume their share of things. When farmers and laborers could not buy, it followed logically that business had lost an equivalent portion of its capacity to sell. Warehouses were clogged with manufactured goods, and massive layoffs resulted.

3. **Agricultural Overexpansion.** Farmers had produced more than they could sell. When produce was too plentiful, farm prices collapsed, farmers went bankrupt and the Great Depression deepened.

4. **Protectionism.** Faced with huge agricultural and industrial surpluses, the Hoover administration responded with the Smoot-Hawley Tariff, the highest in American history. When the United States shut out foreign imports, capitalist countries around the world retaliated with high tariffs against our exports. Agricultural and industrial surpluses then piled up at an accelerated rate.

At the base of the Great Depression was *overproduction* in industry and agriculture and under consumption in depressed farm and labor segments of our economy. In this ironic *depression of abundance*, business had prospered at the expense of other important segments of the economy, and the result was a monumental breakdown in the distribution of money, credit, goods, and services.

The New Deal Response

At the time of the inauguration of Franklin D. Roosevelt, America was in the depths of its worst depression. The crisis called incessantly for government assistance, which was rapidly provided.

One day after the inauguration FDR dealt with his most immediate problem, the banking crises. On March 5, he ordered all banks closed for four days. At the end of this "bank holiday" he pushed an **Emergency Banking Act** through Congress, authorizing healthy banks to reopen with Treasury Department licenses, providing for government management of failed banks, and extending much needed regulatory power over money and banking. Simultaneously the President went on the national airwaves with his first "fireside chat," informing the people of his actions and encouraging them to patronize re-opened banks.

A second banking act was passed in June to create the **Federal Deposit Insurance Corporation.** This government corporation

Franklin D. Roosevelt

Figure 9.3 *A newly elected FDR (1933) poses in a convertible roadster near his home in Hyde Park, New York.*

Courtesy of the Franklin D. Roosevelt Presidential Library and Museum, Hyde Park, NY.

originally insured all bank deposits up to $5,000. It continues to protect savings deposits in the world of the 21st Century.

In an attempt to restore confidence and bring stability into the stock market, Congress passed the Federal Securities Act in 1933. The administration of this act was temporarily assigned to the Federal Trade Commission. In 1934 the Congress dealt with a *basic cause of the stock market crash* when it sharply restricted the purchase of stocks on margin. Next they created the powerful **Securities Exchange Commission.** The Commission was charged with enforcing new rules for investing in securities, and with the protection of investors against fraud. It required the registration of stocks and bonds and mandated that accurate information be furnished to buyers. It continues to protect investors into the new century.

Of immediate concern to New Dealers was the plight of the millions of workers who were without jobs. Since the private sector was incapable of hiring the unemployed, FDR recommended that the Congress create a **Civilian Conservation Corps.** Less than a month after he took office, Congress honored his request. Young men were then encouraged to enlist in the CCC for six months of national service in reforestation, park restoration, and erosion control. If they chose to remain, they could serve a maximum of two years. The pay was $35 per month, and since they received room and board, it was possible for most of them to subsist on $5 per month and send the rest home to their families. By March 31, 1939, over two million CCC boys had contributed 8,500,000 man-hours to the nation's parks, forests, and agricultural lands; 1,575,000 trees had been planted, and140,000 miles of trails and roads had been built.

The needs of older men who were unemployed were served in the **Public Works Administration.** Created in 1933, this agency received federal money for direct work relief and grants in aid to states. PWA workers undertook construction of low cost housing, conservation work, flood control and harbor improvement projects. Over $4 billion was spent on 34,000 projects. The most spectacular achievement of PWA was the Grand Coulee Dam on the Columbia River. This was the largest single construction project since the Great Wall of China.

More federal help for the unemployed came when President Roosevelt issued an executive order on May 6, 1935, creating a federal relief agency called the **Works Progress Administration.** WPA workers built or repaired highways, schools, and public buildings, painted public murals, participated in musical or theatrical performances, and wrote state histories.

Homes and farms were foreclosed at an alarming rate before 1933, so New Dealers responded with two federal agencies designed to save homes and farms. **The Home Owners Loan Corporation** helped desperate families refinance their home mortgages. Eventually HOLC refinanced about one-fifth of all the home mortgages in the United States. **The Farm Credit Administration** did the same for rural Americans who were facing the loss of their farms.

Meanwhile farmers qualified for federal subsidies if they conformed to two **Agricultural Adjustment Acts** and limited production on specified commodities.

Perhaps the most dramatic of the New Deal projects was the **Tennessee Valley Authority.** This federal agency was created by Congress in 1933 to develop the 600 mile Tennessee River, along with its tributaries, for the purposes of flood control, navigation, and the production of hydroelectric power. Thirty five dams were placed in strategic positions, over an area that covered portions of seven states. Workers were given five hour shifts in order to create employment opportunities for the highest number possible. Dormitories were built for single workers. Married couples lived in low rent cottages equipped with the latest electrical appliances and ate in a community cafeteria at a nominal cost.

The waters of the Tennessee River soon flowed over ten high dams turning great turbines that churned out cheap hydroelectric power—electricity that was sold to residents of a seven-state region at half the cost that private companies were charging. In the meantime the TVA strung wire into the remote areas of the region and provided farmers with electricity for the first time. It also provided the stimulus for the development of a prosperous industrial economy in an area that had known only poverty and despair.

In World War II, the TVA was the nucleus of what had become a key industrial hub of the nation. The newly developed region furnished aluminum for the building of airplanes and war materials of all varieties and kinds. TVA also spawned Oak Ridge, Tennessee, where important work was accomplished in the development of the atomic bomb.

President Roosevelt considered the passage of the **Social Security Act** in 1935, the supreme achievement of the New Deal. For more than 70 years this act has provided valuable assistance for the elderly, the blind, and widows and orphans. Since the 1960s, it has included Medicare, a comprehensive system of health coverage for senior citizens.

Federal work relief projects such as WPA, PWA, and CCC were important *temporary* measures, but workers enjoyed *permanent* benefits when the Roosevelt administration passed the **Fair Labor Standards Act of 1938.** The long sought 40-hour work week was now a national mandate; this legislation also provided time-and-a-half pay for overtime work, the abolition of child labor, and a provision for a minimum wage.

The Roots of Change

Employing a three-pronged attack with governmental measures of relief, recovery, and reform, Roosevelt speedily drew upon every tenable correlate which bound the depression experience to the American past. The legacy of Hamilton, the philosophy of Jefferson, the leadership patterns of Jackson, Lincoln, Theodore Roosevelt, and Wilson, the ideas and methods of the Progressives, the experiences of World War I—all of these were consumed and applied. In fact the New Deal was a great consummation and application of American ideas and methods to wage war on the depression and restore old American values.

According to Samuel Rosenman, the New Deal had its "Genesis" in the years 1929–1933, while Governor Roosevelt was fighting the depression in New York State. Rexford G. Tugwell, a key figure in the Roosevelt "brains trust," concurs with this assessment. But Governor Roosevelt's depression-born formulas for a viable economy were not manufactured out of whole cloth. They had deep roots in the American past. The idea that government should play compensatory roles in the economy is as old as the Republic. Alexander Hamilton, our first Secretary of the Treasury, sought a tariff to protect infant industries. In so doing he secured a modification of economic laissez-faire—a modification in which the government underwrote private prosperity and dispersed public revenues for internal improvements.

Alexander Hamilton was also responsible for the creation of the semi-public Bank of the United States. The bank not only served the nation as its treasury, but also as a source of public credit; and the public credit was used to stimulate the private economy and further private ends. Broadus Mitchell has summarized the meaning of this financial planning with the assertion that Hamilton pointed the way to the work of the New Deal.

Charles E. Merriam denies that Hamilton was the true father of the New Deal by characterizing Jefferson as a "national planner," and Dumas Malone and Charles M. Wiltse have argued for the "essentially Jeffersonian" interpretation of the New Deal as well.

While hosts of scholars can legitimately involve themselves in heated polemics over whether the Hamiltonian legacy was more influential than the Jeffersonian tradition in the New Deal, it can be safely assumed that both legacies were present.

That the New Deal had basic roots in the Progressive Era is a well known theme. Arthur Schlesinger, Jr. has noted that it drew significantly from both the New Nationalism and the New Freedom; and Henry Bamford Parkes has lucidly characterized the New Deal as essentially a continuation of the Progressive movement, on a broader scale, and with more intellectual sophistication. While it is true that the political reforms of the Progressive Era did not anticipate the breadth of the New Deal, Parkes' "broader scale" was foreseen by Woodrow Wilson in 1912. Here are his prophetic words: "We are just upon the threshold of a time when the systematic life of this country will be sustained or at least supplemented at every point by governmental activity."

When Wilson became President, he promoted the crossing of the threshold, particularly when his administration undertook extensive roles in the economy during World War I. Congress created the Council of National Defense, an agency which made an inventory of the nation's productive capacity and set up a War Industries Board. Through the WIB all relevant war production was coordinated, materials were allocated, and labor-management relations were supervised.

In March, 1918, Bernard M. Baruch became director of WIB; from this post he "rationalized" industries and standardized sizes of automobile tires, plows, buggy wheels, packages, and other items.

The office of Food Administrator was created in 1917; from this office, Herbert Hoover "managed" the production and distribution of food, farm implements, feed, fertilizer, and fuel.

Woodrow Wilson appointed Harry A. Garfield to be Fuel Administrator in 1917; as a result, marginal mines were made operative, coal production was increased, and coal prices rose.

All rail transportation was put under control of the United States Railroad Administration in 1917; the federal government not only increased railroad efficiency, but also appropriated over $500 million for railroad improvements. But Government spending for railroads was only a pittance when compared to its output for war contracts. Before World War I the annual budget of the federal government never exceeded $750 million; but the average national budget from July 1, 1917, through June 30, 1920, was $12.5 billion. The significance of government spending in World War I, however, is that it brought prosperity, diminished unemployment, and increased the real income of the farmers by about one-fourth. Government spending in World War I created prosperity before it was employed as a strategy to fight the Great Depression.

Increased taxes and borrowing were also integral parts of the World War I economy. In October, 1917, excise taxes were levied on liquor, tobacco, transportation, insurance, automobiles, and other items. Income tax exemptions were lowered to $1,000 for single people, and $2,000 for married couples; 4 percent was designated the normal tax, and a graduated surtax rate went to a maximum of 63 percent. Inheritance taxes for corporations were graduated from 20 to 60 percent.

After the armistice the Wilson administration raised the normal tax to 6 percent, classified incomes over $1 million in the highest bracket, and raised the maximum surtax to 65 percent. This whole tax structure bears striking resemblance to the so called "Wealth Tax Act" of 1935. In the latter, surtax rates on individual incomes above $1 million were graduated steeply to 75 percent, a graduated corporation tax was employed, and an excess profits tax was levied on corporations. It is abundantly clear, therefore, that the emergency of world war furnished precedents for the emergency of depression; and an essentially laissez-faire economy was deemed inadequate in both.

The Objectives of Change

The basic objective of the New Deal, according to President Roosevelt, was to restore balance in our economic system, balance between industry and agriculture, and balance between the employer, the worker, and the consumer. Thus the New Deal fight against the depression was carried on in the name of equity and balance.

By extending the regulative and supportive hands of government into every economic activity, New Dealers were attempting to resolve the problems of the Great Depression. The implied planning, basic to this approach, was not a cynical abandonment of laissez-faire in an attempt to seize power. Rather it was designed to underwrite the well-being of every segment of the American economy, and by so doing it underwrote the pluralism and diversity of American life.

The Extension of Change

In his State of the Union message in January, 1949, President Harry S. Truman reminded the nation that the "business cycle is man-made," and went on to say that "the government is firmly committed to protect business and the people against the dangers of recession and against the evils of inflation."

Truman's Fair Deal proposals for the domestic economy were an extension of the New Deal; and in spite of a coalition of Republicans and Southern Democrats, the President was able to expand New Deal legislation which dealt with minimum wages, continued support of farm prices, and win a new provision for low rent public housing.

Dwight D. Eisenhower

Figure 9.4 *President Eisenhower served as Supreme Allied Commander in World War II. In the post-war era he was Commander of NATO forces and President of Columbia University. Employing an indirect leadership style, he served two quiet terms as president. Peace and prosperity were the hallmarks of the placid Eisenhower years.*

Image courtesy of the Eisenhower Presidential Library & Museum, Abilene, KS.

Under President Eisenhower the essential New Deal was preserved and, in some instances, expanded as well. The government commitment to substantial support for agriculture remained intact. Research programs in agriculture were continued. The Rural Electrification Association announced in 1960 that 97 percent of all American farms had electricity, as compared with 11 percent in 1935. During the late 1950s, the Farmers Home Administration made and insured loans at a rate over $3 million per year, a Rural Development Program had 2,000 local improvement projects underway in 31 states, and through the Agricultural Trade Development and Assistance Act, outright gifts of agricultural surpluses were made to needy nations and needy American families.

Eisenhower gave support to a variety of public works measures. These included funds for flood control projects in the Columbia River Valley, a $1 million appropriation for river and harbor projects, and a huge Colorado River Storage project. Similar storage projects were completed for Texas, Nevada, Oklahoma, California, and the Missouri River Valley; and an agreement was made with the

Mexican government to jointly construct a huge dam and power plant on the Rio Grande River.

If Eisenhower contributed to the idea of keeping public works programs alive, he also secured a new federal program for low-income housing units, a Federal Aid Highway Act, an amendment to the Fair Labor Standards Act increasing the federal minimum wage, and two important amendments expanding the Social Security Act.

During the Eisenhower years federal spending on medical research, hospital construction, and public health climbed from $290 million in 1954 to $971 million in 1961.

On March 2, 1963, the *London Economist* sagely observed that each President since Franklin D. Roosevelt had expanded the New Deal, and that President Kennedy was advocating more New Deal measures in every field in order "to get the country moving again." To the *London Economist,* the planners of the 1930s were "imaginative thinkers" who deserved a great tribute.

These "imaginative thinkers" were also responsible for setting in motion some domestic forces beyond the economic realm as well. It was a Roosevelt Court that began tearing away the Fourteenth Amendment as a protective device for corporations and restoring it as a device to protect racial minorities. These same justices began ruling against discrimination and implementing the principle that all citizens are equal before the law.

As solid as the achievements of the New Deal were (Samuel Eliot Morison has credited the New Deal with saving 20th Century American capitalism), one must recognize that, at best, it was a holding action against complete collapse of American capitalism. The New Deal certainly did not solve the Great Depression. After seven years of the "Roosevelt Revolution," unemployment rates were still high. But most of those who were not listed as gainfully employed, were subsisting on government work relief projects.

In 1940, Selective Service began and World War II presented a solution to the unemployment riddle and put the American economy back on its feet.

Questions for Research and Discussion

1. What were some of the main economic, political, and social trends of the 1920s?

2. Compare the economic policies of the 1920s with those of the 1930s? Why did governmental policies change so drastically?

3. Franklin D. Roosevelt once said that it was his "administration which saved the system of private profit and free enterprise after it had been dragged to the brink of ruin . . ." Do you agree with that statement? Why or why not?

4. Robert A. Taft once said that "New Dealers have a deep-seated distrust of the entire system of individual initiative, free competition, and reward for hard work, ingenuity and daring, which have made America what it is." Do you agree? Why or why not?

5. Did the New Deal seem to have roots in the American past or was it a new departure from American traditions?

Suggested Reading

Samuel Hopkins Adams, *The Incredible Era* (1939); Frederick Lewis Allen, *Only Yesterday* (1931); Joseph Alsop, *FDR, 1882–1945: A Centenary Remembrance* (1982); Bernard Asbell, *The FDR Memoirs* (1973); James M. Burns, *Roosevelt: The Lion and the Fox* (1956); Paul Carter, *The Twenties in America* (1968), and Another *Part of the Twenties* (1976); David M. Chalmers, *Hooded Americanism: The History of the Ku Klux Klan* (1965); Paula Fass, *The Damned and the Beautiful: American Youth in the 1920's* (1977); Robert H. Ferrell, *Harry S. Truman and the Modern American Presidency* (1981); Frank Friedel, *Franklin D. Roosevelt: A Rendezvous with Destiny* (1990); Alonzo I. Hamley, *Beyond the New Deal: Harry S. Truman and American Liberalism* (1973); Herbert Hoover, *Memoirs* (1951); Harvey Klehr, *The Heyday of American Communism: The Depression Decade* (1984); W. E. Leuchtenberg, *The Perils of Prosperity, 1914–1932* (1970); David L. Lewis, *When Harlem was in Vogue* (1981); Frances Perkins, *The Roosevelt I Knew* (1946); Arthur M. Schlesinger, Jr., *The Age of Roosevelt* (multi-volume set-1957); Susan Ware, *Holding Their Own: American Women in the 1930's* (1983); H. G. Warren, *Herbert Hoover and the Great Depression* (1959); William Allen White, *A Puritan in Babylon: The story of calvin coolidge* (1938).

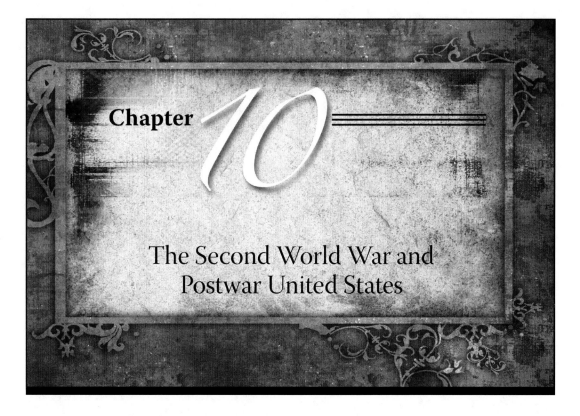

Chapter 10

The Second World War and Postwar United States

World War II emerged largely as an aftermath of the settlements of World War I. Reduced in territory and agricultural, industrial, and mineral wealth, prevented from maintaining an army or an air force, stripped of her chief industrial city, her entire merchant fleet and her overseas possessions, forced to sign the war guilt clause and pay war debts and indemnities, Germany, under the leadership of Adolph Hitler, retaliated. Returning the vengeance of Versailles a thousand-fold, Hitler joined with the Japanese, who had embarked on an ambitious plan of expansion in Asia before Hitler's aggression in Europe, and the Italians, who were led by the Fascist dictator Benito Mussolini.

By 1940 Hitler had conquered France, dominated the western half of Poland, and with Italian help and Spanish cooperation, controlled Western Europe. At this critical juncture, Britain stood alone, reeling under constant German bombardment. Prime Minister Winston Churchill was heroically rallying his people to resist the wave of totalitarian rule that had smothered the continent, but at the same time he was desperately asking President Roosevelt for help.

Franklin D. Roosevelt made some momentous decisions at this time. First, he decided to seek a third term. But before the election he was able to motivate the Congress to expand the army to 2 million men, build 19,000 war planes and add 150 ships to the navy. The fall of France had shocked the American people and broken down much of the isolationist

Franklin D. Roosevelt

Figure 10.1 *President Roosevelt is shown here shortly after his election for a fourth term. The war in Europe would soon end, but the president did not live to witness it.*

Courtesy of the Franklin D. Roosevelt Presidential Library and Museum, Hyde Park, NY.

sentiment that prevailed in the 1930s. Through an executive agreement, Roosevelt quickly traded 50 old destroyers to Great Britain in return for the use of British bases in the Caribbean, Bermuda and Newfoundland, and then, without regard for the political consequences in his bid for a third term, he bravely presided over the first peace-time draft in American history.

In December, 1940, our first third term President-Elect announced that the United States should be the "great arsenal of democracy." In January, 1941, he asked Congress to institute a program that he called Lend-Lease. Explaining that England did not have the cash to buy war material, he persuaded Congress to permit the President to lend or lease supplies to Britain and any country whose defense was vital to United States security. After Germany blitzed into the Soviet Union in June 1941, the Soviets also received Lend-Lease.

After the Japanese attacked Pearl Harbor, President Roosevelt spent the balance of his third term, and a few months of his fourth term, guiding American military forces in a vast European and Asian conflict. He was challenged physically and gave his life in the effort. Vice President Harry S. Truman succeeded FDR and presided over victory in Europe, the founding of the United Nations, and the defeat of Japan.

After the Rome-Berlin-Tokyo Axis was shattered by American, British and Russian forces, the victory became, in some measure, a pyrrhic one. Great allies in war found that it was nearly impossible to become great allies in peace. The clash of East and West emerged as Western powers began to rebuild the war torn Western appendage of Europe along democratic capitalist lines, and the Soviet Union tightened its grip on newly won satellites in Eastern Europe. High hopes for East-West cooperation in the United Nations were shattered when the Soviet Union exercised her veto power in the Security Council on numerous occasions. The Soviet Union also betrayed her Yalta Agreements in regard to free elections in Eastern Europe and assumed a rigid and calculating approach in relation to her former allies in the West.

Soviet designs in Western Europe and the Balkans brought a sharp response in U.S. foreign policy. The Truman Doctrine was announced in March, 1947, giving Greece and Turkey

$400 million dollars in direct aid. In making the request for this appropriation, President Truman noted that Russia was putting pressure on Iran and Turkey, and supporting a civil war against the government of Greece. The Truman Doctrine blocked this Soviet thrust and became the first brick in a capitalist wall of containment.

Before President Truman left office in 1953, the Soviet Union and her satellites had been encircled by the North Atlantic Treaty Organization, a free-world defense pact, and Western Europe had been revived along democratic-capitalist lines through Marshall Plan aid. Point IV aid to underdeveloped countries had helped curb Communist expansion as well.

These bold strokes in the emerging cold war were very successful, and the Truman administration can be credited with halting post-war Communist advances in Europe, but China fell under Communist rule in the same period.

Eleanor Roosevelt

Figure 10.2 *Eleanor Roosevelt awards the Purple Heart in New Caledonia. Despite the fact that her four sons were officers in World War II (FDR Jr. was decorated for bravery in the North African invasion) Mrs. Roosevelt decided to be a "universal mother" in the war. She visited U.S. troops in hospitals and on battlefields throughout the world.*

Courtesy of the Franklin D. Roosevelt Presidential Library and Museum, Hyde Park, NY.

A new challenge to Western security was wrought when Communist North Korea invaded South Korea. A United Nations force, under the command of General Douglas MacArthur, was fielded to "hold the line" and "contain" North Korean aggressors in a peace-keeping, police action.

President Truman eventually relieved General MacArthur of his command in a public dispute over what MacArthur characterized as the "no win" policy of the Truman administration. The Truman years closed with the idea of containment and limited response to Communist aggression very much intact.

An Abortive Crusade

Elected in 1952, President Dwight David Eisenhower threatened the Chinese and the North Koreans with use of atomic weapons, quickly bringing the frustrating police action in Korea to an end. He then embarked on a "crusade" in foreign policy designed to end limited holding actions and "brush-fire" wars. Influenced by advisors who counseled cutbacks in spending, Eisenhower tried to de-emphasize use of costly conventional military forces, while he simultaneously increased the capacity of our nuclear forces.

Eisenhower announced we would replace Truman's foreign policy goal of "containment" with a new objective of "liberation" of the Communist satellites, and Truman's limited holding actions with "massive retaliation," utilizing nuclear weapons. Practicing "brinkmanship," Eisenhower frequently employed clever tactics of bluff, which often worked, notably in the truce settlement in Korea.

When tested in Lebanon, Eisenhower chose to employ a limited response; and when the Hungarian revolution occurred and no U.S. help was forthcoming, the campaign promises of liberation of Communist satellites seemed hollow.

The Eisenhower approach in foreign policy became basically an extension of the Truman approach. For in the age of the hydrogen bomb the possibility of mankind's last war loomed large, and, in spite of his nuclear threats, the need for judicious use of power was evident to the Commander-in-Chief. Peace and prosperity became the hallmarks of the placid Eisenhower years.

The New Frontier

In 1961 John F. Kennedy assumed the Presidency with the promise of a New Frontier. In foreign affairs this meant new emphasis on the rebuilding of our conventional forces in order that we might become more flexible in our responses to potential adversaries.

The President worked hard for his proposed domestic program, and was able to accomplish part of it. Kennedy expanded the national space program, setting the goal for our moon landing; issued an executive order eliminating racial and religious discrimination in housing built or purchased with government assistance; created the Kennedy Commission on Equal Employment in government positions; obtained increased and expanded coverage of the minimum wage law; helped create over seventy federal judgeships to alleviate crowded dockets; obtained legislation promising women equal pay for equal work; submitted a "Medicare" proposal to Congress, tying it to Social Security; created the Kennedy Commission on Registration and Voter Participation, which recommended abolition of the poll tax and literacy tests, and lowering of the voting age to 18; lent support to Dr. Martin Luther King, Jr. and the civil rights movement, and asked Congress for strong civil rights measures which were passed after his death.

In foreign policy President Kennedy took personal responsibility for a dismal failure in the Bay of Pigs fiasco; escalated our involvement in Vietnam to 16,000 advisors; resolved a difficult crisis in Berlin and forced Soviet missiles out of Cuba; obtained a Moscow "hot line" to prevent accidental nuclear war; obtained the trade expansion bill; started the Peace Corps; started an Alliance for Progress with Latin America; obtained the establishment of the Arms Control and Disarmament Agency, giving impetus to his drive for world peace; obtained the Nuclear Test Ban Treaty of 1963, banning atmospheric testing and resolving a serious radioactive health threat to inhabitants of the planet; and called for the strengthening of the United Nations, creation of a worldwide security system, and the development of world peace through world law.

Since John F. Kennedy's most relevant Senatorial addresses were published under the title, *The Strategy of Peace*, it is not without precedent to portray him as a man who was deeply concerned with human survival, and as a man, in his own words, who would " . . . far prefer world law in the age of self determination, to world war in the age of mass extermination."

Stressing the need for strength and the strategy of the deterrent, Kennedy felt strongly that peace could be preserved temporarily on this basis. But in numerous addresses and press conferences, he counseled that we must look across this world of threats to a disarmed world where the peace could be secured through enforceable world law.

Kennedy believed that we should stay first in the development and stockpiling of effective weaponry in order to convince the Soviet Union she could not win the arms race. He hoped, however, that we might convince Soviet leaders that their own best interests could be served in the development of a worldwide security system in which the world could be made safe for diversity.

John F. Kennedy

Figure 10.3 *President Kennedy served a legendary "Thousand Days" before his tragic assassination, He steered the nation safely through the Cuban missile crisis, the world's first nuclear confrontation, set the national goal for a moon landing, and called for a "grand and global alliance . . . against tyranny, poverty, diseases and war itself."*

President John Fitzgerald Kennedy, 1961–1963. Portrait distributed by the White House. Image courtesy of the John F. Kennedy Presidential Library and Museum, Boston.

What could be more current than JFK's words at the U.N. on September 20, 1963, when he called for a "worldwide program of conservation" and reminded us that "the earth, the sea and the air are the concern of every nation. And science, technology and education can be the ally of every nation?"

When Kennedy spoke these words, the Santa Barbara oil spill and the beginning of environmental consciousness were more than five years away; ozone depletion had not been discovered; the greenhouse effect and global warming were not discussed; the rain forests were largely intact; acid rain was not destroying the forests and lakes of Europe, Northeast United States, and Canada; and Earth Day was not yet established and observed.

Cut down by an assassin after "A Thousand Days," he left a legacy of hope for domestic reform, strong civil rights laws, and a proposed "Grand and Global Alliance" to secure the peace and preserve the environment.

The assassination of President Kennedy threatened a sharp break in the continuity of his proposed program, but it did not produce that break, at least in domestic politics. It was the continuity in the transfer of power which was impressive, not the change.

Within a few months President Lyndon Johnson pushed through almost all of the proposed Kennedy legislative program, and more. The new President's ability to deal with Congress was further enhanced when recalcitrant legislators responded to his call for passage of the Kennedy program as a tribute to the martyred President.

A far-reaching civil rights bill passed Congress by sweeping majorities, as did bills to underwrite federal aid to education at every level, from preschool to graduate school. Medicare and the War on Poverty were parts of President Johnson's tidal wave of welfare legislation, but the consensus which produced the wave—the support from farmers, consumers, big business and big labor—was soon dissipated. A large proportion of this lost support could be accounted for by the President's escalation of the Vietnam War.

The Johnson approach to Vietnam, which the President justified as a logical extension of Truman, Eisenhower, and Kennedy "containment" policies, embroiled the United States in what was by 1968 a very unpopular war.

Emphasizing the need to bring order and claiming to have a secret plan to end the war, Johnson's successor, Richard M. Nixon was swept into office with a smashing 301 to 191 electoral majority over Vice President Hubert Humphrey, but Democrats increased their majority in the Senate, 57 to 43 and maintained a House majority of 255-to-179.

The new President immediately elevated four conservative cabinet members to a position called "Super Cabinet," thus degrading other members of his team. This action also widened the breach with Congress, which felt that its power had been eroded.

Congress repeatedly challenged Nixon's concept of an "Imperial Presidency." Snatching the initiative, our legislative branch ignored the President's program to shift economic burdens to the states and social responsibility to individuals. Mustering two-thirds majorities to override his vetoes, Congress passed a number of bills authorizing sewage disposal systems, hospital construction, federal assistance for schools in slum areas, limitation of the President's war-making powers, and voting rights for 18-year-olds.

When Earl Warren retired in 1969, Nixon appointed Warren Burger as the new Chief Justice of the Supreme Court. He also made three more appointments to the Court, and yet most decisions of the Nixon years were clearly in the liberal tradition. Nixon countered by taking a conservative tack on various issues. He urged Congress to outlaw bussing as a method for achieving racial balance and gave virtually no support to civil rights.

When inflation plagued our economy, Nixon adopted a three-month freeze on wages and prices. The problem persisted into the Ford administration, but President Ford appealed only to self-discipline. Introducing WIN buttons, he urged the public to wear them and join a great national rally to WHIP INFLATION NOW!!

The Subversive Activities Board had been defunct for twenty years. Nixon revived it. Between 1969 and 1971 the President searched for breaches of national security. Some newspaper reporters and government officials had their telephones tapped, and the President began to compile an "enemies" list. Nixon also tried to involve the FBI and the CIA in a program of wire tapping in order to ferret out those who endangered national security.

When J. Edgar Hoover balked, the President organized his "White House Plumbers." Under the supervision of John Ehrlichman, the bugging of private telephones brought litigation, and in 1972 the Supreme Court forbade wire taps without a prior court order. Congress decided to investigate and found that both the FBI and the CIA had been conducting wire-taps and mail inspection to spy on private citizens. When Democratic campaign head-quarters at Washington, DC's Watergate Apartment Complex were burglarized, Nixon aides were indicted. When Nixon came under investigation, James Dean III, a White House Attorney, revealed that the President's conversations with aides had been recorded and pre-served on audiotapes. Attempts to protect the President were thwarted when Dean swore that Nixon was fully aware of the Watergate break-in and the cover-up.

A few Nixon aides received prison sentences, but the President denied involvement in the Watergate break-in. Meanwhile the House Judiciary Committee in July, 1974, recommended the impeachment of Nixon. The Committee insisted that the President had obstructed justice, failed to honor his oath to uphold national laws, and defied legal subpoenas.

Nixon decided not to endure the anguish of an impeachment trial. He resigned the Presidency on August 8, 1974, and his successor, Vice President Gerald Ford, issued a full Presidential pardon for all crimes "he may have committed or taken part in."

President Nixon was the first President to resign his office, and President Ford was the first President to become Vice President and President of the United States without receiving a single vote for either office. This happened because President Nixon had appointed Gerald Ford as his new Vice President, under the authority of the new 25th Amendment, after Vice President Agnew was forced to resign for past corruption and income tax evasion.

President Ford inherited the Nixon strategy for the Vietnam conflict. Nixon had announced in 1969 that his "Vietnamization" program would enable the Vietnamese to defend their country without U.S. ground troops by 1970. Heavy withdrawals continued to April, 1975, when President Ford presided over the withdrawal of the last of the American troops, the forced closing of the American embassy in South Vietnam, and the loss of South Vietnam to the Communists.

Nixon's foreign policy was far more successful on other fronts. His Secretary of State, Henry Kissinger, penetrated the Bamboo Curtain with a secret trip to Peking in July, 1971.

Nixon's own follow-up visit to China on February 21, 1972, opened the way for our official recognition of China in the Carter administration and the admission of the People's Republic to the United Nations.

After President Ford's "caretaker" term, Jimmy Carter, a professed outsider, was elected President in 1976. Carter shunned pretense by walking to his inauguration. He also made himself available to the people in "town meetings" and radio "call-in" shows. He even spent overnight visits with families in order to stay in touch with the people.

While Ford's first Presidential act was to pardon Nixon, Carter's was to pardon all draft evaders in the Vietnam War. He did not, however, pardon deserters.

Carter made no attempt to court Congress. In fact, he vetoed a $35.2 billion defense appropriation bill and a $10.2 billion public works bill which were extremely popular with most Congressmen. Congress responded by giving President Carter part of his request for an economic stimulation plan and part of his plan to revise the Social Security program, but it turned down his proposals for a complete overhaul of the welfare system, his long term tax reform program, and gave cautious and measured support to his energy program.

In foreign affairs Carter engaged in moral persuasion to win human rights for all people of the world. Congress authorized the President to stop military aid and bank credits to any nation that violated the human rights of its citizens. When the Soviets invaded Afghanistan in 1979, Carter reacted by withdrawing the Salt II Treaty for consideration, imposing a stiff grain embargo on Russia, and asking other nations to join the U.S. in boycotting the Moscow Olympics of February, 1980.

Carter and General Torrijos Herrera signed two treaties in 1977 to replace an old 1903 agreement between Panama and the United States. These new treaties provided for Panama's sovereignty and control of the canal at the beginning of the year 2000. These actions were designed to thwart Castro's anti-U.S. propaganda in Latin America. They also reflected Carter's strong determination to square his actions in foreign affairs with his own sense of what seemed morally correct.

President Carter's most spectacular achievement in foreign affairs was the resolution of a serious Israeli-Egyptian impasse. Prime Minister Begin and Egypt's President Sadat were invited to Carter's private retreat, Camp David, for secret negotiations. The resulting Camp David Agreement of September, 1978, was widely hailed as a "Framework for Peace in the Middle East." A follow-up peace treaty was negotiated between Israel and Egypt in April, 1979.

Carter's most dismal failure in foreign affairs occurred when radical Islamic students seized the American embassy in Iran to protest the U.S. acceptance of the exiled Shah for medical treatment. They announced that they would hold the embassy personnel hostage until the Shah was returned to Iran for trial. When diplomatic efforts failed, Carter broke off diplomatic relations with Iran, froze all Iranian assets, and planned a military rescue of the hostages. Secretary of State Cyrus Vance advised the President not to attempt the military rescue. He resigned his post when the plan failed.

Carter finally agreed to unfreeze Iranian assets and the hostages were freed, after 444 days of captivity, on President Reagan's Inauguration day.

Plagued by double-digit inflation, energy crises, and the hostage crisis, the American people replaced President Carter with an affable actor-turned-politician.

Questions for Research and Discussion

1. What were some of the factors which led to tension between the United States and the Soviet Union in the post-war era?

2. How did President Eisenhower's foreign policy objectives differ from President Truman's? What were some of the strong and weak aspects of Eisenhower's record in foreign affairs?

3. Characterize some of President Kennedy's goals in foreign affairs. Do they seem realistic for our period of time?

4. What were the major accomplishments of the Johnson administration? The Nixon administration? The Carter administration?

Suggested Reading

Stephen E. Ambrose, *Nixon* (1987); James M. Burns, *Roosevelt: Soldier of Freedom* (1970); Jimmy Carter, *Keeping Faith* (1982); Robert Dalleck, *Franklin D. Roosevelt and American Foreign Policy, 1932–1945* (1979); Robert A. Divine, *Eisenhower and the Cold War* (1981); John Ehrlichman, *Witness to Power: The Nixon Years* (1982); Hamilton Jordan, *Crisis: The Last Year of the Carter Presidency* (1982); Stanley Karnow, *Vietnam: A History* (1983); Victor Lasky, *Jimmy Carter: The Man and the Myth* (1979); Allen Matusow, *The Unraveling of America: A History of Liberalism in the 1960's* (1984); Clark R. Mollenhoff, *The President Who Failed* (Carter) (1980); Richard M. Nixon, *In The Arena: A Memoir of Victory* (1990), and *RN: The Memories of Richard Nixon* (1978); Imanuel Wexler, *The Marshall Plan Revisited* (1983); Bob Woodward and Carl Bernstein, *All the President's Men* (1974), and *The Final Days* (1976).

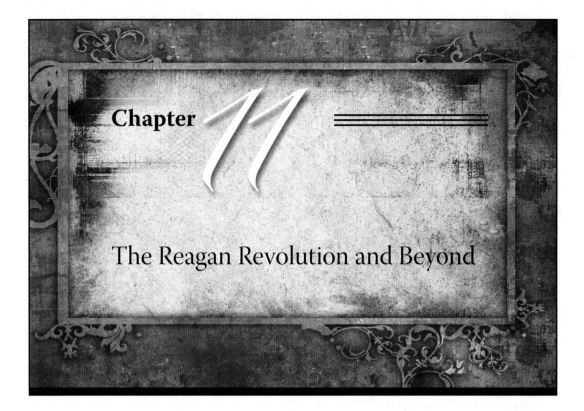

Chapter 11

The Reagan Revolution and Beyond

Ronald Wilson Reagan began his career as a liberal Democrat, supporting Franklin D. Roosevelt and Harry S. Truman. As head of the Screen Actors' Guild, he fought for a few liberal causes, but after his second marriage he was hired by General Electric at a salary of some $150,000 per year to make conservative political speeches throughout the country.

Heading national organizations of Democrats for Eisenhower in the 1950s and Democrats for Nixon in 1960, Reagan soon changed his registration to Republican and was elected to the Governorship of California for two terms.

An opponent of big government, Reagan did not use the Governor's mansion or the state airplane, opting to occupy a home built for him with private money and to fly on a private jet.

When Reagan won the Presidency in 1980, he was the first announced conservative President since the days of Harding, Coolidge, and Hoover. "Government is not the solution to our problems," he said. "Government is the problem."

He promptly hung the picture of Calvin Coolidge in the cabinet room and proceeded to fight for a variety of conservative causes. Among these were abolition of the Department of Education, destruction of the Salt II Accords, opposition to bussing to achieve racial balance in the schools, opposition to the Equal Rights Amendment for women, support for a Constitutional Amendment to end abortion, the line item veto, cuts in government welfare programs, restraints and cuts of government regulations, and increased military spending.

Ronald Reagan

Figure 11.1 *President Reagan raised defense spending from $134 billion in 1980 to $300 billion in 1989. This massive build-up helped convince the Soviet leadership to bid for de-escalation of the arms race. It contributed to the collapse of the Soviet Union as well.*

Official White House photograph, courtesy of the Library of Congress Prints & Photographs Division, LC-USZ62-13040.

Influenced by the Laffer curve and the theories of supply side economists, he made tax cuts the central theme of his "Reagan Revolution." Assuring the American people that tax cuts would create capital surpluses that would result in business expansion and the creation of new jobs, Reagan also insisted that business expansion would ensure that our tax revenues would go up, even with drastically reduced rates. In fact he said we would be able to balance the budget by the end of his first term.

Reagan's Director of the Budget, David Stockman, drafted the first budget message, featuring a five-year $750 billion tax cut which included a 30 percent reduction in federal income taxes over a three-year period.

Trimming Stockman's proposal only slightly, Congress voted a 25 percent income tax cut: 5 percent in 1981, and 10 percent in 1982 and 1983. Conservative Democrats joined Republicans to pass these new tax measures, and they simultaneously cut more than $40 billion from federal spending, mostly in food stamps and federally funded job training centers.

Stockman was delighted until catastrophic federal deficits suddenly materialized. He quickly counseled the President on the need to cut more spending and asked the President for his recommendations on cuts. Stockman found that President Reagan was not willing to recommend deep cuts in Social Security, Medicare, or subsidies to farmers; and where military spending was concerned, the President was in the process of increasing expenditures from 171 billion in 1981 to $300 billion by 1985.

Confused and frustrated, Stockman went public with his concerns about the deficits. Realizing that the President would not recommend further cuts in spending, he suggested an immediate tax hike. Reagan paid no attention to Stockman's advice, or to Walter Mondale's warning in the campaign of 1984 that taxes must be raised.

David Stockman finally resigned his post in 1985 and wrote an important book, titled *The Triumph of Politics: Why the Reagan Revolution Failed.*

Enter George H. W. Bush. He had scoffed at Reaganomics when he was a candidate for the Presidency in 1980, dubbing Reagan's approach "Voodoo Economics"; but in his second try for the Presidency in 1988, "no new taxes" became his trademark phrase.

In the Bush administration, deficit piled upon deficit, and the total mounted until the Reagan-Bush box score included a quadrupling of the outstanding federal debt.

Reagan's appointees were dedicated to his program for deregulation of business. Federal Communications Commission Director Mark Fowler hacked away federal rules that governed the broadcast industry. Secretary of Transportation Drew Lewis emasculated many of the regulations designed to reduce air pollution and improve safety in cars and trucks. Secretary of Interior James Watt, a Christian fundamentalist who believed in the imminent second coming of Jesus Christ, said that there was little point in trying to save the environment for future generations (Watt left office when his outrageous statements and tasteless ethnic humor became a liability). Ann Burford undermined the Environmental Protection Agency's role as a watchdog for corporate polluters and resigned amid a tough Congressional inquiry into the matter, and Reagan appointed as Director of the Occupational Safety and Health Administration, a Florida supporter whose construction company had been cited by OSHA for nearly fifty violations.

Deregulation of the savings and loan industry proved disastrous. Savings and loans institutions had traditionally financed home mortgages, but the Reagan administration designed a new S&L policy that allowed a wide range of highly speculative ventures. As a result, over six hundred S&Ls failed and the taxpayer bail out has been pegged at approximately $150 billion dollars.

The Reagan administration would not support the idea that the Housing and Urban Development agency should house the needy. Regulators and inspectors at HUD were dismissed, and, from 1980 to 1989, HUD's budget was reduced from $34 billion to $15 billion. This gutting of the agency left a wide open field for influence peddlers. Prominent people with influence in Washington were paid hundreds of thousands of dollars for calling HUD in behalf of business clients.

The HUD scandal culminated in misuse of about $8 billion. Some projects even included country clubs. Perhaps Congressman Tom Lantos, Chairman of the Congressional committee that investigated the HUD scandals, said it best. "Failing to kill it [HUD], you [the Reagan administration] decided to milk it."

Foreign Affairs

President Reagan felt that Carter's Human Rights crusade was an ill conceived strategy. Reagan's foreign policy approach emphasized the need to deal decisively with the expansionist aims of the "evil empire." He believed that peace was to be achieved through strength, but his strategy of deterrence finally gave way to the theory of a technological fix called the Strategic Defense Initiative.

Popularly dubbed "star wars" the basic concept behind SDI was the development of an anti-missile system to protect against nuclear missiles. Once we developed this expensive new defense shield, Reagan said we could give the technology to potential adversaries as well.

President Reagan felt obliged to send 2,000 Marines to Lebanon as part of a multinational peacekeeping force in 1982. Soon thereafter Muslims began to fire on our Marines. The horrible climax came on October 23, 1983, when a Muslim terrorist drove a truck filled with explosives into Marine barracks at the Beirut Airport. This suicide bomber killed over 200 Marines, but the President, who had criticized Jimmy Carter for the hostage crisis, failed to explain how this brutally exposed deployment served American interests, why the barracks were so poorly guarded, and what we intended to do to gain release of new hostages that had been seized.

Forty-eight hours later the entire incident was obliterated when 2,000 Marines invaded Grenada, overthrowing a Marxist regime and installing a government friendly to the United States. New headlines drew the attention of the American public away from the Middle East as the President began to quietly withdraw Marines from Lebanon.

In 1986 Reagan reacted sharply to a terrorist attack on U.S. servicemen in a West Berlin discotheque. Blaming Libya for the incident, he ordered a lightening air strike on that country in reprisal.

Shortly afterward, news broke that American diplomats had secretly arranged arms sales in Iran in exchange for Iranian aid in gaining release of hostages in Lebanon. Meanwhile money garnered from the sale of arms was diverted to "contras" in Nicaragua who were fighting against the Sandinista regime. These acts were a clear violation of a Congressional military ban on aid to the Contras and Reagan's solemn commitment never to negotiate with terrorists. The administration responded that it was dealing with moderate elements in Iran and that President Reagan had no knowledge of anything that was happening.

Criminal indictments were brought against Lt. Colonel Oliver North for obstructing a Congressional inquiry, destroying documents, and accepting money from arms dealers. North was fined $150,000 and sentenced to 1200 hours of community service, but by this time he was making up to $200,000 per month on the lecture circuit.

Admiral John Poindexter took the brunt of the Iran-Contra scandal when he claimed he personally ordered the diversion of funds to the Contras and shielded the President from any knowledge of the matter. Published memoirs of Secretary of State George Schultz imply, however, that President Reagan was informed and involved.

The summit meetings between Ronald Reagan and Soviet leader Mikhail Gorbachev at Geneva in 1985 and Reykjavik, Iceland, in 1986 were increasingly successful. At first Gorbachev insisted on United States abandonment of Star Wars as the price for arms-control agreements. In 1987, however, a dramatic warming in Soviet-American relations took place. Plagued by a failing economy and an entrenched bureaucracy at home, Gorbachev chose to compromise on the international level in order to gain some breathing space to pursue *glasnost* and *perestroika* (openness and restructuring) on the domestic front.

The Intermediate Nuclear Forces (INF) Treaty was signed in December, 1987, removing 2,500 Soviet and American missiles from Europe. For the first time in history, an entire class of existing nuclear weapons was destroyed with provision for on-site inspection to verify compliance. This was a splendid beginning, but 95 percent of the world's nuclear arsenal is still in place.

When President Reagan visited Moscow in May, 1988, he addressed students at Moscow University. Asked about his 1983 remark characterizing the Soviet Union as "an evil empire," he replied that he was referring to an earlier period of history, not Gorbachev's Russia. Ironically Reagan, the conservative cold warrior, the denouncer of earlier arms control agreements, and the champion of massive military spending, became Reagan, the man of peace.

In the election of 1988, Vice President Bush defeated Governor Michael Dukakis of Massachusetts. Bush made new proposals to cut military spending by $2.7 billion dollars and to slash SDI research by 22 percent. Bush and Congress also agreed to provide ten months of non-military funding designed to reintegrate Contras back into mainstream Nicaraguan life.

Other departures from the Reagan tradition included a Bush proposal for a strengthened Clean Air Act to combat acid rain and toxic air pollution. In the balance, however, Bush fell far short of his own announced goal to become the environmental President. He not only abandoned federal support for alternative fuels (his own fortune was made in oil and his family is directly and personally involved in Middle East oil), but he also failed to provide strong leadership on environmental issues at the international level.

President Bush's promise to become the Education President was sheer campaign rhetoric, his Education Summit, notwithstanding.

George H. W. Bush

Figure 11.2 *When Saddam Hussein directed an invasion of Kuwait, President Bush orchestrated a world-wide response to contain Iraqi aggression. Operating under the authority of unanimous Security Council resolutions, the first Gulf War was conducted with a universally supported mission statement. It was a brief, shared encounter with few casualties and a minimum of expense.*

Official White House photograph by David Valdez, courtesy of the Library of Congress Prints & Photographs Division, LC-USZ62-98302.

He proposed $3 billion less for the Department of Education than the amount in the final Reagan budget.

President Bush responded quickly when Iraq invaded Kuwait. He masterminded the assemblage of a world coalition that effectively curbed Iraqi aggression in the Persian Gulf. Operating under the authority of U.N. Security Council Resolutions, proceeding in cooperation with the Russians, Arabs, Israelis, and other improbable combinations, President Bush orchestrated "Desert Storm" and made the United Nations work.

Seizing the opportunity afforded by the dismantling of the Soviet Union and the collapse of the cold war, Bush's *New World Order* was an imaginative step beyond containment. It furnished an important precedent for the development of order, stability, and world law.

In the election of 1992, Bill Clinton defeated George Herbert Walker Bush. In his first two years as President, Clinton was able to work with a Democratic majority in Congress, increasing taxes on the wealthy, cutting military expenditures, creating a surplus, and making strides toward paying down the national debt.

Federal money was also allocated to buttress community police ranks to fight crime, and the Brady Bill was enacted to control the use of handguns.

Clinton's biggest setback was the failure to pass a comprehensive national health care plan. Conservatives rallied to block this effort and to issue a "Contract with America" as their campaign agenda in the election of 1994. The "Contract" promised an all-out assault on budget deficits and welfare programs.

In the election of 1994 the Republicans gained control of the Congress. They began to investigate the Clintons' role in a land development scheme of the Whitewater Land Corporation. This evolved into investigations of President Clinton's private life. The latter became the essential work of the Republican majority for the balance of President Clinton's two terms.

In the fall of 1998, Republican leaders started impeachment proceedings against President Clinton. The House of Representatives approved two Articles of Impeachment and forwarded them to the Senate. The Constitution requires a 2/3 Senate majority to convict and remove the President from office. When it came to the formal trial and the verdict, the Republican controlled Senate "caved in." *Article One* indicted the President for committing perjury before the Federal Grand Jury. It failed by a vote of 45 to 55. *Article Two* charged that the President had obstructed justice in the Paula Jones case. It also failed to garner a simple majority with a final count of 50-to-50.

Questions for Research and Discussion

1. Compare and contrast Reaganomics with economics policies of the 1920s. Describe the twin deficits of the 1980s (the growth of our national debt and the international trade deficit). How can these ominous trends be curbed?

2. Over 800 prominent historians participated in the Murray-Blessing poll of 1982. They were asked to rank the Presidents of the United States. Abraham Lincoln, Franklin D. Roosevelt, George Washington, and Thomas Jefferson were ranked in the "Great" category. In an update survey published in Time magazine, April 15, 1991, President Reagan was placed 28th on the Presidential list in the "Below Average" category. Does President Reagan deserve this ranking? Why or why not?

Suggested Reading

George Bush, *Looking Forward* (1987); Lou Cannon, *President Reagan: The Role of a Lifetime* (1991); Bill Clinton, *My Life* (2004) Robert Dalleck, Ronald *Reagan: The politics of Symbolism* (1984); Michael Deaver, *Behind the Scenes* (1987); Michael Duffy, *Marching in Place: The Status Quo President* (1992); Joe Klein, *The Natural: The Misunderstood Presidency of Bill Clinton* (2003); Jonathan Lash, *A Season of Spoils: The Story of the Reagan Administration's Attack on the Environment* (1984); Bob Schieffer, *The Acting President* (1989); George Schultz, *Turmoil and Triumph: My Years as Secretary of State* (1993); Geoffrey Smith, *Reagan and Thatcher* (1991); Jean Edward Smith, *George Bush's War* (1992); Larry Speakes, *Speaking Out* (1988); Gary Wills, *Reagan's America* (1987).

Three

Crisis Dialogues:

Four Historical Debates
with Lessons for Today

Debate One

The Nullification Crisis: Two Views
of the Federal Union

Historical Notes

The United States History Abstract: Major Crises in American History *features a chapter on four major confrontations between North and South. One of those confrontations was the nullification crisis of the early 1830s. In this dispute, southerners insisted that sovereign states had created the Union and they could therefore nullify federal legislation and even choose to secede. Northerners denied that the Union was a compact made by sovereign states, insisting instead, that the people had created a Union, in Daniel Webster's words, that was "one and inseparable."*

While the Northern and Southern perspectives on the nature of the Union are eloquently presented in the Webster-Hayne debate, there is not much material that indicates why Senator Daniel Webster supported nationalism, and why his opponent Senator Robert Hayne supported states rights. Perhaps a brief summary of a few factors that led to the nullification crisis could supply those answers.

In the earliest days of the new Republic, Secretary of the Treasury Alexander Hamilton introduced a financial plan that encompassed, among other things, a Bank of the United States, a tariff, and excise taxes. Through the tariff the federal government gave protection to Northern industries. The tariff also provided federal revenues that were dispersed chiefly in the North, for the construction of roads and canals, thus enhancing Northern industry and commerce. In addition, the federal government collected a burdensome excise tax on the whiskey produced by farmers in the west. Southerners and Westerners, therefore, became increasingly convinced that the federal government was underwriting the prosperity of the industrial North at their expense.

In the struggle to curb the power of the federal government, the weapon of choice for Southerners was states' rights. Thomas Jefferson and James Madison had provided the model in 1798, when they led the fight to interpose state authority against federal Alien and Sedition laws, so in the nullification crisis, John C. Calhoun and others tried to use state authority to nullify the hated federal tariff. In this national crisis, Senators Webster and Hayne made their classic statements on the Northern and Southern perspectives of the nature of the Union.

Daniel Webster: The Union Is "One and Inseparable"[1]

Excerpts from the Webster-Hayne Debate in the United States Senate, January 19–27, 1830

I must now beg to ask, Sir, Whence is this supposed right of the States derived? Where do they find the power to interfere with the laws of the Union? Sir, the opinion which the honorable gentleman maintains is a notion founded in a total misapprehension, in my judgment, of the origin of this government, and of the foundation on which it stands. I hold it to be a popular government, erected by the people; those who administer it, responsible to the people; and itself capable of being amended and modified, just as the people may choose it should be. It is as popular, just as truly emanating from the people, as the State governments. It is created for one purpose; the State governments for another. It has its own powers; they have theirs. There is no more authority with them to arrest the operation of a law of Congress, than with Congress to arrest the operation of their laws. We are here to administer a Constitution emanating immediately from the people, and trusted by them to our administration. It is not the creature of the State governments . . .

But, Sir, the people have wisely provided, in the Constitution itself, a proper, suitable mode and tribunal for settling questions of constitutional law. There are in the Constitution grants of powers to Congress, and restrictions on these powers. There are, also, prohibitions on the States. Some authority must, therefore, necessarily exist, having the ultimate jurisdiction to fix and ascertain the interpretation of these grants, restrictions, and prohibitions. The Constitution has itself pointed out, ordained, and established that authority. How has it accomplished this great and essential end? By declaring, Sir, that *"the Constitution, and the laws of the United States made in pursuance thereof, shall be the supreme law of the land, anything in the Constitution or laws of any State to the contrary notwithstanding."* . . .

For myself, Sir, I do not admit the competency of South Carolina, or any other State, to prescribe my constitutional duty; or to settle, between me and the people, the validity of laws of Congress for which I have voted. I decline her umpirage. I have not sworn to support the Constitution according to her construction of its clauses. I have not stipulated, by my oath of office or otherwise, to come under any responsibility, except to the people, and those whom appointed to pass upon the question, whether laws, supported by my votes, conform to the Constitution of the country. And, Sir, if we look to the general nature of the case, could anything have been more preposterous, than to make a government for the whole Union, and yet leave its powers subject, not to one interpretation, but to thirteen or twenty-four interpretations? Instead of one tribunal, established by all, responsible to all, with power to decide for all, shall constitutional questions be left to four-and-twenty popular bodies, each at liberty to decide for itself, and none bound to respect the decisions of others,— and each at liberty, too, to give a new construction on every new election of its own members? Would any thing, with such a principle in it, or rather with such a destitution of all principle, be fit to be called a government? No, Sir. It should not be denominated a Constitution. It should be called, rather, a collection of topics for everlasting controversy; heads of debate for a disputatious people. It would not be a government. It would not be adequate to any practical good, or fit for any country to live under . . .

Let it be remembered, that the Constitution of the United States is not unalterable. It is to continue in its present form no longer than the people who established it shall choose to continue it. If they shall become convinced that they have made an injudicious or inexpedient partition and distribution of power between the State governments and the general government, they can alter that distribution at will . . .

If anything be found in the national Constitution, either by original provision or subsequent interpretation, which ought not to be in it, the people know how to get rid of it. If any construction, unacceptable to them, be established, so as to become practically a part of the Constitution, they will amend it, at their own sovereign pleasure. But while the people choose to maintain it as it is, while they are satisfied with it, and refuse to change it, who has given, or who can give, to the State legislatures a right to alter it, either by interference, construction, or otherwise? Gentlemen do not seem to recollect that the people have any power to do anything for themselves. They imagine there is no safety for them, any longer than they are under the close guardianship of the State legislatures. Sir, the people have not trusted their safety, in regard to the general Constitution, to these hands. They have required other security, and taken other bonds. They have chosen to trust themselves, first, to the plain words of the instrument, and to such construction as the government themselves, in doubtful cases, should put on their own powers, under their oaths of office, and subject to their responsibility, to them just as the people of a State trust their own State governments with a similar power. Secondly, they have reposed their trust in the efficacy of frequent elections, and in their own power to remove their own servants and agents whenever they see cause. Thirdly, they have reposed trust in the judicial power, which, in order that it might be trustworthy, they have made as respectable, as disinterested, and as independent as was practicable. Fourthly, they have seen fit to rely, in case of necessity, or high expediency, on their known and admitted power to alter or amend the Constitution, peaceably and quietly, whenever experience shall point out defects or imperfections. And, finally, the people of the United States have at no time, in no way, directly or indirectly, authorized any State legislature to construe or interpret *their* high instrument of government; much less, to interfere by their own power, to arrest its course and operation.

If, Sir, the people in these respects had done otherwise than they have done, their Constitution could neither have been preserved, nor would it have been worth preserving. And if its plain provisions shall now be disregarded, and these new doctrines interpolated in it, it will become as feeble and helpless a being as its enemies, whether early or more recent, could possibly desire. It will exist in every State but as a poor dependent on State permission. It must borrow leave to be; and will be, no longer than State pleasure, or State discretion, sees fit to grant the indulgence, and to prolong its poor existence.

But, Sir, although there are fears, there are hopes also. The people have preserved this, their own chosen Constitution, for forty years, and have seen their happiness, prosperity, and renown grow with its growth, and strengthen with its strength. They are now, generally, strongly attached to it. Overthrown by direct assault, it cannot be; evaded, undermined, NULLIFIED, it will not be, if we and those who shall succeed us here, as agents and representatives of the people, shall conscientiously and vigilantly discharge the two great branches of our public trust, faithfully to preserve, and wisely to administer it . . .

Sir, in my career hitherto, I have kept steadily in view the prosperity and honor of the whole country, and the preservation of our Federal Union. It is to that Union we owe our safety at home, and our consideration and dignity abroad. It is to that Union that we are chiefly indebted for whatever makes us most proud of our country. That Union we reached only by the discipline of our virtues in the severe school of adversity. It had its origin in the necessities of disordered finance, prostrate commerce, and ruined credit. Under its benign influences, these great interests immediately awoke, as from the dead, and sprang forth with newness of life. Every year of its duration has teemed with fresh proofs of its utility and its blessings; and although our territory has stretched out wider and wider, and our population spread farther and farther, they have not outrun its protection or its benefits. It has been to us all a copious fountain of national, social, and personal happiness.

I have not allowed myself, Sir, to look beyond the Union, to see what might lie hidden in the dark recess behind. I have not coolly weighed the chances of preserving liberty when the bonds that unite us together shall be broken asunder. I have not accustomed myself to hang over the precipice of disunion, to see whether, with my short sight, I can fathom the depth of the abyss below; nor could I regard him as a safe counsellor in the affairs of this government, whose thoughts should be mainly bent on considering, not how the Union may be best preserved, but how tolerable might be the condition of the people when it should be broken up and destroyed. While the Union lasts, we have high, exciting, gratifying prospects spread out before us, for us and our children. Beyond that I seek not to penetrate the veil. God grant that, in my day, at least, that curtain may not rise! God grant that on my vision never may be opened what lies behind! When my eyes shall be turned to behold for the last time the sun in heaven, may I not see him shining on the broken and dishonored fragments of a once glorious Union; on States dissevered, discordant, belligerent; on a land rent with civil feuds, or drenched, it may be, in fraternal blood! Let their last feeble and lingering glance rather behold the gorgeous ensign of the republic, now known and honored throughout the earth, still full high advanced, its arms and trophies streaming in their original luster, not a stripe erased or polluted, nor a single Star obscured, bearing for its motto, no such miserable interrogatory as "What is all this worth?" nor those other words of delusion and folly, "Liberty first and Union afterwards"; but everywhere, spread all over in characters of living light, blazing on all its ample folds, as they float over the sea and over the land, and in every wind under the whole heavens, that other sentiment, dear to every true American heart,—Liberty *and* Union, now and forever, one and inseparable!

Questions for Research and Discussion

1. What are the main points Senator Webster makes in support of Union (nationalism)?

2. Name some prominent advocates of nationalism from 1789 to 1865. These should include prominent members of the Federalist party, the National Republicans, the Whigs, and the Republicans.

3. Webster characterizes the phrase "Liberty first and Union afterward" as delusion and folly. Do you agree with that assessment?

4. Which political party is most closely identified with nationalism in modern times? Explain fully.

5. What seems to be the future of American federalism? Read section Four of this textbook, *The Significance of American History and evaluate* American federalism as a model for a world security system.

Robert Hayne: The Union Is a Compact Made by Sovereign States[2]

Excerpts from the Webster-Hayne Debate in the United States Senate
January 19–27, 1830

In (Thomas Jefferson's) letter to Mr. Giles, he says,—

"I see as you do, and with the deepest affliction, the rapid strides with which the federal branch of our government is advancing towards the usurpation of all the rights reserved to the states, and the consolidation in itself of all powers, foreign and domestic, and that too by constructions which leave no limits to their powers, &c. Under the power to regulate commerce, they assume, indefinitely, that also over agriculture and manufactures, &c. Under the authority to establish post roads, they claim that of cutting down mountains for the construction of roads, and digging canals, &c. And what is our resource for the preservation of the constitution. Reason and argument? You might as well reason and argue with the marble columns encircling them, &c. Are we then to stand to our arms with the hot-headed Georgian? No; [and I say no, and South Carolina has said no;] that must be the last resource. We must have patience and long endurance with our brethren, &c., and separate from our companions only when the sole alternatives left are a dissolution of our Union with them, or submission to a government without limitation of powers. Between these two evils, when we must make a choice, there can be no hesitation."

Such, sir, are the high and imposing authorities in support of "the Carolina doctrine," which is, in fact, the doctrine of the Virginia Resolutions of 1798.

Sir, at that day the whole country was divided on this very question. It formed the line of demarcation between the federal and republican parties; and the great political revolution which then took place turned upon the very questions involved in these resolutions. That question was decided by the people, and by that decision the Constitution was, in the emphatic language of Mr. Jefferson, "saved at its last gasp." I should suppose, sir, it would require more self-respect than any gentleman here would be willing to assume, to treat lightly doctrines derived from such high resources.

Resting on authority like this, I will ask gentlemen whether South Carolina has not manifested a high regard for the Union, when under a tyranny ten times more grievous than the Alien and Sedition laws, she has hitherto gone no further than to petition, remonstrate, and to solemnly protest against a series of measures which she believes to be wholly unconstitutional and utterly destructive of her interests. Sir, South Carolina has not gone one step further than Mr. Jefferson himself was disposed to go, in relation to the present subject of our present complaints—not a step further than the statesmen from New England were disposed to go, under similar circumstances; no further than the senator from Massachusetts himself once considered as within "the limits of a constitutional opposition." The doctrine that it is the right of a state to judge of the violations of the Constitution on the part of the federal government, and to protect her citizens from the operations of unconstitutional laws, was held by the enlightened citizens of Boston, who assembled in Faneuil Hall, on the 25th of January, 1809. They state in that celebrated memorial, that "they looked only to the state legislature, who were competent to devise relief against the unconstitutional acts of the general government. That your power (say they) is adequate to that object, is evident from the organization of the confederacy."

Thus it will be then, Mr. President, that the South Carolina doctrine is the republican doctrine of '98—that it was promulgated by the fathers of the faith—that it was maintained by Virginia and Kentucky in the worst of times—that it constituted the very pivot on which the political revolution of that day turned—that it embraces the very principles, the triumph of which, at that time, saved the constitution at its last gasp, and which New England statesmen were not unwilling to adopt, when they believed themselves to be the victims of unconstitutional legislation. Sir, as to the doctrine that the federal government is the exclusive judge of the extent as well as the limitations of its powers, it seems to me to be utterly subversive of the sovereignty and independence of the states. It makes but little difference, in my estimation, whether Congress or Supreme Court are invested with this power. If the federal government, in all, or any, of its departments, is to prescribe the limits of its own authority. and the states are bound to submit to the decision, and are not to be allowed to examine and decide for themselves, when the barriers of the Constitution shall be overleaped, this is practically government without limitation of powers." The states are at once reduced to mere petty corporations and the people are entirely at your mercy. I have but one word more to add.

In all the efforts that have been made by South Carolina to resist the unconstitutional laws which Congress has extended over them, she has kept steadily in view the preservation of the Union, by the only means by which she believes it can be long preserved—a firm, manly, and steady resistance against usurpation. The measures of the federal government have, it is true, prostrated her interests, and will soon involve the whole South in irretrievable ruin. But even this evil, great as it is is not the chief ground of our complaints. It is the principle involved in the contest—a principle which, substituting' the discretion of Congress for the limitations of the Constitution, brings the states and the people to the feet of the federal government, and leaves them nothing they can call their own. Sir, if the measures of the federal government were less oppressive, we should still strive against this usurpation. The South is acting on a principle she has always held sacred—resistance to unauthorized taxation. These, sir, are the principles which induced the immortal Hampden to resist the payment of a tax of twenty shillings. Would twenty shillings have ruined his fortune? No! But the payment of half-twenty shillings, on the principle on which it was demanded, would have made him a slave. Sir, if acting on these high motives—if animated by that ardent love of liberty which has always, been the most prominent trait in the Southern character—we should be hurried beyond' the **bounds of a cold** and calculating prudence, who is there, with one *noble* and generous sentiment in his bosom, that would not be disposed, in the language of Burke, to exclaim, "You must pardon something to the spirit of liberty"?

Questions for Research and Discussion

1. List Senator Hayne's reasons for favoring states' rights? Are there additional unstated reasons for employing this strategy?

2. On April 13, 1830, at a dinner in honor of Jefferson's birthday, President Andrew Jackson toasted the Union. Vice President Calhoun responded by toasting "the Union, next to our liberties most dear." What were some of the liberties that Vice President Calhoun meant to preserve?

3. Name some prominent advocates of states' rights from 1800 to 1860.

4. Which modern political party favors a states' rights approach? List some modern reasons for this states' rights strategy. How do these reasons compare with those of Senator Haynes and Vice President Calhoun?

Debate Two

The Crisis of Economic Collapse: Advocates of a New Deal vs. The Defenders of the Status Quo

Historical Notes

Chapter nine of The United States History Abstract: Major Crises in American History contains a description of the economic policies of the 1920s, the basic causes of the Great Depression, and the New Deal response to the collapse.

In the depths of the Great Depression. well over 5,000 banks had failed, farm foreclosures had exceeded 1000 per day, the unemployment rate had risen to 25%, and one in three families had no income at all.

This section of Crisis Dialogues features the arguments, advanced in the depths off the Great Depression, by leading advocates of a New Deal as well as the defenders of the status quo.

Franklin D. Roosevelt: American Business Is Moving Ahead[3]

A Campaign Address Delivered in Chicago, Illinois
October 14, 1936

I seem to have been here before. Four years ago I dropped into this city from the airways—an old friend came in a new way—to accept in this hall the nomination for the presidency of the United States. I came to a Chicago fighting with its back to the wall—factories closed, markets silent, banks shaky, ships and trains empty. Today those factories sing the song of industry; markets hum with bustling movement; banks are secure; ships and trains are running full. Once again it is Chicago as Carl Sandburg saw it—"The City of the big shoulders"—the city that smiles. And with Chicago a whole Nation that had not been cheerful for years is full of cheer once more.

On this trip through the Nation I have talked to farmers, I have talked to miners, I have talked to industrial workers; and in all that I have seen and heard one fact has been clear as crystal—that they are part and parcel of a rounded whole, and that none of them can succeed in his chosen occupation if those in the other occupations fail in their prosperity. I have driven home that point.

Tonight, in this center of business, I give the same message to the businessmen of America—to those who make and sell the processed goods the Nation uses and to the men and women who work for them.

To them I say:

Do you have a deposit in the bank? It is safer today than it has ever been in our history. It is guaranteed. Last October 1st marked the end of the first full year in fifty-five years without a single failure of a national bank in the United States. Is that not on the credit side of the Government's account with you?

Are you an investor? Your stocks and bonds are up to five- and six-year high levels.

Are you a merchant? Your markets have the precious lifeblood of purchasing power. Your customers on the farms have better incomes and smaller debts. Your customers in the cities have more jobs, surer jobs, better jobs. Did not your Government have something to do with that?

Are you in industry? Industrial earnings, industrial profits are the highest in four, six, or seven years! Bankruptcies are at a new low. Your Government takes some credit for that.

Are you in railroads? Freight loadings are steadily going up. Passenger receipts are steadily going up—have in some cases doubled—because your Government made the railroads cut rates and make money.

Are you a middleman in the great stream of farm products? The meat and grain that move through your yards and elevators have a steadier supply, a steadier demand and steadier prices than you have known for years. And your Government is trying to keep it that way.

Some people say that all this recovery has just happened. But in a complicated modern world recoveries from depressions do not just happen. The years from 1929 to 1933, when we waited for recovery just to happen, prove the point.

But in 1933 we did not wait. We acted. Behind the growing recovery of today is a story of deliberate Government acceptance of responsibility to save business, to save the American system of private enterprise and economic democracy—a record unequaled by any modern Government in history.

What had the previous administration in Washington done for four years? Nothing. Why? For a very fundamental reason. That Administration was not industrially-minded or agriculturally-minded or business-minded. It was high-finance-minded—manned and controlled by a handful of men who in turn controlled and by one financial device or another took their toll from the greater part of all other business and industry.

Let me make one simple statement. When I refer to high finance I am not talking about all great bankers, or all great corporation executives, or all multimillionaires—any more than Theodore Roosevelt, in using the term "malefactors of great wealth," implied that all men of great wealth were "malefactors." I do not even imply that the majority of them are bad citizens. The opposite is true.

Just in the same way, the overwhelming majority of businessmen in this country are good citizens and the proportion of those who are not is probably about the same proportion as in the other occupations and professions of life.

When I speak of high finance as a harmful factor in recent years, I am speaking about a minority which includes the type of individual who speculates with other people's money—and you in Chicago know the kind I refer to—and also the type of individual who says that popular government cannot be trusted and, therefore, that the control of business of all kinds and, indeed, of Government itself should be vested in the hands of one hundred or two hundred all-wise individuals controlling the purse-strings of the Nation.

High finance of this type refused to permit Government credit to go directly to the industrialist, to the businessman, to the homeowner, to the farmer. They wanted it to trickle down from the top, through the intricate arrangements which they controlled and by which they were able to levy tribute on every business in the land.

They did not want interest rates to be reduced by the use of Government funds, for that would affect the rate of interest which they themselves wanted to charge. They did not want Government supervision over financial markets through which they manipulated their monopolies with other people's money.

And in the face of their demands that Government do nothing that they called "unsound," the Government, hypnotized by its indebtedness to them, stood by and let the depression drive industry and business toward bankruptcy.

America is an economic unit. New means and methods of transportation and communication have made us economically as well as politically a single Nation.

Because kidnappers and bank robbers could in high-powered cars speed across state lines, it became necessary, in order to protect our people, to invoke the power of the Federal Government. In the same way speculators and manipulators from across State lines, and regardless of State laws, have lured the unsuspecting and the unwary to financial destruction. In the same way across State lines, there have been built up intricate corporate structures, piling bond upon stock and stock upon bond—huge monopolies which were stifling independent business and private enterprise.

There was no power under Heaven that could protect the people against that sort of thing except a people's Government at Washington. All that this Administration has done, all that it proposes to do—and this it does propose to do—is to use every power and authority of the Federal Government to protect the commerce of America from the selfish forces which ruined it.

Always, month in and month out, during these three and a half years, your Government has had but one sign on its desk—"Seek only the greater good of the greater number of Americans." And in appraising the record, remember two things. First, this Administration was called upon to act after a previous Administration and all the combined forces of private enterprise had failed. Secondly, in spite of all the demand for speed, the complexity of the problem and all the vast sums of money involved, we have had no Teapot Dome.

We found when we came to Washington in 1933, that the business and industry of the Nation were like a train which had gone off the rails into a ditch. Our first job was to get it out of the ditch and start it up the track again as far as the repair shops. Our next job was to make repairs—on the broken axles which had gotten it off the road, on the engine which had been worn down by gross misuse.

What was it that the average businessman wanted Government to do for him—to do immediately in 1933?

1. Stop deflation and falling prices—and we did it.

2. Increase the purchasing power of his customers who were industrial workers in the cities—and we did it.

3. Increase the purchasing power of his customers on the farms—and we did it.

4. Decrease interest rates, power rates and transportation rates—and we did it.

5. Protect him from the losses due to crime, bank robbers, kidnappers, blackmailers—and we did it.

How did we do it? By a sound monetary policy which raised prices. By reorganizing the banks of the Nation and insuring their deposits. By bringing the businessmen of the Nation together and encouraging them to pay higher wages, to shorten working hours, and to discourage that minority among their own members who were engaging in unfair competition and unethical business practices.

Through the A.A.A., through our cattle-buying program, through our program of drought relief and flood relief, through the Farm Credit Administration, we raised the income of the customers of business who lived on the farms. By our program to provide work for the unemployed, by our C.C.C. camps, and other measures, greater purchasing power was given to those who lived in our cities.

Money began going round again. The dollars paid out by Government were spent in the stores and stops of the Nation; and spent again to the wholesaler; and spent again to the factory; and spent again to the wage earner; and then spent again in another store and shop. The wheels of business began to turn again; the train was back on the rails.

Mind you, it did not get out of the ditch itself; it was hauled out by your Government.

And we hauled it along the road. P.W.A, W.P.A., both provided normal and useful employment for hundreds of thousands of workers. Hundreds of millions of dollars got into circulation when we liquidated the assets of closed banks through the Reconstruction Finance Corporation; millions more when we loaned money for home building and home financing through the Federal Housing program; hundreds of millions more in loans and grants to enable municipalities to build needed improvements; hundreds of millions more through the C.C.C. camps.

I am not going to talk tonight about how much our program to provide work for the unemployed meant to the Nation as a whole. That cannot be measured in dollars and cents. It can be measured only in terms of the preservation of the families of America.

But so far as business goes, it can be measured in terms of sales made and goods moving.

The train of American business is moving ahead.

But you people know what I mean when I say it is clear that if the train is to run smoothly again, the cars will have to be loaded more evenly. We have made a definite start in getting the train loaded more evenly, in order that axles may not break again.

For example, we have provided a sounder and cheaper money market and a sound banking and securities system. You businessmen know how much legitimate business you lost in the old days because your customers were robbed by fake securities or impoverished by shaky banks.

By our monetary policy we have kept prices up and lightened the burden of debt. It is easier to get credit. It is easier to repay.

We have encouraged cheaper power for the small factory owner to lower his cost of production.

We have given the businessman cheaper transportation rates.

But above all, we have fought to break the deadly grip which monopoly has in the past been able to fasten on the business of the Nation.

Because we cherished our system of private property and free enterprise and were determined to preserve it as the foundation of our traditional American system, we recalled the warning of Thomas Jefferson that "widespread poverty and concentrated wealth cannot long endure side by side in a democracy."

Our job was to preserve the American ideal of economic as well as political democracy, against the abuse of concentration of economic power that had been insidiously growing up among us in the past fifty years, particularly during the twelve years of preceding Administrations. Free economic enterprise was being weeded out at an alarming pace.

During those years of false prosperity and during the more recent years of exhausting depression, one business after another, one small corporation after another, their resources depleted, had failed or had fallen into the lap of a bigger competitor.

A dangerous thing was happening. Half of the industrial corporate wealth of the country had come under the control of less than two hundred huge corporations. That is not all. These huge corporations in some cases did not even try to compete with each other. They themselves were tied together by interlocking directors, interlocking bankers, interlocking lawyers.

This concentration of wealth and power has been built upon other people's money, other people's business, other people's labor. Under this concentration independent business was allowed to exist only by sufferance. It has been a menace to the social system as well as to the economic system which we call American democracy.

There is no excuse for it in the cold terms of industrial efficiency.

There is no excuse for it from the point of view of the average investor.

There is no excuse for it from the point of view of the independent businessman.

I believe, I have always believed, and I will always believe in private enterprise as the backbone of economic well-being in the United States.

But I know, and you know, and every independent businessman who has had to struggle against the competition of monopolies knows, that this concentration of economic power in all-embracing corporations does not represent private enterprise as we Americans cherish it and propose to foster it. On the contrary, it represents private enterprise which has become a kind of private government, a power unto itself—a regimentation of other people's money and other people's lives.

Back in Kansas I spoke about bogey-men and fairy tales which the real Republican leaders, many of whom are part of this concentrated power, are using to spread fear among the American people.

You good people have heard about these fairy tales and bogey-men too. You have heard about how antagonistic to business this Administration is supposed to be. You have heard all about the dangers which the business of America is supposed to be facing if this Administration continues.

The answer to that is the record of what we have done. It was this Administration which saved the system of private profit and free enterprise after it had been dragged to the brink of ruin by these same leaders who now try to scare you.

Look at the advance in private business in the last three and a half years; and read there what we think about private business.

Today for the first time in seven yeas the banker, the storekeeper, the small factory owner, the industrialist, can all sit back and enjoy the company of their own ledgers. They are in the black. That is where we want them to be; that is where our policies aim them to be; that is where we intend them to be in the future.

Some of these people really forget how sick they were. But I know how sick they were. I have their fever charts. I know how the knees of all our rugged individualists were trembling four years ago and how their hearts fluttered. They came to Washington in great numbers. Washington did not look like a dangerous bureaucracy to them then. Oh, no! It looked like an emergency hospital. All of the distinguished patients wanted two things—a quick hypodermic to end the pain and a course of treatment to cure the disease. They wanted them in a hurry; we gave them both. And now most of the patients seem to be doing very nicely. Some of them are even well enough to throw their crutches at the doctor.

The struggle against private monopoly is a struggle for, and not against, American business. It is a struggle to preserve individual enterprise and economic freedom.

I believe in individualism. I believe in it in the arts, the sciences and professions. I believe in it in business. I believe in individualism in all of these things—up to the point where the individualist starts to operate at the expense of society. The overwhelming majority of American businessmen do not believe in it beyond that point. We have all suffered in the past from individualism run wild. Society has suffered and business has suffered.

Believing in the solvency of business, the solvency of farmers and the solvency of workers, I believe also in the solvency of Government. Your Government is solvent.

The net Federal debt today is lower in proportion to the income of the Nation and in proportion to the wealth of the Nation than it was on March 4, 1933.

In the future it will become lower still because with the rising tide of national income and national wealth, the very causes of our emergency spending are starting to disappear. Government expenditures are coming down and Government income is going up. The opportunities for private enterprise will continue to expand.

The people of America have no quarrel with business. They insist only that the power of concentrated wealth shall not be abused.

We have come through a hard struggle to preserve democracy in America. Where other Nations in other parts of the world have lost that fight, we have won.

The businessmen of America and all other citizens have joined in a firm resolve to hold the fruits of that victory, to cling to the old ideals and old fundamentals upon which America has grown great.

Questions for Research and Discussion

1. President Roosevelt credits the New Deal recovery programs with the saving of American capitalism. Is that a fair assessment?

2. Did the New Deal solve the Great Depression or did it just hold the line against economic collapse?

3. List the claims FDR made about New Deal benefits for businessmen. Was he correct?

4. The second Agricultural Adjustment Act and the Fair Labor Standards Act were passed after FDR made this speech. How did each of these impact the economic crisis?

5. Compare government spending during the Great Depression and World War II. What was the impact of war spending on the economy?

6. Many critics accused FDR of attempting to replace traditional American business models, yet Roosevelt closes his speech by affirming his identification with "old ideals and old fundamentals." Is this affirmation credible?

Marriner S. Eccles: Government Spending Is Sound: Balancing the Budget Is Not Essential[4]

An Address by the Chairman of the Federal Reserve Board On the National Broadcasting Network Monday, January 23, 1939

A week ago tonight Senator Byrd of Virginia spoke over this station on "Government Spending." I am grateful to the National Radio Forum, conducted under the auspices of the *Washington Evening Star*, for this opportunity to speak to you on the same general subject.

What I say represents my own viewpoint as it is now and as it has been consistently for more than eight years. I do not speak for the Board of Governors or for the Federal Reserve System. I speak merely as one who has had more than twenty years of practical experience in banking as well as in various business and agricultural enterprises, and who happens to occupy a public office concerned with banking, fiscal and monetary problems. These are economic problems and I have always approached them from an economic rather than from a political standpoint. In fact, I cannot approach these questions from any other standpoint for I have never taken an active part in politics and I have never sought a public office.

The greatest of all domestic problems before this country today is to find steady jobs in private enterprise for all of our unemployed who are able and willing to work.

The fundamental issue between Senator Byrd and myself is whether the Government can and should contribute to bringing about an increase in private employment by borrowing idle money, and lending and spending it, at a time like the present when there are millions of people who cannot find jobs in private industry, when there is an abundance of natural resources, unused productive facilities of all kinds, and billions of savings and of bank credit waiting to be used.

In the limited time at my disposal tonight, I cannot deal with all of the misconceptions of my position under which Senator Byrd evidently labored in his recent statements on this subject. This I expect to do by letter at an early date. The issue between the Senator and myself is not personal, and I ascribe to him, as he does to me, the fullest degree of sincerity.

At the outset, I want to clear away some of the more glaring misconceptions of my views. I *do not* believe in government spending at any time for spending's sake. I *do* believe in government deficit-spending in depression periods as a supplement and stimulant to private spending, using only the man power, materials, and money that otherwise would be idle, and using them only in a way that avoids competition with private enterprise. I believe that inefficiency and waste should be eliminated. Government should get the maximum value for the money it spends, recognizing the size and inherent difficulties of the unemployment and relief problem—the objective always being a maximum of private employment. I abhor politics and favoritism in any phase of government expenditures. I am as anxious as anyone to see the Federal budget balanced. In my judgment this cannot be accomplished until the national income is higher than it will be this year. I do not believe it can be done at this time either by reducing government expenditures or by increasing Federal taxes, particularly those that bear most heavily upon consumption. I believe that the only way the budget can be brought into balance is through increased Federal revenue from an increased national income.

I am just as much against inflation as I am against deflation. However, we do not want to stay in a perpetual deflation because of fear of inflation. Inflation can and should be prevented, and this can be done by giving adequate powers to the Treasury and the Federal Reserve System. I do not see how it would be possible to have a dangerous general inflation so long as we have a large amount of idle men and unused resources. Long before inflation could develop, we would have a volume of business activity that would increase the national income to a point where the budget could easily be balanced. I do not believe, and I have never said, that the Federal debt should continue to grow indefinitely and no part of it ever paid. I do believe that it cannot safely be reduced except when national income is high and when private debt is expanding. Reduction of government debt at such a time would tend to counteract any trend toward inflation that might develop, just as expansion of the government debt during depression tends to offset deflationary developments.

I realize that government spending is not a cure-all or a remedy for all of our problems or for special conditions that may be retarding private employment and investment. Everything should be done to bring about a prompt solution of these problems. In the meantime, I can see no practical alternative except to sustain purchasing power through public employment until private employment substantially increases.

The viewpoint which I have outlined relative to the need for government spending is strongly opposed by Senator Byrd, by most of the press, and by many of the bankers and large business interests of the country today. Most of them still demand, as they did at the bottom of the depression in 1932, that government expenditures be cut and that the Federal budget be brought into balance in order to re-establish confidence. Only in this way, they believe, will jobs be provided in private enterprise.

I quite understand why so many of our bankers and businessmen have this viewpoint, for I did also until about 1929. I knew from experience that private investment had led the way out of past depressions without government spending.

In the face of fundamental changes that have come over our economy—changes that I think many of our businessmen and bankers either have not fully perceived or fully appraised—I can no longer bring myself to believe that the nation can risk stopping its support to the unemployed in the hope or expectation that, upon doing so, private enterprise will move forward on any scale sufficient to give them jobs.

To discuss these fundamental changes adequately, would take more time than I have on the air. I can only remind you that we are no longer a nation with rapidly expanding markets at home and abroad, as we were through most of our history. We are no longer pushing our frontiers westward and opening up vast new territories to settlement. We no longer have great incoming tides of immigration. The day has passed when millions can follow Horace Greeley's advice and go West when they fail to find employment or opportunity in the populous eastern centers. The era of railroad expansion has come to an end.

We no longer have expanding foreign markets. We are now a creditor and not a debtor nation, as we were before the war. We are no longer willing to lend billions of dollars abroad, as we did in the '20's, to enable foreigners to absorb American products.

The rapid growth of the automobile and related industries, which were important factors in the expansion of the '20's, has been greatly slowed down. There are not immediate visible vast markets awaiting production by existing industry. Nor does new invention and new industry, which I should especially like to see encouraged and stimulated, hold out prospects for enough investment and employment to absorb great numbers of the unemployed at this time.

If I felt that the government were risking a dangerous inflation, or that it could not afford the expenditures, because of the size of the national debt, I would not advocate a continuance of the present stimulus—on the basis of a deficit. I do not share these fears. I do not agree with those who believe, as Senator Byrd does, that the government is like an individual in its fiscal affairs and, therefore, should not spend more than its income, but should always balance its budget and keep out of debt.

I do not scorn the old precepts of thrift and frugality, as the Senator has said. One of the most familiar of these time-honored sayings is: "neither a borrower nor a lender be." Admirable as these maxims are for the individual, they cannot be applied, realistically to business or to the nation. If there were no borrowing or lending in the business world, there would be no business except by the primitive methods of barter. Borrowing and lending means creating debt. We have never had a period of prosperity without an expansion of debt. Conversely, we have never had a period of deflation without a contraction of debt.

I would like to see more equities and fewer debt forms in our economy, but it operates now very largely by the process of debts being created and extinguished. To recognize that debt expands with prosperity, which we all favor, does not mean that one is in favor of debt, but only that under our system we cannot have the prosperity which we all want without the debts which we all dislike.

It is beyond dispute, I think, that as debt contracts or expands, business activity rises and falls and that national income increases or decreases in relatively greater volume. Thus from 1929 to 1933, total debts, both public and private, contracted by 14 percent. Yet at the same time national income fell by more than 50 percent. As a result, the private debt structure, even though contracted, was so large in relation to the diminished national income that debts became insupportable. Hence, our entire financial structure collapsed and general economic paralysis resulted.

Had the government been like an individual, nothing could have been to help the situation. We ultimately found that only the government, under such conditions as existed, was able by its lending and spending to stop the tide of deflation and bring about the upturn that we have since had, though it is still far short of the goal of full recovery. However, acting on the advice of the business and financial leaders of the country, the government did attempt to act like an individual from 1930 until the end of 1933 on the theory that the government could not afford to do otherwise, and that in order to maintain confidence and keep money sound, it must balance the budget. Most of you haven't forgotten the results.

Of course, the government could not balance its budget because the incomes and profits of the taxpayers continued to fall or to disappear. Therefore, the government's revenues fell faster than it was possible to reduce expenses. Consequently, it had a total deficit of more than $7 billions for the calendar years of 1931, 1932, and 1933, while it was pursuing the policy advocated by those who believe as Senator Byrd does. And, mind you, all this happened during the period when everything was being done that business leaders thought would encourage business, even to the extent of setting up the RFC to provide money to support the private financial structure. At the same time, the same business and financial leaders, some of whom were the beneficiaries of government lending, contended that the government's credit was such that it could not afford to come to the financial assistance of millions of unemployed through creation of beneficial public work in the absence of private work.

The deficits incurred in 1931, 1932, and 1933 cannot be considered as being of what Senator Byrd chooses to call the "pump-priming" variety, because they resulted largely from decreased Federal revenues rather than from increased government expenditures. During this period we had no increase in the national income. In fact, during this period the sum of the annual losses in the national income, compared with the 1929 level, amounted to $120 billions. This staggering loss, to which Senator Byrd makes no reference, resulted from our failure to utilize our idle human and material resources. This is the kind of waste that the nation can ill afford. We had no increase in the national income until a comprehensive lending and spending program was launched, beginning in 1934, giving aid to farmers and home owners and creating jobs through relief and public works.

Let us now consider the years 1934–1937, inclusive. In this period, the government made cash loans and expenditures, including the soldiers' bonus, of $11 billions more than it collected, including payroll taxes. This largely resulted from a deliberate policy of stimulating recovery in private activity. During this period, the national income rose from approximately $40 billions in 1933 to about $70 billions in 1937. the combined increases in the national income for these four years, as compared with 1933, aggregated $70 billions, or more than six times the government's cash deficit of $11 billions for the same period.

And then what happened? During the year 1937, the government contributed about $3 billions less to the buying power of the public than it did in the year 1936, so that its cash receipts were only about $400 millions less than it spent. This too rapid withdrawal of the government's stimulus was accompanied by other important factors, including sharply increased construction costs, large scale speculative inventory buying, a too rapid expansion of short-term installment credit, serious conflicts between capital and labor, and a widening spread between agricultural and industrial prices. The result was another period of rapid deflation in the fall of 1937, which continued until the present spending program of the government was begun last summer. The national income has been rising steadily ever since that time.

In the light of this record of the last nine years—a record which Senator Byrd denounces as one of "fiscal insanity"—does it seem reasonable to believe that, as the Senator said in his letter to me—and I quote—"For every dollar the government borrows and spends in pump-priming, private enterprise is deterred from spending two"? If Senator Byrd really believes this, he should be exerting all of his influence in fighting for an immediate, instead of a gradual, balancing of the budget, in order to reduce government expenditures by at least $3 billions. Such a reduction, according to his unequivocal statement, would bring about an expansion in spending by private enterprise of $6 billions a year. I am convinced that the exact opposite is true. Accordingly,

I believe that the country can well afford to have the government continue its stimulus to consumption and thus to business at this juncture.

We might have had about the same results with less government spending had some of it been directed into other channels or had it been better timed, or if private activity had not felt that there were deterrents due to government policy, but of one thing I am certain—whatever the deterrents have been, government spending has not been one of them.

As to the burden of the government debt on our children and our children's children, which also disturbs the Senator, if they reduce the national debt it will probably be because their national income justified the reduction, and it will be no more of a burden on them than was the reduction of nine billions of the war debt during the '20's. In fact, we could have paid off much more of the war debt, if we had not had three major income tax reductions which helped to encourage stock market speculation and the making of uncollectible foreign loans.

Why not worry also about the burden of all of the private debts on our children and their children, because these debts will also be passed along to future generations who will have to pay the cost of servicing or paying these debts just as in the case of the government debt. We should know that all debts, both public and private, are passed along from one generation to the next, just as all assets, both public and private, are handed down from one generation to the next. It may be that Senator Byrd would be less worried if there were no debts, but in that case, there would be no banks, insurance companies, or other financial institutions.

The Senator has warned you that the total debt of all public bodies in the United States now amounts to $430 for every man, woman and child, that it is a mortgage on you and your property, and that your children and grandchildren will have to pay off this mortgage. But he failed to tell you who owns the mortgage. You, of course know that it is owned by all of the people and amounts to an average of exactly $430 owed to every man, woman, and child. In other words, all of the people are borrowing through their public bodies from all of the people.

The whole problem of internal debt, public and private, must be considered in relationship to the total real wealth of the nation. Our total debts are great or small, depending upon total national income. The British public debt a century ago was equal to $4 billions. At the present time it is $40 billions, or ten times greater. Their debt has grown, but the income of the British people has grown much faster than the debt. While doubtless it would be better for them if they had less public debt, it cannot be said that the debt has either bankrupted or impoverished the British nation, because their standard of living has increased during this entire period.

Now make no mistake, I am not advocating ever-increasing debt, but I am merely pointing out that we should see the problem of debt in its true perspective. I do not think that alarmist talk about it is calculated to help recovery or to induce private capital to go to work.

As to the argument that the British achieved recovery by balancing their budget, it would be well for those who cite this to remember that while our national income was falling 50 percent, their government never permitted theirs to fall more than 10 percent, and that British rates of taxation, if applied to the United States, would very likely balance our budget. Their balanced budget is not due to the fact that they spend proportionately less than we do, but because their income and inheritance taxes are relatively much higher.

Individuals and corporations may become bankrupt, but no nation, having the human and material resources of the United States, need impoverish itself by borrowing from itself. The only way that we can impoverish ourselves is by failing to utilize our idle man power, resources, productive facilities, and money in the production of real wealth.

I have been talking so far about the economic aspects of the problem of government fiscal policy. In conclusion, I would like to say a word about the human or fundamental aspect of this problem.

We did not hesitate to have the government borrow billions of dollars to protect this country against a foreign enemy during the World War. In one year alone we created a deficit of $13 billions, as much as the entire cash deficit of the government during the past five years. We are again proposing to spend billions for preparedness. Yet at the same time, many are quibbling about 150 million dollars necessary to help protect our human resources.

The same government credit than can be used to protect human lives in time of war against the encroachment of a foreign enemy can also be used in times of peace to protect these human lives against demoralization and despair. There is no more limitation upon a government's ability to fight a depression than there is to fight a war. Both depend upon our human and material resources, brains, and courage—and upon nothing else.

The danger for the future of democracy comes from within as well as from without. The leadership of this country, both in government and in business, must realize that if the American liberal tradition is to be preserved, then, for the millions of our citizens, the right to work must also be preserved.

Questions for Research and Discussion

1. Is Marriner Eccles correct when he asserts that government spending is sound in protecting the lives of individuals in a crisis of economic collapse? Why or why not?

2. In the economic crisis of 2008–2010, Paul Krugman, Nobel Prize economist, criticized President Obama for spending far too little in the economic stimulus package. Was he correct?

3. What statistical data is basic in determining if stimulus spending should be increased?

4. How did government spending to fight the Great Depression compare with spending to fight the Rome-Berlin-Tokyo Axis?

5. Did government spending in World War II solve the Great Depression?

6. If we express WW II spending in terms of current dollars, how many trillions were spent?

7. Describe trends in government spending during the Reagan, George H. W. Bush, Clinton, and George W. Bush years. Does our huge national debt limit our capacity to help the homeless, the elderly, and the unemployed in the economic crisis of 2008?

Defenders of the Status Quo

Herbert Hoover: A Holy Crusade for Liberty[5]

An Address by the Former President of the United States
At the Republican National Convention, Cleveland, Ohio
June 10, 1936

In this room rests the greatest responsibility that has come to a body of Americans in three generations. In the lesser sense this is a convention of a great political party. But in the larger sense it is a convention of Americans to determine the fate of those ideals for which this nation was founded. That far transcends all partisanship.

There are elemental currents which make or break the fate of nations. There is a moral purpose in the universe. Those forces which affect the vitality and the soul of a people will control its destinies. The sum of years of public service in these currents is the overwhelming conviction of their transcendent importance over the more transitory, even though difficult, issues of national life.

I have given about four years to research into the New Deal, trying to determine what its ultimate objectives were, what sort of a system it is imposing on this country.

To some people it appears to be a strange interlude in American history in that it has no philosophy, that it is sheer opportunism, that it is a muddle of a spoils system, of emotional economics, of reckless adventure, of unctuous claims to a monopoly of human sympathy, of greed for power, of a desire for popular acclaim and an aspiration to make the front pages of the newspapers. That is the most charitable view.

To other people it appears to be a cold-blooded attempt by starry-eyed boys to infect the American people by a mixture of European ideas, flavored with our native predilection to get something for nothing.

You can choose either one you like best. But the first is the road of chaos which leads to the second. Both of these roads lead over the same grim precipice that is the crippling and possibly the destruction of the freedom of men.

Which of these interpretations is accurate is even disputed by alumni of the New Deal who have graduated for conscience's sake or have graduated by request.

In Central Europe the march of Socialist or Fascist dictatorships and their destruction of liberty did not set out with guns and armies. Dictatorships began their ascent to the seats of power through the elections provided by liberal institutions.

Their weapons were promise and hate. They offered the mirage of Utopia to those in distress. They flung the poison of class hatred. They may not have maimed the bodies of men, but they maimed their souls.

The 1932 campaign was a pretty good imitation of this first stage of European tactics. You may recall the promises of the abundant life, the propaganda of hate.

Once seated in office the first demand of these European despotisms was for power and "action." Legislatures were told they "must" delegate their authorities. Their free debate was suppressed. The powers demanded are always the same pattern. They all adopt planned economy. They regimented industry and agriculture. They put the Government into business. They engaged in gigantic Government expenditures. They created vast organizations of spoils henchmen and subsidized dependents. They corrupted currency and credit. They drugged the thinking of the people with propaganda at the people's expense.

If there are any items in this stage in the march of European collectivism that the New Deal has not imitated it must have been an oversight.

But at this point this parallel with Europe halts—at least for the present. The American people should thank Almighty God for the Constitution and the Supreme Court. They should be grateful to a courageous press.

You might contemplate what would have happened if Mr. Roosevelt could have appointed enough Supreme Court justices in the first year of his administration. Suppose these New Deal acts had remained upon the statute books. We would have been a regimented people. Have you any assurance that he will not have the appointments if he is re-elected?

The succeeding stages of violence and outrage by which European despotisms have crushed all liberalism and all freedom have filled our headlines for years.

But what comes next in the United States? Have the New Dealers dropped their ideas of centralization of government? Have they abandoned the notion of regimenting the people into a planned economy? Has that greed for power become cooled by the resistance of a people with a heritage of liberty? Will they resume if they are re-elected?

When we examine the speeches of Tugwell, Wallace, Ickes, and others, we see little indications of repentance.

Let me say this: America is no monarchy where the chief of state is not responsible for his ministers. It has been traditional in our Government since the beginning that the important officials appointed by the President speak in tune with his mind. That is imperative if there is to be intellectual honesty in government. President Roosevelt finds no difficulty in disciplining his officials. Witness the prompt dismissal of those who did not publicly agree with him. The President will not discharge these men on whom his New Deal is dependent. No matter what the new platform of the New Deal party may say, the philosophy of collectivism and that greed for power are in the blood of some part of these men. Do you believe that if re-elected they intend to stand still among the wreckage of their dreams? In the words of Mr. Hopkins, perhaps we are too profanely dumb to understand.

So much for the evidence that the New Deal is a definite attempt to replace the American system of freedom with some sort of European planned existence. But let us assume that the explanation is simply hit-and-run opportunism, spoils system, and muddle.

We can well take a moment to explore the prospects of American ideals of liberty and self-government under that philosophy. We may take only seven short examples:

The Supreme Court has reversed some ten or twelve of the New Deal major enactments. Many of these acts were a violation of the rights of men and of self-government. Despite the sworn duty of the executive and Congress to defend these rights, they have sought to take them into their own hands. That is an attack on the foundations of freedom.

More than this, the independence of Congress, the Supreme Court, and the Executive are pillars at the door of liberty. For three years the word "must" has invaded the independence of Congress. And the Congress has abandoned its responsibility to check even the expenditures of money. They have turned open appropriations into personal power. These are destructions of the very safeguards of free people.

We have seen these gigantic expenditures and this torrent of waste pile up a national debt which two generations cannot repay. One time I told a Democratic Congress that "you cannot spend yourselves into prosperity." You recall that advice did not take then. It hasn't taken yet. Billions have been spent to prime the economic pump. It did employ a horde of paid officials upon the pump handle. We have seen the frantic attempts to find new taxes on the rich. Yet three-quarters of the bill will be sent to the average man and the poor. He and his wife and his grandchildren will be giving a quarter of all their working days to pay taxes. Freedom to work for himself is changed into a slavery of work for the follies of government.

We have seen an explosive inflation of bank credits by this government borrowing. We have seen varied steps toward currency inflation that have already enriched the speculator and deprived the poor. If this is to continue, the end result is the tears and anguish of universal bankruptcy and distress. No democracy in history has survived its final stages.

We have seen the building up of a horde of political officials, we have seen the pressures upon the helpless and destitute to trade political support for relief. Both are a pollution of the very fountains of liberty.

We have seen the most elemental violation of economic law and experience. The New Deal forgets it is solely by production of more goods and more varieties of goods and services that we advance the living and security of men. If we constantly decrease costs and prices and keep up earnings the production of plenty will be more and more widely distributed. These laws may be re-stitched in new phrases so that they are the very shoes of human progress. We had so triumphed in this long climb of mankind toward plenty that we had reached Mount Pisgah where we looked over the promised land of abolished poverty. Then men began to quarrel over the division of the goods. The depression produced by war destruction temporarily checked our march toward the promised land.

Then came the little prophets of the New Deal. They announce the striking solution that the way out is to produce less and to increase prices so the people can buy less. They have kept on providing some new restriction or burden or fright down to a week ago.

At least it has enabled the New Deal to take a few hundred thousand earnest party workers to the promised land. It takes the rest of us for a ride into the wilderness of unemployment.

Can democracy stand the strain of Mother Hubbard economics for long?

Any examination of the economic muddle of the past three years shows the constant thread of price fixing, restriction of production, and drive against small business. That is the soul of monopoly. That has maintained from the N.R.A. to the last tax bill. These are old tricks in new disguise which put shackles upon the freedom of men.

In desperate jumping from one muddle to another we have seen repeated violation or morals and honor in government. Do I need recall the repudiation of obligations, the clipping of the coin, the violation of trust to guard the Constitution and the coercion of the voter? When the standards of honor and morals fail in government, they fail in the people.

There are some moral laws written in a great book. Over all there is the gospel of brotherhood. For the first time in the history of America we have heard the gospel of class hatred preached from the White House. That is human poison far more deadly than fear. Every reader of the history of democracy knows that is the final rock upon which all democracies have been wrecked.

There is the suggestion in the Gospels that it is the meek who will inherit the earth. The New Deal will have little inheritance. There are recommendations as to righteousness for righteousness' sake only. I will not elaborate that.

If all this is the theory and practice of muddle, where has it brought us, even now? We have spent $15,000,000,000 more than the last Republican Administration. We have a debt ten billions greater than even the great war debt. After three years we still have the same number of unemployed that we had at the election of November, 1932. These actions are bringing injury to the well-being of people it purports to serve. It has produced gross reactionarism in the guise of liberalism. And, above all, the New Deal has brought that which George Washington called "alterations which may impair the energy of the system and thus overthrow that which cannot be directly overthrown."

Republicans! After a hundred and fifty years, we have arrived at that hour.

Here where the tablets of human freedom were first handed down, their sacred word has been flouted. Today the stern task is before the Republican party to restore the ark of that covenant to the temple in Washington.

The New Deal may be a revolutionary design to replace the American system with despotism. It may be the dream stuff of a false liberalism. It may be the valor of muddle. Their relationship to each other, however, is exactly the sister ship of the witches who brewed the cauldron of powerful trouble for Macbeth. Their product is the poisoning of Americanism.

The President has constantly reiterated that he will not retreat. For months, to be sure, there has been a strange quiet. Just as the last campaign was fought on promises that have been broken so apparently this campaign is to be slipped through by evasion.

But the American people have the right to know now, while they still have power to act. What is going to be done after election with these measures which the Constitution forbids and the people by their votes have never authorized? What do the New Dealers propose to do with these unstable currencies, unbalanced budgets, debts, and taxes? Fifty words would make it clear. Surely the propaganda agencies which emit half a million words a day could find room for these fifty. I noticed they recently spent three hundred words on how to choose a hat. It is slightly more important to know the fate of a nation.

You have the duty to determine the principles upon which the Republican party will stand. You make the laws of the party. Whether it is within the party or a government, our system is a government of laws and not of men. This party holds its promises.

The immediate task is to set the country on the road of genuine recovery from the paths of instability. We have enough inventions and enough accumulated needs to start the physical rebuilding of America. The day the Republican party can assure right principles we can turn this nation from the demoralization of relief to the contentment of constructive jobs. Herein—and herein alone—is a guaranty of jobs for the 11,000,000 idle based upon realities and not on political claptrap. In the meantime the party which organized efficient relief of the unemployed three years before the New Deal was born will not turn from those in need. That support to distress comes from the conscience and sympathy of a people, not from the New Deal.

Four years ago I stated that the Republican party must undertake progressive reforms from evils exposed by the boom and depression. But I stated our first job was to restore men to work. The New Deal has attempted many reforms. They have delayed recovery. Parts of them are good. Some have failed. Some are tainted with collective ideas. That task must be undertaken anew by the Republican party.

A new danger is created to the republic in that the swing from the foolishness of radicalism will carry us to the selfishness of reaction.

The Republican party must achieve true social betterment. But we must produce measures that will not work confusion and disappointment. We must propose a real approach to social ills, not the prescription for them, by quacks of poison in place of remedy.

Questions for Research and Discussion

1. List former President Hoover's main criticisms of the New Deal. Does he characterize the objectives of the New Deal fairly?

2. Why do you think Hoover uses words such as the "Ark of the Covenant.?" Why does he suggest that New Dealers should repent? Why does he quote from the Gospels?

3. How does Hoover's critique of the New Deal compare to the conservative critiques of the Obama administration?

Robert A. Taft: A Declaration of Republican Principles[6]

An Address by Senator Taft at the National Republican Club
March 18, 1939

The Republican Party today is still the minority party, but the general impression in Washington and throughout the country is that the New Deal tide is rapidly receding, and that the people are again looking to the Republican Party for leadership. It is most important that the Republicans, even though they are still in the opposition, formulate their program on which to appeal to the people for a change of administration, and the Frank Committee has been working on a declaration of Republican principles.

We find an overwhelmingly difficult problem before us. After six years of New Deal rule, after every kind of experiment, and the addition of twenty billion dollars to the national debt, the fundamental problems are still unsolved. More than ten million people are unemployed in the United States today, about three million of them receiving a bare subsistence from W.P.A. Twenty million people are looking to the government for food. Millions more are receiving inadequate wages, and fall in that underprivileged class for whom New Dealers have shed tears in every speech, and to whom they have repeatedly promised prosperity and security. And yet there are more people underprivileged today, more people who have barely enough to live on, or not enough to live on, than there have been at any time except at the very bottom of the depression.

The national income in 1938 was not much more than sixty billion dollars. If we go back ten years, we find a national income of eighty billion dollars, and ten million fewer people among whom to divide it. The average income per individual is thirty percent less than it was in 1928. Of course times are hard.

There can be no absolute proof that this condition has been created or prolonged by the policies of the present Administration, but we have come out of every past depression more quickly, to a higher standard of income, and to greater employment, without measures of the New Deal character. Certainly there is no doubt that the New Deal policies have utterly failed in their objectives.

There can be only one main purpose in any intelligent program today—that it is to improve the conditions of the millions of unemployed, and the other millions who are below a reasonable standard of life. If that problem cannot be solved, our whole republican form of government must admit itself a failure. When we see the conditions which exist in some of our cities, and I have seen them in Ohio as you have seen them in New York, we very quickly lose our pride in the statistics which show a higher average standard of living in the United States than elsewhere. When you see the conditions which social workers see every day, you cannot be surprised that they are eager to adopt any measure which seems to furnish direct assistance to the bitter conditions their charges face, no matter what the other consequences of those measures.

It is a problem which challenges the Yankee ingenuity of the American people, and of course we Republicans claim a little more of that Yankee ingenuity, particularly from Maine and Vermont, than is possessed by the Democrats. The New Deal must have credit for trying every possible remedy which anyone suggested, sound or unsound, and through experimentation they have eliminated a considerable number of their favorite panaceas; at least they have eliminated them in the minds of all reasonable men, even if they themselves are unwilling to abandon them.

The New Deal is such a conglomeration of all kinds of measures that it is interesting for a moment to try to analyze just what it really is. Its objectives undoubtedly were to help the nation, and particularly the lower income groups, but from the beginning it has been motivated apparently by a complete distrust of our entire economic and business system, extending almost to every individual businessman. The assumption was that because a great depression occurred, all of the former principles accepted as the cause for American leadership in the world should be discarded, and this in spite of the fact that the depression was worldwide, and affected many other nations where an entirely different business system existed. There has been no real interest in trying to restore private industry, and the assumption has been that the government could do everything better than it was done before.

This critical attitude extended to the most accepted fiscal principles, such as the belief (which has inspired every past President, Republican and Democratic), that there is a moral obligation to hold government expenses down to revenues, and conduct the United States Government on the same sound business principles which are necessary to avoid bankruptcy in private industry and ultimate repudiation by government.

The President even abandoned the sound currency ideas which have always guided the United States, devalued the dollar under the almost childish Warren theory that this would increase domestic prices, and flirted with the idea of an inflation of the currency. There is no doubt that the New Dealers have a deep-seated distrust of the entire system of individual initiative, free competition, and reward for hard work, ingenuity and daring, which have made America what it is.

They have relied on three types of government activity. The first type consists of direct relief, in different forms, to the lower income groups. Beginning with assistance to the States, which were building up a very satisfactory method of handling relief, a combination of direct and work relief under public-spirited citizen boards, cooperating with private agencies, the New Deal suddenly decided that no one could do the job as well as they could, and as a condition of the financial assistance which was necessary, insisted on complete administrative control. Finding this too much of a job, they returned the unemployables to the States, and undertook to provide work relief for all employables. That job has never been completely done, and the expense is so tremendous that it probably never will be. The attempt to administer from Washington a great work relief program throughout the entire United States has resulted in inefficiency, politics, and a vast expense which threatens a complete bankruptcy of the federal government. Other relief measures are the C.C.C., the N.Y.A., the Farm Security Administration, and other minor agencies.

The second type of New Deal activity includes the government regulatory measures, which attempt to raise the income of this group or that group by controlling prices, wages, hours and practices throughout the United States. Such were the N.R.A. and the A.A.A. Such are the laws regulating agriculture today, the Guffey Coal Act, the Wage-Hour Law. This type of law has completely failed in its purpose. Farm prices are as low today as they were five and one-half years ago, before the agricultural control measures began. The administration of the Guffey Coal Act for two years has done no more than impose expense on the industry. The Wage-Hour Law threatens to drive hundreds of people out of small business, and may do more harm than good. Attempts to fix prices have been frequent in history throughout the world. Without questioning the wisdom of the purposes sought, experience has shown, as in the case of the Brazil coffee control and the East Indian rubber control, that such attempts are doomed to failure. Our own experience does not contradict that conclusion.

Furthermore, this type of law is one of the most discouraging to private enterprise. No man can tell when the government may step into his business, and nullify all of the effort and energy and ingenuity he may have shown in developing that business. He is hounded by inspectors, excessive regulation, reports, and red tape. Many have gone out of business, and many have stayed out of business because they could not feel certain that with all this government regulation they might not be utterly wasting their time and their money.

The other type of New Deal experiment is direct government business activity in fields where the government thinks that private enterprise has fallen down on its job. Of this character are the T.V.A., the Rural Electrification Administration, the lending agencies extending government credit to homeowners and farm owners, the building of canals and other self-liquidating public works. Unquestionably some of this activity is justified, though usually the reason that private capital has failed to enter the field is because the enterprise is unprofitable in spite of the glowing prospectus of some government department.

But there are some unprofitable things which a government should start, and governments always have done something of this kind. It is a question of degree. It is very doubtful in my mind whether the T.V.A. ever was justified in view of the development of public utilities in the Tennessee Valley, but now we have it, and have to operate it to the best advantage. Private capital could not under-take the building of canals, but neither should the government unless they are economically sound, and justified by the tolls which can be collected.

The lending of funds to stimulate the building industry under the F.H.A. seems to be justified as an emergency matter. And so also the Federal Farm Loan Banks fill a need which for one reason or another private capital could not reach. In this lending field, however, the government, as far as possible, should create a set-up which can be taken over by private lending agencies under government supervision, and in general there should be no further extension of government activity and competition unless it is absolutely necessary.

I have pointed out that the New Deal seemed to be inspired with a hostility to the entire pre-existing American economic system. The result is that these three types of measures which I have described have not been administered with any special care to preserve the best features of private industry, and encourage it to bring about recovery. The relief measures have been inefficient and expensive. They have resulted in a tremendous burden of taxation, which bears down on the man who is trying to make his own living. There has been no effort to preserve conditions under which a man, striving for a private job and doing his job well, shall be encouraged and preferred to the man on W.P.A. The other two types of measures, government regulation and government competition, have directly discouraged private activity of every kind. More men have gone out of business in the last five years than have gone into business, because of the complete uncertainty whether they can survive a constant government interference.

Now we are told that everything has changed, and the administration is going to treat business like human beings. The very adoption of a so-called policy of appeasement admits that American businessmen and men who would like to go into business have been badgered and discouraged to an extent which requires an absolute reversal of government policy. Secretary Hopkins made a speech in Des Moines, and Secretary Morgenthau is having mottoes hung in the offices of the Treasury Department with the legend "Does it help recovery?"

But, as the old saying goes, "fine words butter no parsnips." The appeasement policy is like the famous "breathing spell for business," only a smoke-screen to conceal the real policies of the Administration. It cannot be sincere. Whenever any question of action arises, the President is just as determined in his previous policies as he ever has been before.

Within the last few days Secretary Morgenthau and Secretary Wallace have argued for a continuation of the President's power to devalue the dollar, although a stable currency is one of the greatest necessities for mental reassurance to American business. The President himself has indicated that he wishes a continuation of his power to issue three billion dollars in greenbacks, a power which he says is a convenient club in his closet. A club against whom? Against Congress? Against the economic royalists, in case the President chooses to blame them for depressed prices? Nothing would be more calamitous to business revival than the sudden decision of the President to issue billions of paper greenbacks with no property whatever behind them. How easy for the President to give up these monetary powers, which hang over the business world like the sword of Damocles!

Businessmen are agreed that the amendment of the National Labor Relations Act would do much to reassure manufacturers, and stimulate additional investment in plant. The American Federation of Labor has demanded an immediate hearing on its amendments. Yet up to this time the President and the C.I.O. have successfully prevented the setting of any date even for hearings on the amendments already introduced before the Committee on Education and Labor of the Senate.

If taxes cannot be reduced, at least an increase can be prevented. The payroll tax is today the most burdensome tax on business, and incidentally a bonus to get rid of labor and install machinery and increase unemployment. The tax is already five percent of the payroll, and goes up to six percent the first of next January. This increase is wholly unnecessary except to build up an imaginary reserve to astronomical figures, and provide the New Deal with cash to pay deficits. Senator Vandenberg has introduced an amendment to suspend the going into effect of this increase, but the Administration is definitely opposed.

The S.E.C. still takes the attitude that businessmen are presumptively crooks. Only this week a committee suggesting minor modifications in the Securities Law, the merit of which I do not know, was met by a blast from Mr. Douglas, characterizing their plan as a "phony," and implying that their only interest was to line their own pockets at the expense of the investors. The S.E.C. is still pressing for a bill giving it additional regulatory powers over the drafting of trust indentures and the private business negotiations involved in such indentures. The appeasement policy is completely insincere. The present administration has no confidence in the efficacy of private business activity. While their policy continues, it is impossible to achieve any real progress towards the elimination of unemployment.

What then should be the Republican program? It must combine a policy of encouragement to private industry, which can put millions of men to work, with sincere and effective administration of relief measures to assist directly the lower income groups. It must recognize the absolute necessity of relief measures in this country for many years to come. Before the great depression it was reasonable to hope that our economic system had reached a point where government help was unnecessary except in cases of misfortune. It was reasonable to hope that a man who worked diligently during his active life could provide a home and an income for his old age. But the depression of 1929 to 1932 showed us that our system had not reached that point. Even if we eliminated unemployment, the fact remains that many people must work at poor jobs, the product of which is of so little value that the rest of the population will not pay them an adequate living. And so we must assist the lower income groups by direct relief, by work relief, by old age pensions, by unemployment insurance, and by some form of housing subsidy.

But the administration of this relief must be carried on with the greatest care, that it may not destroy our entire American system, and put the whole population on relief. It must be carried on with economy, because the cost of supporting those who do not work is undoubtedly borne by those who are working. The return from capital will never support but a small proportion of the population. The greatest part of the cost of relief can only come from the income of those who are actually working, and if we impose too heavy a burden on that income, there will no longer be any incentive to work, and certainly no incentive to put other men to work.

I think we must recognize, after all, that relief will never do more than provide a bare living, and will never be a satisfactory substitute for real work in private industry. Old age pensions can never be so high as to be a satisfactory substitute for a house and a reasonable income, saved by the effort of the family which has worked successfully. We see today that we have reached the limit of popular approval of further expenditures for W.P.A., and if we were raising by taxation our entire budget, we would find the popular opposition even stronger. And it is right that it should be so, because the burden of supporting those who do not work cannot be allowed to grow to a point at which it will discourage all initiative and all effort on the part of the other two-thirds of the population.

For the same reason, the relief agencies must be administered so that those on relief are not better off than the people who are working. A man who has saved and built his home should certainly be better off than the man who has saved nothing. He should be better off than the man who has the good fortune to live in a subsidized apartment house built by the government.

In short, in administering relief, we must recognize that it is only a palliative, only a stop-gap, and that it is not an end in itself, as many of our New Deal friends seem to think.

In the second place, we must take every possible measure to cure the unemployment problem. It can only be cured by more jobs in private industry. We must, therefore, take every possible measure to encourage people to put their time and money again into the development of private industry. We must see that there is an incentive and a reward for initiative, hard work, and persistence. The problem is partly psychological and partly practical. The people must feel again that the making of a deserved profit is not a crime, but a merit. They must feel again that the government is interested in the prosperity of the businessman. They must feel again that the government does not regard every businessman as a potential crook.

But there must be more than mental reassurance. There must be an abandonment as far as possible of government fixing of prices, wages, and business practices. Americans must be assured that they will not be met by government competition in their field of business activity. They must feel that government activity will be confined to keeping their markets open, free and competitive, so that they will have an equal chance with their little neighbor or their big neighbor. They must feel that government expenses will be held down as far as possible, so that the tax burdens may not deprive them of the fruits of their most successful efforts. They would like to know that the currency is stable, the government's fiscal policy sound, and all danger of inflation of the currency removed.

If we can restore business activity to the conditions which existed in 1928, we would have a national income of ninety billion dollars, nearly fifty percent more than we have today. If it could be done then, why can't it be done now? If there were any such increase in income in this country, millions of men would be employed, not only in manufacture, but in transportation, in distribution, in agriculture, and in mining. Certainly the greater part of those unemployed today would reach the goal of real jobs. Taxes can be reduced. We can reduce the payroll tax today, and still take care of all present requirements. We can cut down the cost of every government department, and eliminate a reasonable number or make them self-supporting. The return of relief to local administration, with a liberal federal grant, will still cost the federal government much less than the present W.P.A. expenditure, amounting to more than two billion dollars this year. I do not underestimate the difficulty of doing it, and it is almost impossible for Congress to do it against the opposition of an extravagant executive, whose party still controls both branches of Congress and is opposed to cutting down the present expanded functions of the federal government. Its cost can certainly be reduced to seven billion dollars, twice what it was in the days of Hoover, and a reasonable increase of prosperity would provide the taxes to balance the budget.

But prosperity can only be brought about by increased production. This country was built up by millions of men, starting new enterprises, putting their time and money into some machine shop, or store, or farm, or any one of a thousand commercial activities. Perhaps they could employ two men, then ten men, then hundreds, and in the case of the great industries, finally thousands or hundreds of thousands. Employment increased steadily for one hundred and fifty years, not by arbitrary building up of consumers' purchasing power, but by encouraging production and putting men to work. The theory that relief payments stimulate production is disproved by our own experience.

We hear a good deal today about the necessity of lending more money to little business and railroads and other enterprises; but it isn't loans that are needed by any business enterprise I know of. If they are entitled to borrow, they can borrow today from the banks. What they need is more capital, more people willing to put their money into stocks, more people willing to put their time and energy and money into building up new enterprises and developing new products, more people willing to abandon the low fixed return from government bonds for the chance of a material profit from business enterprise.

This was the way America was built up, and the only way to resume it is to assure people again that government will not interfere with their normal and reasonable efforts to make a living, and raise themselves and their families to a condition a little better than that of their neighbors; that government will not take away from them the profit which they make; that reasonable success will receive the recognition it deserves, at least from their friends and neighbors.

If we can stop spending money now, if we can stop tremendous expansion of government activity, regulation and taxation, it is not too late to resume the progress which made this country the envy of the world; but if we continue for six years more the course which we have pursued, it is a bold man who will say that we can restore then prosperity under a democratic form of government.

Questions for Research and Discussion

1. What did Senator Taft say Republican principles were?

2. What were the most convincing parts of Taft's speech, his critique of the New Deal, or his enunciation of Republican principles?

3. Taft said that New Dealers had a "deep seated distrust" of the American system. Is that true?

4. Senator Taft attempted to win the Republican nomination for President in 1940. Republicans nominated Wendell Willkie in that year. Why do you think they chose Willkie over Taft?

Debate Three

The Crisis of McCarthyism: Three Views on Defeating Communism

Historical Notes

On January 20, 1950, Senator Joseph R. McCarthy delivered his first speech in the Senate on alleged Communists in the State Department.

On March 21, 1950, Senator McCarthy called Owen Lattimore, former State Department adviser, a top Russian agent.

In a speech on the Senate floor, June 14, 1951, McCarthy charged that Secretary of State George C. Marshall was an instrument of the Soviet conspiracy.

On August 31, 1953, McCarthy shifted his investigative focus from the State Department to the Army. The Army-McCarthy hearings ended on June 17, 1954.

On December 2, 1954, the U. S. Senate voted to condemn Senator McCarthy with the word "censure" removed from the final resolution.

On May 2, 1957, McCarthy died at Bethesda Naval Hospital, of acute hepatitis, a condition exacerbated by heavy drinking. He is buried in St Mary's Cemetery at Appleton, Wisconsin.

Joseph R. McCarthy: Communists in the State Department Must Be Rooted Out[7]

The Senator's First Speech on Communists in the State Department
Delivered in the United States Senate
January 20, 1950

Mr. McCARTHY. Mr. President, I wish to discuss a subject tonight which concerns me more than does any other subject I have ever discussed before this body, and perhaps more than any other subject I shall ever have the good fortune to discuss in the future. It not only concerns me, but it disturbs and frightens me.

About 10 days ago, at Wheeling, W. Va., in making a Lincoln Day speech, I made the statement that there are presently in the State Department a very sizable group of active Communists. I made the further statement, Mr. President, that of one small group which had been screened by the President's own security agency, the State Department refused to discharge approximately 200 of those individuals.

The Secretary of State promptly denied my statement and said there was not a single Communist in the State Department. I thereafter sent a telegram to the President, which I should like to read at this time:

President Harry S. Truman,

White House, Washington, D.C.:

In the Lincoln Day speech at Wheeling Thursday night I stated that the State Department harbors a nest of Communists and Communist sympathizers who are helping to shape our foreign policy. I further stated that I have in my possession the names of 57 Communists who are in the State Department at present. A State Department spokesman promptly denied this, claiming that there is not a single Communist in the Department. You can convince yourself of the falsity of the State Department claim very easily. You will recall that you personally appointed a board to screen State Department employees for the purpose of weeding out fellow travelers—men whom the board considered dangerous to the security of this Nation. Your board did a painstaking job, and named hundreds which had been listed as dangerous to the security of the Nation, because of communistic connections.

While the records are not available to me, I know absolutely of one group of approximately 300 certified to the Secretary for discharge because of communism. He actually only discharged approximately 80. I understand that this was done after lengthy consultation with the now-convicted traitor, Alger Hiss. I would, suggest, therefore, Mr. President, that you simply pick up your phone and ask Mr. Acheson how many of those whom your board had labeled as dangerous Communists he failed to discharge. The day the House Un-American Activities Committee exposed Alger Hiss as an important link in an international Communist spy ring you signed an order forbidding the State Department's giving any information in regard to the disloyalty or the communistic connections of anyone in that Department to the Congress.

Despite this State Department blackout, we have been able to compile a list of 57 Communists in the State Department. This list is available to you but you can get a much longer list by ordering Secretary Acheson to give you a list of those whom your own board listed as being disloyal and who are still working in the State Department. I believe the following is the minimum which can be expected of you in this case.

1. That you demand that Acheson give you and the proper congressional committee the names and a complete report on all of those who were placed in the Department by Alger Hiss, and all of those still working in the State Department who were listed by your board as bad security risks because of their communistic connections.

2. That you promptly revoke the order in which you provided under no circumstances could a congressional committee obtain any information or help in exposing Communists.

Failure on your part will label the Democratic Party of being the bedfellow of international communism. Certainly this label is not deserved by the hundreds of thousands of loyal American Democrats throughout the Nation, and by the sizable number of able loyal Democrats in both the Senate and the House.

Mr. President, the only answer I have received to this telegram was the statement by the President at his press conference to the effect that there was not a word of truth in the telegram.

Subsequently, the Democratic leader of the Senate—at least, the alleged leader—made a speech in Chicago in which he repeated substantially what the President said, except that he went one step further and stated:

If I had said the nasty things that McCarthy has about the State Department, I would be ashamed all my life.

He also said there was not a word of truth in my charge. I think it is unfortunate, not because I am concerned with what the senior Senator from Illinois happens to think, but because he occupies such an important position. I believe, if we are going to root out the fifth column in the State Department, we should have the wholehearted cooperation of both Democrats and Republicans—

Mr. LUCAS. Mr. President, will the Senator yield?

Mr. McCARTHY. Wait until I finish. If the Senator will stay with me for the next few hours, he will learn a great many facts. I have never refused to yield to any Senator, and I do not intend to refuse. The Senator from Illinois will have full time in which to answer any question he wishes to ask, but let me first finish my sentence.

I started to say that I think it is especially bad because it indicates a pre-conceived decision not to work with us in attempting to ferret out communists. I do not feel that the Democratic Party has control of the executive branch of the Government any more. If it had, with the very able Members on the other side of the aisle, we would not find the picture which I intend to disclose. I think a group of twisted-thinking intellectuals have taken over the Democratic Party.

I shall be glad now to yield to the Senator from Illinois.

Mr. LUCAS. Mr. President, I should like to say to the Senator that there is no one in the Senate or in the country who is any more opposed to Communist domination of any nation or Communist infiltration into any country than is the Senator from Illinois. What I am asking the Senator to do— and I hope he will do it, and the country wants him to do it—is to follow through with the speech which he made in Wheeling, W. Va., in which he stated more than 200 persons working in the State Department were known to the Secretary of State to be members of the Communist Party. If the Senator made that statement—and that is what has been reported—I want him to name those Communists. If there are card-carrying Communists in the State Department, the Senator from Illinois will go along with the Senator from Wisconsin in any way possible to remove those Communists from the rolls.

The Senator does not have to do as he did in Salt Lake City and say, "I am not charging these four people with being Communists." The Senator is privileged to name them all in the Senate, and if those people are not Communists he will be protected. That is all I want the Senator to do. If the Senator names those 205 card-carrying Communists, and he proves to be right, the Senator from Illinois will apologize for anything he has said about the Senator from Wisconsin.

Mr. McCARTHY. I wish to thank the distinguished Senator from Illinois for his views, but I should like to assure him that I will not say anything on the Senate floor which I will not say off the floor. On the day when I take advantage of the security we have on the Senate floor, on that day I will resign from the Senate. Anything I say on the floor of the Senate at any time will be repeated off the floor.

Mr. LUCAS. Mr. President, will the Senator yield?

Mr. McCARTHY. Not until I have finished answering the question of the Senator from Illinois. The Senator called my attention to something, and I am glad he did; otherwise I might have over-looked it. Incidentally, the speech in Reno, Nev., and that in Wheeling, W. Va., were recorded, so there is no question about what I said. I do not believe I mentioned the figure 205. I believe I said "over 200." The President said, "It is just a No. There is nothing to it."

I have before me a letter which was reproduced in the CONGRESSIONAL RECORD on August 1, 1946, at page A4892. It is a letter from James F. Byrnes, former Secretary of State. It deals with the screening of the first group, of about 3,000. There were a great number of subsequent screenings. This was the beginning.

Mr. LUCAS. Mr. President, will the Senator yield?

Mr. McCARTHY. Please let me finish. The senator will have all the time in the world to ask questions, and I shall be very glad to yield to the Senator for that purpose, and he can even make short speeches and take all the time he wants.

Mr. LUCAS. Mr. President, the Senator from Illinois—

Mr. McCARTHY. I do not yield at this time.

The PRESIDING OFFICER. The Senator from Wisconsin declines to yield.

Mr. McCARTHY. The letter deals with the first group of 3,000 which was screened. The President—and I think wisely so—set up a board to screen the employees who were coming to the State Department from the various war agencies of the War Department. There were thousands of unusual characters in some of those war agencies. Former Secretary Byrnes in his letter, which is reproduced in the CONGRESSIONAL RECORD, says this:

Pursuant to Executive order, approximately 4,000 employees have been transferred to the Department of State from various war agencies such as the OSS, FEA, OWI, OIAA, and so forth. Of these 4,000 employees, the case histories of approximately 3,000 have been subjected to a preliminary examination as a result of which a recommendation against permanent employment has been made in 285 cases by the screening committee to which you refer in your letter.

In other words, former Secretary Byrnes said that 285 of those men are unsafe risks. He goes on to say that of that number only 79 have been removed. Of the 57 I mentioned some are from the group of 205, and some are from subsequent groups which have been screened but not discharged.

I might say in that connection that the investigative agency of the State Department has done an excellent job. The files show that they went into great detail labeling Communists as such. The only trouble is that after the investigative agency had properly labeled these men Communists, the State Department refused to discharge them. I shall give detailed cases. . . .

Questions for Research and Discussion

1. What were some of Senator McCarthy's charges against the Roosevelt and Truman administrations? How did Truman respond? Was Truman's response to McCarthy effective?

2. What were some of Senator McCarthy's charges against the Eisenhower administration? How did Eisenhower respond?

3. Was Senator McCarthy's characterizations of General George C. Marshall justified?

4. Was Senator Joseph McCarthy a credible figure?

Franklin D. Roosevelt: Facing Communism: The True Conservative Is Liberal[8]

An Address at the New York State Democratic Convention at Syracuse
September 29, 1936

Historical Note

This is the response, in the election of 1936, by Franklin D. Roosevelt, to those who called him he a Marxist, a Socialist, or a Communist.

Even though FDR had passed away before the era of McCarthyism, Senator McCarthy made serious charges that reflected on the Roosevelt and-Truman administrations. FDR's response, to those who called him names in 1936, is also an answer to Senator McCarthy as well.

Tonight you and I join forces for the 1936 campaign. We enter it with confidence. Never was there greater need for fidelity to the underlying conception of Americanism than there is today. And once again it is given to our party to carry the message of that Americanism to the people.

The task on our part is twofold: First, as simple patriotism requires, to separate the false from the real issues; and secondly, with facts and without rancor, to clarify the real problems for the American public.

There will be—there are—many false issues. In that respect, this will be no different from other campaigns.

Partisans, not willing to face realities, will drag out red herrings, as they have always done, to divert attention from the trail of their own weaknesses.

This practice is as old as our democracy. Avoiding the facts, fearful of the truth, a malicious opposition charged that George Washington planned to make himself king under a British form of government; that Thomas Jefferson planned to set up a guillotine under a French revolution-ary form of government; that Andrew Jackson soaked the rich of the Eastern seaboard and planned to surrender American democracy to the dictatorship of a frontier mob. They called Abraham Lincoln a Roman emperor; Theodore Roosevelt a destroyer; Woodrow Wilson a self-constituted messiah.

In this campaign another herring turns up. It has been British and French, and a variety of other things. This year it is Russian. Desperate in mood, angry at failure, cunning in purpose, individu-als and groups are seeking to make communism an issue in an election where communism is not a controversy between the two major parties.

Here and now, once and for all, let us bury that red herring and destroy that false issue. You are familiar with my background; you know my heritage. And you are familiar, especially in the State of New York, with my public service extending back over a quarter of a century.

For nearly four years I have been President of the United States. A long record has been written. In that record, both in this state and in the national capital, you will find a simple, clear, and consistent adherence not only to the letter but to the spirit of the American form of government.

To that record, my future and the future of my administration will conform. I have not sought, I do not seek, I repudiate the support of any advocate of communism, or of any other alien "ism" which would by fair means or foul change our American democracy.

That is my position. It always has been my position. It always will be my position.

There is no difference between the major parties as to what they think about communism.

There is a very great difference between the two parties in what they do about communism.

Communism is a manifestation of the social unrest which always comes with widespread economic maladjustment. We in the Democratic party have not been content merely to denounce this menace. We have been realistic enough to face it. We have been intelligent enough to do something about it. And the world has seen the results of what we have done.

In the spring of 1933 we faced a crisis which was the ugly fruit of twelve years of neglect of the causes of economic and social unrest. It was a crisis made to order for all those who would overthrow our form of government. Do I need to recall to you the fear of those days—the reports of those who piled supplies in their basements, who laid plans to get their fortunes across the border, who got themselves hide-aways in the country against the impending upheaval?

Do I need to recall the law-abiding heads of peaceful families who began to wonder, as they saw their children starve, how they could get the bread they saw in the bakery window? Do I need to recall the homeless boys who were traveling in bands through the country seeking work and food—desperate because they could find neither?

Do I need to recall the farmers who banded together with pitchforks to keep the sheriff from selling the farm home under foreclosure? Do I need to recall the powerful leaders of industry and banking who came to me in Washington in those early days of 1933 pleading to be saved?

Most people in the United States remember today the fact that starvation was averted, that homes and farms were saved, that banks reopened, that crop prices rose, that industry revived, and that the dangerous forces subversive of our form of government were turned aside.

A few people—and few only—unwilling to remember, seem to have forgotten those days.

In the summer of 1933, a nice old gentleman wearing a silk hat fell off the end of a pier. He was unable to swim. A friend ran down the pier, dived overboard and pulled him out, but the silk hat floated off with the tide. After the old gentleman had been resuscitated, he was effusive in his thanks. He praised his friend for saving his life. Today, three years later, the old gentlemen is berating his friend because the silk hat was lost.

Why did the crisis of 1929 to 1932 pass without disaster? The answer is found in the record of what we did. Early in the campaign of 1932 I said: "To meet by reaction that danger of radicalism is to invite disaster.

"The way to meet that danger is to offer a workable program of reconstruction, and the party to offer it is the party with the clean hands."

We met the emergency with emergency action. But, far more important than that, we went to the roots of the problem and attacked the cause of the crisis. We were against revolution. Therefore, we waged war against those conditions which make revolutions—against the inequalities and resentments which breed them.

In America in 1933 the people did not attempt to remedy wrongs by overthrowing their institutions. Americans were made to realize that wrongs could and would be set right within their institution. We proved that democracy can work.

I have said that there is a very great difference between the two parties in what they do about communism. Conditions congenial to communism were being bred and fostered throughout this nation up to the very day of March 4, 1933. Hunger was breeding it, loss of homes and farms was breeding it, closing banks were breeding it, a ruinous price level was breeding it. Discontent and fear were spreading through the land. The previous national administration, bewildered, did nothing.

In their speeches they deplored it, but by their actions they encouraged it. The injustices, the inequalities, the downright suffering out of which revolutions come—what did they do about these things? Lacking courage, they evaded. Being selfish, they neglected. Being short-sighted, they ignored.

When the crisis came, as these wrongs made it sure to come, America was unprepared. Our lack of preparation for it was best proved by the cringing and the fear of the very people whose indifference helped to make the crisis. They came to us pleading that we should do, overnight, what they should have been doing through the years.

And the simple causes of our unpreparedness were two; first, a weak leadership, and secondly, an inability to understand the reasons for social unrest—the tragic plight of 90 percent of the men, women, and children who made up the population of the United States.

It has been well said: "Every empire that has crashed has come down primarily because its rulers did not know what was going on in the world and were incapable of learning."

It is for that reason that our American form of government will continue to be safest in Democratic hands. The real, actual, undercover Republican leadership is the same as it was four years ago. That leadership will never comprehend the need for a progress of social justice and of regard for the well-being of the masses of our people.

I have been comparing leadership in Washington. This contrast between Democratic and Republican leadership holds through throughout the length and breadth of the State of New York. As far back as the year 1910, the Black Horse Cavalry in Albany was failing to meet changing social conditions by appropriate social legislation.

Here was a State noted for its industry and noted for its agriculture—a State with the greatest mixture of population—where the poorest and the richest lived, literally within a stone's throw of each other—in short a situation made to order for unrest. And yet in this situation the best the Republican leaders of those days could say was: "let them eat cake."

What would have happened if that reactionary domination had continued through all of these hard years?

Starting in 1911, a Democratic leadership came into power, and with it a new philosophy of government. I had the good fortune to come into public office at that time. I found other young men in the Legislature—men who had the same philosophy. One of them was Bob Wagner, another was Al Smith. We were all joined in a common cause. We did not look on government as something apart from the people. We thought of it as something to be used by the people for their own good.

New factory legislation setting up decent standards of safety and sanitation, limitation of the working hours of women in industry, a workmen's compensation law, a one day rest in seven law, a full train crew law, a direct primary law—these laws and many more were passed which were then called radical and alien to our form of government. Would you or any other Americans call them radical or alien today?

In later years, the first under Governor Smith, then during my Governorship, this program of practical intelligence was carried forward over the typical and unswerving opposition of Republican leaders throughout the State.

Today the great tradition of a liberal, progressive Democratic party has been carried still further by your present Governor, Herbert H. Lehman. He has begun a program of insurance to remove the spectre of unemployment from the working people of the State. He has broadened our labor legislation. He has extended the supervision of public utility companies. He has proved himself an untiring seeker for the public good; a doer of social justice; a wise, conscientious, clear-headed, and businesslike administrator of the executive branch of our government.

And be it noted that his opponents are led and backed by the same forces and the same individuals who, for a quarter of a century, have tried to hamstring progress within our State. The overwhelming majority of our citizens, regardless of party, propose to return him and his administration to Albany for another two years.

His task in Albany, like my task in Washington, has been to maintain contact between statecraft and reality. In New York and in Washington, government which has rendered more than lip service to our constitutional democracy has done a work for the protection and preservation of our institutions that could not have been accomplished by repression and force.

Let me warn you and let me warn the nation against the smooth evasion which says: "Of course we believe all these things; we believe in social security; we believe in work for the unemployed; we believe in saving homes. Cross our hearts and hope to die, we believe in all these things; but we do not like the way the present administration is doing them. Just turn them over to us. We will do all of them—we will do more of them—we will do them better; and, most important of all, the doing of them will not cost anybody anything."

But, my friends, these evaders are banking too heavily on the shortness of our memories. No one will forget that they had their golden opportunity—twelve long years of it.

Remember, too, that the first essential of doing a job well is to want to see the job done. But make no mistake about this; the Republican leadership today is not against the way we have done the job. The Republican leadership is against the job being done.

Look to the source of the promises of the past. Governor Lehman knows and I know how little legislation in the interests of the average citizen would be on the statute books of the State of New York and of the Federal Government if we had waited for the Republican leaders to pass it.

The same lack of purpose of fulfillment lies behind the promises of today. You cannot be an Old Guard Republican in the East and a New Deal Republican in the West. You cannot promise to repeal taxes before one audience and promise to spend more of the taxpayers' money before another audience. You cannot promise tax relief for those who can afford to pay and at the same time promise more of the taxpayers' money for those who are in need. You simply cannot make good in both promises at the same time.

Who is there in America who believes that we can run the risk of turning back our government to the old leadership which brought it to the brink of 1933? Out of the strains and stresses of these years we now come to see that the true conservative is the man who has a real concern for injustices and takes thought against the day of reckoning.

The true conservative seeks to protect the system of private property and free enterprise by correcting such injustices and inequalities as rise from it. The most serious threat to our institutions comes from those who refuse to face the need for change. Liberalism becomes the protection for the far-sighted conservative.

Never has a nation made greater strides in the safeguarding of democracy than we have made during the past three years. Wise and prudent men, intelligent conservatives, have long known that in a changing world worthy institutions can be conserved only by adjusting them to the changing time. In the words of the great essayist, "The voice of great events is proclaiming to us: reform if you would preserve."

I am that kind of a conservative because I am that kind of a liberal.

Questions for Research and Discussion

1. What is FDR's central point about fighting communism?

2. Compare FDR's approach to eliminating subversives to that of Senator McCarthy. Which approach is the most effective?

Margaret Chase Smith: A Declaration of Conscience[9]

Statement of the Republican Senator from Maine
Delivered on the Floor of the United States Senate
June 1, 1950

Historical Note

Senator Margaret Chase Smith, Republican of Maine, was the first person to speak out against McCarthyism, but she does it indirectly, without the use of names.

"Mr. President:

I would like to speak briefly and simply about a serious national condition. It is a national feeling of fear and frustration that could result in national suicide and the end of everything that we Americans hold dear. It is a condition that comes from the lack of effective leadership in either the Legislative Branch or the Executive Branch of our Government.

That leadership is so lacking that serious and responsible proposals are being made that national advisory commissions be appointed to provide such critically needed leadership.

I speak as briefly as possible because too much harm has already been done with irresponsible words of bitterness and selfish political opportunism. I speak as simply as possible because the issue is too great to be obscured by eloquence. I speak simply and briefly in the hope that my words will be taken to heart.

I speak as a Republican, I speak as a woman. I speak as a United States Senator. I speak as an American.

The United States Senate has long enjoyed worldwide respect as the greatest deliberative body in the world. But recently that deliberative character has too often been debased to the level of a forum of hate and character assassination sheltered by the shield of congressional immunity.

It is ironical that we Senators can in debate in the Senate directly or indirectly, by any form of words impute to any American, who is not a Senator, any conduct or motive unworthy or unbecoming an American—and without that non-Senator American having any legal redress against us—yet if we say the same thing in the Senate about our colleagues we can be stopped on the grounds of being out of order.

It is strange that we can verbally attack anyone else without restraint and with full protection and yet we hold ourselves above the same type of criticism here on the Senate Floor. Surely the United States Senate is big enough to take self-criticism and self-appraisal. Surely we should be able to take the same kind of character attacks that we dish out to outsiders.

I think that it is high time for the United States Senate and its members to do some soul searching—for us to weigh our consciences—on the manner in which we are performing our duty to the people of America—on the manner in which we are using or abusing our individual powers and privileges.

I think that it is high time that we remembered that we have sworn to uphold and defend the Constitution. I think that it is high time that we remembered; that the Constitution, as amended, speaks not only of the freedom of speech but also of trial by jury instead of trial by accusation.

Whether it be a criminal prosecution in court or a character prosecution in the Senate, there is little practical distinction when the life of a person has been ruined.

Those of us who shout the loudest about Americanism in making character assassinations are all too frequently those who, by our own words and acts, ignore some of the basic principles of Americanism—

The right to criticize;

The right to hold unpopular beliefs;

The right to protest;

The right of independent thought.

The exercise of these rights should not cost one single American citizen his reputation or his right to a livelihood nor should he be in danger of losing his reputation or livelihood merely because he happens to know some one who holds unpopular beliefs. Who of us doesn't? Otherwise none of us could call our souls our own. Otherwise thought control would have set in.

The American people are sick and tired of being afraid to speak their minds lest they be politically smeared as "Communists" or "Fascists" by their opponents. Freedom of speech is not what it used to be in America. It has been so abused by some that it is not exercised by others. The American people are sick and tired of seeing innocent people smeared and guilty people whitewashed. But there have been enough proved cases to cause nation-wide distrust and strong suspicion that there may be something to the unproved, sensational accusations.

As a Republican, I say to my colleagues on this side of the aisle that the Republican Party faces a challenge today that is not unlike the challenge that it faced back in Lincoln's day. The Republican Party so successfully met that challenge that it emerged from the Civil War as the champion of a united nation—in addition to being a Party that unrelentingly fought loose spending and loose programs.

Today our country is being psychologically divided by the confusion and the suspicions that are bred in the United States Senate to spread like cancerous tentacles of "know nothing, suspect everything" attitudes. Today we have a Democratic Administration that has developed a mania for loose spending and loose programs. History is repeating itself—and the Republican Party again has the opportunity to emerge as the champion of unity and prudence.

The record of the present Democratic Administration has provided us with sufficient campaign issues without the necessity of resorting to political smears. America is rapidly losing its position as leader of the world simply because the Democratic Administration has pitifully failed to provide effective leadership.

The Democratic Administration has completely confused the American people by its daily contradictory grave warnings and optimistic assurances—that show the people that our Democratic Administration has no idea of where it is going.

The Democratic Administration has greatly lost the confidence of the American people by its complacency to the threat of communism here at home and the leak of vital secrets to Russia through key officials of the Democratic Administration. There are enough proved cases to make this point without diluting our criticism with unproved charges.

Surely these are sufficient reasons to make it clear to the American people that it is time for a change and that a Republican victory is necessary to the security of this country. Surely it is clear that this nation will continue to suffer as long as it is governed by the present ineffective Democratic Administration.

Yet to displace it with a Republican regime embracing a philosophy that lacks political integrity or intellectual honesty would prove equally disastrous to this nation. The nation sorely needs a Republican victory. But I don't want to see the Republican Party ride to political victory on the Four Horsemen of Calumny—Fear, Ignorance, Bigotry and Smear.

I doubt if the Republican Party could—simply because I don't believe the American people will uphold any political party that puts political exploitation above national interest. Surely we Republicans aren't that desperate for victory.

I don't want to see the Republican Party win that way. While it might be a fleeting victory for the Republican Party, it would be a more lasting defeat for the American people. Surely it would ultimately be suicide for the Republican Party and the two-party system that has protected our American liberties from the dictatorship of a one party system.

As members of the Minority Party, we do not have the primary authority to formulate the policy of our Government. But we do have the responsibility of rendering constructive criticism, of clarifying issues, of allaying fears by acting as responsible citizens.

As a woman, I wonder how the mothers, wives, sisters and daughters feel about the way in which members of their families have been politically mangled in Senate debate—and I use the word 'debate' advisedly.

As a United States Senator, I am not proud of the way in which the Senate has been made a publicity platform for irresponsible sensationalism. I am not proud of the reckless abandon in which unproved charges have been hurled from this side of the aisle. I am not proud of the obviously staged, undignified countercharges that have been attempted in retaliation from the other side of the aisle.

I don't like the way the Senate has been made a rendezvous for vilification, for selfish political gain at the sacrifice of individual reputations and national unity. I am not proud of the way we smear outsiders from the Floor of the Senate and hide behind the cloak of congressional immunity and still place ourselves beyond criticism on the Floor of the Senate.

As an American, I am shocked at the way Republicans and Democrats alike are playing directly into the Communist design of "confuse, divide and conquer." As an American, I don't want a Democratic Administration "white wash" or "cover up" any more than I want a Republican smear or witch hunt.

As an American, I condemn a Republican "Fascist" just as much as I condemn a Democrat "Communist." I condemn a Democrat "fascist" just as much as I condemn a Republican "Communist." They are equally dangerous to you and me and to our country. As an American, I want to see our nation recapture the strength and unity it once had when we fought the enemy instead of ourselves.

It is with these thoughts I have drafted what I call a "Declaration of Conscience." I am gratified that Senator Tobey, Senator Aiken, Senator Morse, Senator Ives, Senator Thye and Senator Hendrickson, have concurred in that declaration and have authorized me to announce their concurrence."

Questions for Research and Discussion

1. Was Senator Smith correct in her assessment that McCarthyism came about as a result of lack of leadership in the executive and legislative branches?

2. Was Senator Smith's indirect style effective in defeating Communism?

Debate Four

The Crises of Thermonuclear and Environmental Threats: Five Survival Perspectives

Historical Notes

This section of Crisis Dialogues features four survival perspectives. President Kennedy sought a world security system to control nuclear weapons and a worldwide program of conservation to curb environmental deterioration.

President George H. W. Bush spoke eloquently of a New World Order When Iraq attacked Kuwait he organized the entire world (Communists and capitalists, Arabs and Jews, and other unlikely combinations) to curb Iraqi aggression in an engagement he called Desert Storm.

Senator Barry Goldwater and President George W. Bush each favored a foreign policy that favored national interest over cooperative collectivism.

John F. Kennedy was the most dedicated of all advocates for the development of a world security system.. He first called for the pursuit of world law in two important speeches as a United States Senator. As a candidate for the presidency, he and his New Frontiersmen charted a bold pathway when they developed the following plank in.

The Democratic Party Platform of 1960[10]

The United Nations

To all our fellow members of the United Nations: We shall strengthen our commitments in this, our great continuing institution for conciliation and the growth of a world community.

Through the machinery of the United Nations, we shall work for disarmament, the establishment of an international police force, the strengthening of the World Court, and the establishment of world law.

We shall propose the bolder and more effective use of the specialized agencies to promote the world's economic and social development.

Great Democratic Presidents have taken the lead in the effort to unite the nations of the world in an international organization to assure world peace with justice under law.

The League of Nations, conceived by Woodrow Wilson, was doomed by Republican defeat of United States participation.

The United Nations, sponsored by Franklin Roosevelt, has become the one place where representatives of the rival systems and interests which divide the world can and do maintain continuous contact.

The United States' adherence to the World Court contains a so-called "self-judging reservation" which, in effect, permits us to prevent a Court decision in any particular case in which we are involved. The Democratic Party proposes its repeal.

To all these endeavors so essential to world peace, we, the members of the Democratic Party, will bring a new urgency, persistence, and determination, born of the conviction that in our thermonuclear century all of the other Rights of Man hinge on our ability to assure man's right to peace.

John F. Kennedy: One World, One Human Race with One Common Destiny[11]

An Address by the President before the General Assembly of the United Nations
September 20, 1963

. . . We meet again in the quest for peace.

Twenty-four months ago, when I last had the honor of addressing this body, the shadow of fear lay darkly across the world. The freedom of West Berlin was in immediate peril. Agreement on a neutral Laos seemed remote. The mandate of the United Nations in the Congo was under fire. The financial outlook for this organization was in doubt. Dag Hammarskjold was dead. The doctrine of troika was being pressed in his place, and atmospheric nuclear tests had been resumed by the Soviet Union.

Those were anxious days for mankind, and some men wondered aloud whether this organization could survive. But the Sixteenth and Seventeenth General Assemblies achieved not only survival but progress. Rising to its responsibility, the United Nations helped reduce the tensions and helped to hold back the darkness.

Today the clouds have lifted a little so that new rays of hope can break through. The pressures on West Berlin appear to be temporarily eased. Political unity in the Congo has been largely restored. A neutral coalition in Laos, while still in difficulty, is at least in being. The integrity of the United Nations Secretariat has been reaffirmed. A United Nations Decade of Development is under way. And, for the first time in seventeen years of effort, a specific step has been taken to limit the nuclear arms race.

I refer, of course, to the treaty to ban nuclear tests in the atmosphere, outer space and underwater, concluded by the Soviet Union, the United Kingdom and the United States, and already signed by nearly one hundred countries. It has been hailed by people the world over who are thankful to be free from the fears of nuclear fallout, and I am confident that on next Tuesday at ten-thirty o'clock in the morning it will receive the overwhelming endorsement of the Senate of the United States.

The world has not escaped from the darkness. The long shadows of conflict and crisis envelop us still. But we meet today in an atmosphere of rising hope at a moment of comparative calm. My presence here today is not a sign of crisis, but of confidence. I am not here to report on a new threat to the peace or new signs of war. I have come to salute the United Nations and to show the support of the American people for your daily deliberations.

For the value of this body's work is not dependent on the existence of emergencies, nor can the winning of peace consist only of dramatic victories. Peace is a daily, a weekly, a monthly process, gradually changing opinions, slowly eroding old barriers, quietly building new structures. And however undramatic the pursuit of peace, that pursuit must go on.

Today we may have reached a pause in the Cold War, but that is not a lasting peace. A test ban treaty is a milestone, but it is not the millennium. We have not been released from our obligations; we have been given an opportunity. And if we fail to make the most of this moment and this momentum, if we convert our new-found hopes and understandings into new walls and weapons of hostility, if this pause in the Cold War merely leads to its renewal and not to its end, then the indictment of posterity will rightly point its finger at us all. But if we can stretch this pause into a period of cooperation, if both sides can now gain new confidence and experience in concrete collaborations for peace, if we can now be as bold and farsighted in the control of deadly weapons as we have been in their creation, then surely this first small step can be the start of a long and fruitful journey.

The task of building the peace lies with the leaders of every nation, large and small. For the great powers have no monopoly on conflict or ambition. The Cold War is not the only expression of tension in this world, and the nuclear race is not the only arms race. Even little wars are dangerous in a nuclear world. The long labor of peace is an undertaking for every nation, and in this effort none of us can remain unaligned. To this goal none can be uncommitted.

The reduction of global tension must not be an excuse for the narrow pursuit of self-interest. If the Soviet Union and the United States, with all their global interests and clashing commitments of ideology, and with nuclear weapons still aimed at each other today, can find areas of common interest and agreement, then surely other nations can do the same—nations caught in regional conflicts, in racial issues or in the death throes of old colonialism. Chronic disputes which divert precious resources from the needs of the people or drain the energies of both sides serve the interests of no one, and the badge of responsibility in the modern world is a willingness to seek peaceful solutions.

It is never to early to try; and it is never too late to talk; and it is high time that many disputes on the agenda of this Assembly were taken off the debating schedule and placed on the negotiating table.

The fact remains that the United States, as a major nuclear power, does have a special responsibility in the world. It is, in fact, a threefold responsibility: a responsibility to our own citizens, a responsibility to the people of the whole world who are affected by our decisions, and to the next generation of humanity. We believe the Soviet Union also has these special responsibilities, and that those responsibilities require our two nations to concentrate less on our differences and more on the means of resolving them peacefully. For too long both of us have increased our military budgets, our nuclear stockpiles and our capacity to destroy all life—human, animal, vegetable—without any corresponding increase in our security.

Our conflicts, to be sure, are real. Our concepts of the world are different. No service is performed by failing to make clear our disagreements. A central difference is the belief of the American people in self-determination for all people.

We believe that the people of Germany and Berlin must be free to reunite their capital and their country.

We believe that the people of Cuba must be free to secure the fruits of the revolution that has been betrayed from within and exploited from without.

In short, we believe that all the world—in Eastern Europe as well as Western, in Southern Africa as well as Northern, in old nations as well as new—people must be free to choose their own future, without discrimination or dictation, without coercion or subversion.

These are the basic differences between the Soviet Union and the United States, and they cannot be concealed. So long as they exist, they set limits to agreement, and they forbid the relaxation of our vigilance. Our defense around the world will be maintained for the protection of freedom, and our determination to safeguard that freedom will measure up to any threat or challenge.

But I would say to the leaders of the Soviet Union, and to their people, that if either of our countries is to be fully secure, we need a much better weapon than the H-bomb, a weapon better than ballistic missiles or nuclear submarines, and that better weapon is peaceful cooperation.

We have, in recent years, agreed on a limited test ban treaty, on an emergency communications link between our capitals, on a statement of principles for disarmament, on an increase in cultural exchange, on cooperation in outer space, on the peaceful exploration of the Antarctic, and on tempering last year's crisis over Cuba.

I believe, therefore, that the Soviet Union and the United States, together with their allies, can achieve further agreements—agreements which spring from our mutual interest in avoiding mutual destruction.

There can be no doubt about the agenda of further steps. We must continue to seek agreements on measures which prevent war by accident or miscalculation. We must continue to seek agreement on safeguards against surprise attack, including observation posts at key points. We must continue to seek agreement on further measures to curb the nuclear arms race, by controlling the transfer of nuclear weapons, converting fissionable materials to peaceful purposes and banning underground testing, with adequate inspection and enforcement. We must continue to seek agreement on a freer flow of information and people from East to West and West to East.

We must continue to seek agreement, encouraged by yesterday's affirmative response to this proposal by the Soviet Foreign Minister, on an arrangement to keep weapons of mass destruction out of outer space. Let us get our negotiators back to the negotiating table to work out a practicable arrangement to this end.

In these and other ways, let us move up the steep and difficult path toward comprehensive disarmament, securing mutual confidence through mutual verification and building the institutions of peace as we dismantle the engines of war. We must not let failure to agree on all points delay agreements where agreement is possible. And we must not put forward proposals for propaganda purposes.

Finally, in a field where the United States and the Soviet Union have a special capacity—in the field of space—there is room for new cooperation, for further joint efforts in the regulation and exploration of space. I include among these possibilities a joint expedition to the moon. Space offers no problems of sovereignty. By resolution of this Assembly, the members of the United Nations have forsworn any claim to territorial rights in outer space or on celestial bodies, and declared that international law and the United Nations Charter will apply. Why, therefore, should man's first flight to the moon be a matter of national competition? Why should the United States and the Soviet Union, in preparing for such expeditions, become involved in immense duplications of research, construction, and expenditures? Surely we should explore whether the scientists and the astronauts of our two countries—indeed, of all the world—cannot work together in the conquest of space, sending someday in this decade to the moon not the representatives of a single nation but the representatives of all our countries.

All these and other new steps toward peaceful cooperation may be possible. Most of them will require on our part full consultation with our allies, for their interests are as much involved as our own, and we will not make an agreement at their expense. Most of them will require long and careful negotiation. And most of them will require a new approach to the Cold War—a desire not to "bury" one's adversary, but to compete in a host of peaceful arenas: in ideas, in production and ultimately in service to all mankind.

The contest will continue—the contest between those who see a monolithic world and those who believe in diversity—but it should be a contest in leadership and responsibility instead of destruction, a contest in achievement instead of intimidation. Speaking for the United States of America, I welcome such a contest. For we believe that truth is stronger than error, and that freedom is more enduring than coercion. And in the contest for a better life, all the world can be a winner.

The effort to improve the conditions of man, however, is not a task for a few. It is the task of all nations, acting along, acting in groups, acting in the United Nations; for plague and pestilence, and plunder and pollution, the hazards of nature and the hunger of children are the foes of every nation. The earth, the sea and the air are the concern of every nation. And science, technology and education can be the ally of every nation.

Never before has man had such capacity to control his own environment—to end thirst and hunger, to conquer poverty and disease, to banish illiteracy and massive human misery. We have the power to make this the best generation of mankind in the history of the world or to make it the last.

The United States since the close of the war has sent over $100 billion worth of assistance to nations seeking economic viability. And two years ago this week we formed a Peace Corps to help interested nations meet the needs for trained manpower. Other industrialized nations whose economies were rebuilt not so long ago with some help from us are now in turn recognizing their responsibility to the less developed nations.

The provision of development assistance by individual nations must go on. But the United Nations also must play a larger role in helping bring to all men the fruits of modern science and industry. A United Nations conference on this subject held earlier this year at Geneva opened new vistas for the developing countries. Next year a United Nations Conference on Trade will consider the needs of these nations for new markets. And more than four-fifths of the entire United Nations system can be found today mobilizing the weapons of science and technology for the United Nations' Decade of Development.

But more can be done.

A world center for health communications under the World Health Organization would warn of epidemics and the adverse effects of certain drugs, as well as transmit the results of new experiments and new discoveries.

Regional research centers could advance our common medical knowledge and train new scientists and doctors for new nations.

A global system of satellites could provide communication and weather information for all corners of the earth.

A world-wide program of conservation could protect the forest and wild game preserves now in danger of extinction for all time, improve the marine harvest of food from our oceans, and prevent the contamination of air and water by industrial as well as nuclear pollution.

And, finally, a world-wide program of farm productivity and food distribution, similar to our country's "Food for Peace" program, could now give every child the food he needs.

But man does not live by bread alone, and members of this organization are committed by the Charter to promote and respect human rights. Those rights are not respected when a Buddhist priest is driven from his pagoda, when a synagogue is shut down, when a Protestant church cannot open a mission, when a cardinal is forced into hiding or when a crowded church service is bombed. The United States of America is opposed to discrimination and persecution on grounds of race and religion anywhere in the world, including our own nation. We are working to right the wrongs of our own country.

Through legislation and administrative action, through moral and legal commitment, this government has launched a determined effort to rid our nation of discrimination which has existed too long—in education, in housing, in transportation, in employment, in the Civil Service, in recreation and in places of public accommodation. And therefore, in this or any other forum, we do not hesitate to condemn racial or religious injustice, whether committed or permitted by friend or foe.

I know that some of you have experienced discrimination in this country. But I ask you to believe me when I tell you that this is not the wish of most Americans, that we share your regret and resentment, and that we intend to end such practices for all time to come, not only for our visitors but for our own citizens as well.

I hope that not only our nation but all other multiracial societies will meet these standards of fairness and justice. We are opposed to apartheid and all forms of human oppression. We do not advocate the rights of black Africans in order to drive out white Africans. Our concern is the right of all men to equal protection under the law; and since human rights are indivisible, this body cannot stand aside when those rights are abused and neglected by any member state.

New efforts are needed if this Assembly's Declaration of Human Rights, now fifteen years old, is to have full meaning. And new means should be found for promoting the free expression and trade of ideas, through travel and communication, and through increased exchanges of people and books and broadcasts. For as the world renounces the competition of weapons, competition in ideas must flourish, and that competition must be as full and as fair as possible.

The United States delegation will be prepared to suggest to the United Nations initiatives in the pursuit of all the goals. For this is an organization for peace, and peace cannot come without work and progress.

The peace-keeping record of the United Nations has been a proud one, though its tasks are always formidable. We are fortunate to have the skills of our distinguished Secretary General and the brave efforts of those who have been serving the cause of peace in the Congo, in the Middle East, in Korea and Kashmir, in West New Guinea and Malaysia. But what the United Nations has done in the past is less important than the tasks for the future. We cannot take its peace-keeping machinery for granted. That machinery must be soundly financed, which it cannot be if some members are allowed to prevent it from meeting its obligations by failing to meet their own. The United Nations must be supported by all those who exercise their franchise here. And its operations must be backed to the end.

Too often a project is undertaken in the excitement of a crisis, and then it begins to lose its appeal as the problems drag on and the bills pile up. But we must have the steadfastness to see every enterprise through.

It is, for example, most important not to jeopardize the extraordinary United Nations gains in the Congo. The nation which sought this organization's help only three years ago has now asked the United Nations' presence to remain a little longer. I believe this Assembly should do what is necessary to preserve the gains already made and to protect the new nation in its struggle for progress. Let us complete what we have started, for "No man who puts his hand to the plow and looks back," as the Scriptures tell us, "No man who puts his hand to the plow and looks back is fit for the Kingdom of God."

I also hope that the recent initiative of several members in preparing stand-by peace forces for United Nations call will encourage similar commitments by others. This nation remains ready to provide logistic and other material support.

Policing, moreover, is not enough without provision for pacific settlement. We should increase the resort to special missions of fact-finding and conciliation, make greater use of the International Court of Justice and accelerate the work of the International Law Commission.

The United Nations cannot survive as a static organization. Its obligations are increasing as well as its size. Its charter must be changed as well as its customs. The authors of that charter did not intend that it be frozen in perpetuity. The science of weapons and war has made us all, far more than eighteen years ago in San Francisco, one world and one human race, with one common destiny. In such a world absolute sovereignty no longer assures us of absolute security. The conventions of peace must pull abreast and then ahead of the inventions of war. The United Nations, building on its successes and learning from its failures, must be developed into a genuine world security system.

But peace does not rest in charters and covenants alone. It lies in the hearts and minds of all people. And in this world no act, no pact, no treaty, no organization can hope to preserve it without the support of the wholehearted commitment of all people. So let us not rest all our hopes on parchment and on paper. Let us strive to build peace, a desire for peace, a willingness to work for peace, in the hearts and minds of all our people. I believe that we can. I believe the problems of human destiny are not beyond the reach of human beings.

Two years ago I told this body that the United States had proposed, and was willing to sign, a limited test ban treaty. Today that treaty has been signed. It will not put an end to war. It will not remove basic conflicts. It will not secure freedom for all. But it can be a lever, and Archimedes, in explaining the principles of the lever, was said to have declared to his friends: "Give me a place where I can stand, and I shall move the world."

My fellow inhabitants of this planet, let us take our stand here in this Assembly of nations. And let us see if we, in our own time, can move the world to a just and lasting peace.

Questions for Research and Discussion

1. Are President Kennedy's proposals realistic and practical?

2. Would President Kennedy's proposals elevate American ideals to the international level or would they surrender American sovereignty? Could the three branches of the UN be fashioned into a world security system with checks and balances against tyranny?

3. President Kennedy talks about the UN Assembly's Declaration of Human Rights. He suggests that they should have full meaning. Could the Universal Declaration of Human Rights be codified into enforceable world law in the same manner that the American Bill of Rights has been codified into national law?

Barry M. Goldwater: The National Interest Must Be Our First Priority[12]

An Address by Senator Goldwater
Delivered on the Floor of the United States Senate
March 15, 1960

American Freedom has always depended, to an extent, on what is happening beyond our shores. Even in Ben Franklin's day, Americans had to reckon with foreign threats. Our forbearers knew that keeping a republic meant, above all, keeping it safe from foreign transgressors; they knew that a people cannot live and work freely, and develop national institutions conducive to freedom, except in peace and with independence.

In those early days the threat to peace and independence was very real. We were a fledgling nation, and the slightest misstep—or faint hearts—would have laid us open to the ravages of predatory European powers. It was only because wise and courageous men understood that defense of freedom required risks and sacrifice, as well as their belief in it, that we survived the crisis of national infancy. As we grew stronger, and as the oceans continued to interpose a physical barrier between ourselves and European militarism, the foreign danger gradually receded. Though we always had to keep a weather eye on would-be conquerors, our independence was acknowledged and peace, unless we chose otherwise, was established. Indeed, after the Second World War, we were not only a master of our own destiny; we were a master of the world. With a monopoly of atomic weapons, and with a conventional military establishment superior to any in the world, America was—in relative and absolute terms—the most powerful Nation the world had ever known. American freedom was as secure as at any time in our history.

Now, a decade and a half later, we have come full circle and our national existence is once again threatened as it was in the early days of the Republic. Though we are still strong physically, we are in clear and imminent danger of being overwhelmed by alien forces. We are confronted by a revolutionary world movement that possesses not only the will to dominate absolutely every square mile of the globe, but increasingly the capacity to do so: a military power that rivals our own, political welfare, and propaganda skills that are superior to ours, an international fifth column that operates conspiratorially in the heart of our defenses, an ideology that imbues its adherents with a sense of historical mission; and all of these resources controlled by a ruthless despotism that brooks no deviation from the revolutionary course. This threat, moreover, is growing day by day. And it has now reached the point where American leaders, both political, and intellectual, are searching desperately for means of 'appeasing' or 'accommodating' the Soviet Union as the price of national survival. The American people are being told that, it is even more important to live. A craven fear of death is entering the American consciousness; so much so that many recently felt that honoring the chief despot himself was the price we had to pay to avoid nuclear destruction.

The temptation is strong to blame the deterioration of America's fortunes on the Soviet Union's acquisition of nuclear weapons. But this is self-delusion. The rot had set in, the crumbling of our position was already observable, long before the Communists detonated their first atom bomb.

Even in the early 1950's, when America still held unquestioned nuclear superiority, it was clear that we were losing the cold war. Time and again in my campaign speeches of 1952 I warned my fellow Arizonians that 'American foreign policy has brought us from a position of undisputed power, in 7 short years, to the brink of possible disaster.' And in the succeeding 7 years, that trend, because its cause remains, has continued.

The real cause of the deterioration can be simply stated. Our enemies have understood the nature of the conflict, and we have not. They are determined to win the conflict, and we are not.

I hesitate to restate the obvious—to say again what has been said so many times before by so many others: That the Communists' aim is to conquer the world. I repeat it because it is the beginning and the end of our knowledge about the conflict between East and West. I repeat it because I fear that however often we have given lip service to this central political fact of our time, very few of us have believed it. If we had, our entire approach to foreign policy over the past 14 years would have been radically different, and the course of world events radically changed.

If an enemy power is bent on conquering you, and proposes to turn all of its resources to that end, he is at war with you; and you—unless you contemplate surrender—are at war with him. Moreover—unless you contemplate treason—your objective, like his, will be victory. Not peace, but victory. Now, while traitors—and perhaps cowards—have at times occupied key positions in our Government, it is clear that our national leadership over the past 14 years has favored neither surrender nor treason. It is equally clear, however, that our leaders have not made victory the goal of American policy. And the reason they have not done so, I am saying, is that they have never believed deeply that the Communists are in earnest.

Our avowed national objective is peace. We have, with great sincerity, waged peace, while the Communists wage war. We have sought settlements, while the Communists seek victories. We have tried to pacify the world. The Communists mean to own it. Here is why the contest has been an unequal one, and why, essentially, we are losing it.

Peace, to be sure, is a proper goal for American policy—as long as it is understood that peace is not all we seek. For we do not want the peace of surrender. We want a peace in which freedom and justice will prevail, and that—given the nature of communism—is a peace in which Soviet power will no longer be in a position to threaten us and the rest of the world. A tolerable peace, in other words, must follow victory over communism. We have been 14 years trying to bury that unpleasant fact. It cannot be buried, and any foreign policy that ignores it will lead to our extinction as a Nation.

We do not, of course, want to achieve victory by force of arms. If possible, overt hostilities should always be avoided; especially is this so when a shooting war may cause the death of many millions of people, including our own. But we cannot, for that reason, make the avoidance of a shooting war our chief objective. If we do that—if we tell ourselves that it is more important to avoid shooting than to keep our freedom—we are committed to a course that has only one terminal point: surrender. We cannot, by proclamation, make war 'unthinkable.' For it is not unthinkable to the Communists: naturally, they would prefer to avoid war, but they are prepared to risk it, in the last analysis, to achieve their objectives. We must, in our hearts, be equally dedicated to our objectives. If war is unthinkable to us but not to them, the famous 'balance of terror' is not a balance at all, but an instrument of blackmail. And it cannot be long before a universal Communist Empire sits astride the globe.

The rallying cry of an appeasement organization, portrayed in a recent novel on American politics, was 'I would rather crawl on my knees to Moscow than die under an atom bomb.' This sentiment, of course, repudiates everything that is courageous and honorable and dignified in the human being. We must—as the first step toward saving American freedom—affirm the contrary view and make it the cornerstone of our foreign policy: that we would rather die than lose our freedom. There are ways which I will suggest later on—not easy ways, to be sure—in which we may save both our freedom and our lives; but all such suggestions are meaningless and vain unless we first understand what the objective is. We want to stay alive, of course; but more than that we want to be free. We want to have peace; but before that we want to establish the conditions that will make peace tolerable. 'Like it or not,' Eugene Lyons has written, 'the great and inescapable task of our epoch is not to end the cold war but to win it.'

Support of the United Nations, our leaders earnestly proclaim, is one of the cornerstones of American foreign policy. I confess to being more interested in whether American foreign policy has the support of the United Nations.

Here, again, it seems to me that our approach to foreign affairs suffers from a confusion in objectives. Is the perpetuation of an international debating forum, for its own sake, the primary objective of American policy? If so, there is much to be said for our past record of subordinating our national interest to that of the United Nations. If, on the other hand, our primary objective is victory over communism, we will, as a matter of course, view such organizations as the U.N. as a possible means to that end. Once the question is asked—Does America's participation in the United Nations help or hinder her struggle against world communism"—it becomes clear that our present commitment to the U.N. deserves reexamination.

The United Nations, we must remember, is part of a Communist organization. The Communists always have at least one seat in its major policymaking body, the Security Council; and the Soviet Union's permanent veto power in that body allows the Kremlin to block any action, on a substantial issue, that is contrary to its interests. The Communists also have a sizable membership in the U.N.'s other policymaking body, the General Assembly. Moreover, the U.N.'s working staff, the Secretariat, is manned by hundreds of Communist agents who are frequently in a position to sabotage those few U.N. policies that are contrary to Communist interests. Finally, a great number of non-Communist United Nations are sympathetic to Soviet aims—or, at best, are unsympathetic to ours.

We therefore should not be surprised that many of the policies that emerge from the deliberations of the United Nations are not policies that are in the best interest of the United States. United Nations policy is, necessarily, the product of many different views—some of them friendly, some of them indifferent to our interests, some of them mortally hostile. And the result is that our national interests usually suffer when we subordinate our own policy to the U.N.'s. In nearly every case in which we have called upon the United Nations to do our thinking for us, and to make our policy for us—whether during the Korean war, or in the Suez crisis, or following the revolution in Iraq—we have been a less effective for of communism than we otherwise might have been.

Unlike America, the Communists do not respect the United Nations and do not permit their policies to be affected by it. If the 'opinion of mankind,' as reflected by a United Nations resolution, goes against them, they, in effect tell mankind to go fly a kite. Not so with us: We would rather be approved than succeed, and so are likely to adjust our own views to conform with a United Nations majority. This is not the way to win the cold war. I repeat, communism will not be beaten by a policy that is the common denominator of the foreign policies of 80-odd nations, some of which are our enemies, nearly all of which are less determined than we to save the world from Communist domination. Let us, then, have done with submitting major policy decisions to a forum where the opinions of the Sultan of Yemen count equally with ours; where the vote of the United States can be canceled out by the likes of Byelorussia.

I am troubled by several other aspects of our United Nations commitment. First—and here again our cold war interests are damaged—the United Nations provides a unique forum for Communist propaganda. We, too, of course, can voice our views at the United Nations; but the Communists' special advantage is that their lies and misrepresentations are elevated to the level of serious international debate. By recognizing the right of Communist regimes to participate in the United Nations as equals, and by officially acknowledging them as peace loving, we grant Communist propaganda a presumption of reasonableness and plausibility it otherwise would not have.

Second, the United Nations places an unwarranted financial burden on the American taxpayer. The Marxist formula, 'from each according to his ability'—under which contributions to the United Nations and its specialized agencies are determined—does not tally with the American concept of justice. The United States is currently defraying roughly a third of all United Nations expenses. That assessment should be drastically reduced. The U.N. should not operate as a charity. Assessments should take into account the benefits received by the contributor nation.

Finally, I fear that our involvement in the United Nations may be leading to an unconstitutional surrender of American sovereignty. Many U.N. activities have already made strong inroads against the sovereign powers of member nations. This is neither the time nor place to discuss the merits of yielding sovereign American rights—other than to record my unequivocal opposition to the idea. It is both the time and place, however, to insist that any such discussion take place within the framework of a proposed constitutional amendment—and not, clandestinely, in the headquarters of some U.N. agency.

Withdrawal from the United Nations is probably not the answer to these problems. For a number of reasons that course is unfeasible. We should make sure, however, that the nature of our commitment is such as to advance American interests; and that will involve changes in some of our present attitudes and policies toward the U.N. Let the U.N.-firsters—of whom there are many in this country—put their enthusiasm for international cooperation in proper perspective. Let them understand that victory over communism must come before the achievement of lasting peace. Let them, in a word, keep their eyes on the target.

Questions for Research and Discussion

1. Was Senator Goldwater's approach in foreign affairs realistic and practical? Explain.

2. Compare Senator Goldwater's foreign policy views with those of President George W. Bush.

3. Can you explain the differences between President Kennedy and Senator Goldwater in foreign affairs?

George H. W. Bush: Excerpt from "The Possibility of a New World Order: Unlocking the Possibility of Freedom."[13]

Delivered at Maxwell Air Force Base, Montgomery, Alabama
April 13, 1991.

. . . Here at Air University it's your business to read the lessons of the past with an eye on the far horizon. And that's why I wanted to speak to you today about the new world taking shape around us, about the prospects for a new world order now within our reach. For more than four decades we've lived in a world divided. East from West: a world locked in a conflict of arms and ideas called the Cold War. Two systems, two superpowers, separated by mistrust and unremitting hostility.

For more than four decades, America's energies were focused on containing the threat to the free world from the forces of communism. That war is over. East Germany has vanished from the map as a separate entity. Today in Berlin, the wall that once divided a continent, divided a world in two, has been pulverized, turned into souvenirs. And the sections that remain standing are but museum pieces. The Warsaw Pact passed into the pages of history last week. Not with a bang, but with a whimper, its demise reported in a story on page A16 of *The Washington Post*.

In the coming weeks I'll be talking in some detail about the possibility of a New World Order emerging after the Cold War. And in recent weeks I have been focusing not only on the Gulf, but on free trade, on the American Free Trade agreement, the Uruguay round trade negotiations, and the essentially of obtaining from the United States Congress a renewal of Fast-Track authority to achieve our goals. But today I want to discuss another aspect of that order, our relations with Europe and the Soviet Union.

Twice this century, a dream born on the battlefields of Europe died after the shooting stopped. The dream of a world in which major powers worked together to insure peace: to settle their disputes through cooperation, not confrontation. Today a transformed Europe stands closer than ever before to its free and democratic destiny. At long last, Europe is moving forward, moving toward a new world of hope.

At the same time, we and our European allies have moved beyond containment to a policy of active engagement in a world no longer driven by Cold War tensions and animosities. You see, as the Cold War drew to an end, we saw the possibilities of a new order in which nations worked together to promote peace and prosperity. I'm not talking here of a blueprint that will govern the conduct of nations or some supernatural structure or institution. The new order does not mean surrendering our national sovereignty or forfeiting our interests. It really describes a responsibility imposed by our successes. It refers to new ways of working with other nations to deter aggression and to achieve stability, to achieve prosperity, and above all, to achieve peace. It springs from hopes for a world based on a shared commitment among nations large and small, to a set of principles that undergird our relations. Peaceful settlements of disputes, solidarity against aggression, reduced and controlled arsenals, and just treatment of all peoples.

This order, this ability to work together, got its first real test in the Gulf War. For the first time, a regional conflict, the aggression against Kuwait, did not serve as a proxy for superpower confrontation. For the first time the United Nations Security Council, free from the clash of Cold War ideologies, functioned as its designers intended, a force for conflict resolution in collective security . . .

We must build on the successes of Desert Storm to give new shape and momentum to this new world order, to use force wisely and extend the hand of compassion wherever we can. Today we welcome Europe's willingness to shoulder a large share of this responsibility. This new sense of responsibility on the part of our European allies is most evident and most critical in Europe's eastern half.

The nations of Eastern Europe, for so long the other Europe, must take their place now alongside their neighbors to the west. Just as we've overcome Europe's political division, we must help to ease crossover from poverty into prosperity.

The United States will do its part; we always have. As we have already in reducing Poland's official debt burden to the United States by 70 percent, increasing our assistance this year to Eastern Europe by 50 percent. But the key, the key to helping these new democracies develop, is trade and investment.

The new entrepreneurs of Czechoslovakia and Poland and Hungary aren't looking to government, their own or others, to shower them with riches. They're looking for new opportunities, a new freedom for the productive genius strangled by forty years of state control . . .

We recognize that new roles and even new institutions are natural outgrowths of the new Europe. Whether it's the European community or a broadened mandate for CSCE, the U.S. supports all efforts to forge a European approach to common challenges on the continent and in the world beyond, with the understanding that Europe's long term security is intertwined with America's, and that NATO remains the best means to assure it.

And we look to Europe to act as a force for stability outside its own borders. In a world as interdependent as ours, no industrialized nation can maintain membership in good standing in the global community without assuming its fair share of responsibility for peace and security.

But even in the face of such welcome change, Americans will remain in Europe in support of history's most successful alliance, NATO. America's commitment is the best guarantee of a secure Europe, and a secure Europe is vital to American interests and vital to world peace. This is the essential logic of the Atlantic alliance which anchors America in Europe.

This century's history shows that America's destiny and interests cannot be separate from Europe's. Through the long years of Cold War and conflict, the United States stood fast for freedom in Europe. And now, as Eastern Europe is opening up to democratic ideals, true progress becomes possible . . .

The Soviet Union managed its own dramatic transformation. The policies of confrontation abroad, like the discredited dogma of communism from which those policies sprang, lies dormant, if not mortally wounded. Much has changed. The path of international cooperation fostered by President Gorbachev and manifested most clearly in the Persian Gulf marks a radical change in Soviet behavior. And yet the course of change within the Soviet Union is far less clear.

Economic and political reform there is under severe challenge. Soviet citizens, facing the collapse of the old order while the new still struggles to be born, confront desperate economic conditions, their hard-won freedoms in peril. Ancient ethnic enmities, conflict between republics and between republics and the central government add to these monumental challenges that they face.

America's policy toward the Soviet Union in these troubled times is, first and foremost, to continue our efforts to build the cooperative relationship that has allowed our nations and so many others to strengthen international peace and stability. At the same time, we will continue to support a reform process within the Soviet Union aimed at political and economic freedom. A process we believe must be built on peaceful dialogue and negotiation. This is a policy that we will advocate steadfastly, both in our discussions with the central Soviet government and with all elements active in Soviet political life.

Let there be no misunderstanding. The path ahead for the Soviet Union will be difficult and, at times, extraordinarily painful. History weighs heavily upon all the peoples of the USSR, liberation from 70 years of communism, from a thousand years of autocracy. Its going to be slow. There will be setbacks. But this process of reform, this transformation from within must proceed. If external cooperation and our progress toward true international peace is to endure, it must succeed. Only when the transformation is complete will we be able to take full measure of the opportunities presented by this new and evolving world order.

The New World Order really is a tool for addressing a new world of possibilities. This order gains its mission and shape, not just from shared interests, but from shared ideals. And the ideals that have spawned new freedom throughout the world have received their boldest and clearest expression in our great country, the United States. Never before has the world looked more to the American example. Never before have so many of millions drawn hope from the American idea. And the reason is simple: Unlike any other nation in the world, as Americans, we enjoy profound and mysterious bonds of affection and idealism. We eel our deep connections to community, to families, and to our faiths.

But what defines this nation? What makes us America is not our ties to a piece of territory or bonds of blood: What makes us America is our allegiance to the idea that all people everywhere must be free. This idea is as old and enduring as this nation itself, as deeply rooted, and what we are as a promise implicit to all the world in the words of the Declaration of Independence.

The new world facing us, and I wish I were your age, it's a wonderful world of discovery. A world devoted to unlocking the promise of freedom. It's no more structured than a dream; no more regimented than an innovator's burst of inspiration. If we trust ourselves and our values; if we retain the pioneer's enthusiasm for exploring the world beyond our shores; if we strive to engage in the world that beckons us, then and only then, will America be true to all that is best in us.

May God bless our great nation, the United States of America. And thank you all for what you have done for freedom and for our fundamental values.

Questions for Research and Discussion

1. Would President George H. W. Bush's emphasis on his New World Order unlock the promise of freedom in the world? Why do you think that President Bush believed that it would?

2. What part did Brent Scofield and other advisers have in shaping George H. W. Bush's foreign policy approach?

3. Compare the George H. W. Bush and the George W. Bush engagements in Iraq, in terms of: mission statements, UN involvement, ,participation and support, lengths of engagement, and total cost of each operation.

George W. Bush: Remarks on the War on Terror[14]

Delivered at the Pentagon
March 19, 2008

On this day in 2003, the United States began Operation Iraqi Freedom. As the campaign unfolded, tens and thousands of our troops poured across the Iraqi border to liberate the Iraqi people and remove a regime that threatened free nations.

Five years into this battle, there is an understandable debate over whether the war was worth fighting; whether the fight is worth winning; and whether we can win it. The answers are clear to me: Removing Saddam Hussein from power was the right decision, and this is a fight America can and must win.

The men and women who crossed into Iraq 5 years ago removed a tyrant, liberated a country, and rescued millions from unspeakable horrors. Some of those troops are with us today, and you need to know that the American people are proud of your accomplishment, and so is the Commander in Chief.

I appreciate Admiral Mullen, the Joint Chiefs who are here. Thanks for coming. Secretary Donald Winter of the Navy; Deputy Secretary of State John Negroponte is with us. Admiral Thad Allen of the Coast Guard is with us. Ambassador from Iraq is with us; Mr. Ambassador, we're proud to have you here. Soldiers, sailors, marines, airmen, and coast men—coast guard men, thanks for coming; thanks for wearing the uniform. Men and women of the Department of State are here as well.

Operation Iraqi Freedom was a remarkable display of military effectiveness. Forces from the UK, Australia, Poland, and other allies joined our troops in the initial operations. As they advanced, our troops fought their way through sandstorms so intense that they blackened the daytime sky. Our troops engaged in pitched battles with Fedayeen Saddam, death squads acting on the orders of Saddam Hussein, that obeyed neither the conventions of war nor the dictates of conscience. These death squads hid in schools, and they hid in hospitals, hoping to draw fire against Iraqi civilians. They used women and children as human shields. They stopped at nothing in their efforts to prevent us from prevailing, but they couldn't stop the coalition advance.

Aided by the most effective and precise air campaign in history, coalition forces raced across 350 miles of enemy territory, destroying Republican Guard divisions, pushing through the Karbala Gap, capturing Saddam International Airport, and liberating Baghdad in less than 1 month.

Along the way, our troops added new chapters to the story of American military heroism. During these first weeks of battle, Army Sergeant First Class Paul Ray Smith and his troops came under a surprise attack by about a hundred Republican Guard forces. Sergeant Smith rallied his men. He led a counterattack, killing as many as 50 enemy soldiers before being fatally wounded. His actions saved the lives of more than a hundred American troops and earned him the Medal of Honor.

Today, in light of the challenges we have faced in Iraq, some look back at this period as the easy part of the war. Yet there was nothing easy about it. The liberation of Iraq took incredible skill and amazing courage. And the speed, precision, and brilliant execution of the campaign will be studied by military historians for years to come.

What our troops found in Iraq following Saddam's removal was horrifying. They uncovered children's prisons and torture chambers and rape rooms where Iraqi women were violated in front of their families. They found videos showing regime thugs mutilating Iraqis deemed disloyal to Saddam. And across the Iraqi countryside, they uncovered mass graves of thousands executed by the regime.

Because we acted, Saddam Hussein no longer fills fields with the remains of innocent men, women, and children. Because we acted, Saddam's torture chambers and rape rooms and children's prisons have been closed for good. Because we acted, Saddam's regime is no longer invading its neighbors or attacking them with chemical weapons and ballistic missiles. Because we acted, Saddam's regime is no longer paying the families of suicide bombers in the Holy Land. Because we acted, Saddam's regime is no longer shooting at American and British aircraft patrolling the no-fly zones and defying the will of the United Nations. Because we acted, the world is better and United States of America is safer.

When the Iraqi regime was removed, it did not lay down its arms and surrender. Instead, former regime elements took off their uniforms and faded into the countryside to fight the emergence of a free Iraq. And then they were joined by foreign terrorists who were seeking to stop the advance of liberty in the Middle East and seeking to establish safe havens from which to plot new attacks across the world.

The battle in Iraq has been longer and harder and more costly than we anticipated, but it is a fight we must win. So our troops have engaged these enemies with courage and determination. And as they've battled the terrorists and extremists in Iraq, they have helped the Iraqi people reclaim their nation and helped a young democracy rise from the rubble of Saddam Hussein's tyranny.

Over the past 5 years, we have seen moments of triumph and moments of tragedy. We have watched in admiration as 12 million Iraqis defied the terrorists and went to the polls and chose their leaders in free elections. We watched in horror as Al Qaida beheaded innocent captives and sent suicide bombers to blow up mosques and markets. These actions show the brutal nature of the enemy in Iraq, and they serve as a grim reminder. The terrorists who murder the innocent in the streets of Baghdad want to murder the innocent in the streets of America. Defeating this enemy in Iraq will make it less likely that we will face the enemy here at home.

A little over a year ago, the fight in Iraq was faltering. Extremist elements were succeeding in their efforts to plunge Iraq into chaos. They had established safe havens in many parts of the country. They were creating divisions among the Iraqis along sectarian lines. And their strategy of using violence in Iraq to cause divisions in America was working as pressures built here in Washington for withdrawal before the job was done.

My administration understood that America could not retreat in the face of terror. And we knew that if we did not act, the violence that had been consuming Iraq would worsen and spread and could eventually reach genocidal levels. Baghdad could have disintegrated into a contagion of killing, and Iraq could have descended into full-blown sectarian warfare.

So we reviewed the strategy and changed course in Iraq. We sent reinforcements into the country in a dramatic policy shift that is now known as the surge. General David Petraeus took command with a new mission: Work with Iraqi forces to protect the Iraqi people; pressure the enemy into strongholds; and deny the terrorists sanctuary anywhere in the country. And that is precisely what we have done.

In Anbar, Sunni tribal leaders had grown tired of Al Qaida's brutality and started a popular uprising called the Anbar Awakening. To take advantage of this opportunity, we sent 4,000 additional marines to help these brave Iraqis drive Al Qaida from the Province. As this effort succeeded, it inspired other Iraqis to take up the fight. Soon similar uprisings began to spread across the country. Today, there are more than 90,000 concerned local citizens who are protecting their communities from the terrorists and insurgents and the extremists. The Government in Baghdad has stepped forward with a surge of its own; they've added more than 100,000 new Iraqi soldiers and police during the past year. These Iraqi troops have fought bravely, and thousands have given their lives in this struggle.

Together, these Americans and Iraqi forces have driven the terrorists from many of the sanctuaries they once held. Now the terrorists have gathered in and around the northern Iraqi city of Mosul, and Iraqi and American forces are relentlessly pursuing them. There will be tough fighting in Mosul and areas of northern Iraq in the weeks ahead. But there's no doubt in my mind, because of the courage of our troops and the bravery of the Iraqis, the Al Qaida terrorists in this region will suffer the same fate as Al Qaida suffered elsewhere in Iraq.

As we have fought Al Qaida, coalition and Iraqi forces have also taken the fight to Shi'a extremist groups, many of them backed and financed and armed by Iran. A year ago, these groups were on the rise. Today, they are increasingly isolated, and Iraqis of all faiths are putting their lives on the line to stop these extremists from hijacking their young democracy.

To ensure that military progress in Iraq is quickly followed up with real improvements in daily life, we have doubled the number of Provincial Reconstruction Teams in Iraq. These teams of civilian experts are serving all Iraqi—18 Iraqi Provinces, and they're helping to strengthen responsible leaders and build up local economies and bring Iraqis together, so that reconciliation can happen from the ground up. They're very effective. They're helping give ordinary Iraqis confidence that by rejecting the extremists and reconciling with one another, they can claim their place in a free Iraq and build better lives for their families.

There's still hard work to be done in Iraq. The gains we have made are fragile and reversible. But on this anniversary, the American people should know that since the surge began, the level of violence is significantly down, civilian deaths are down, sectarian killings are down, attacks on American forces are down. We have captured or killed thousands of extremists in Iraq, including hundreds of key Al Qaida leaders and operatives. Our men and women in uniform are performing with characteristic honor and valor. The surge is working. And as a return on our success in Iraq, we've begun bringing some of our troops home.

The surge has done more than turn the situation in Iraq around, it has opened the door to a major strategic victory in the broader war on terror. For the terrorists, Iraq was supposed to be the place where Al Qaida rallied Arab masses to drive America out. Instead, Iraq has become the place where Arabs joined with Americans to drive Al Qaida out. In Iraq, we are witnessing the first large-scale Arab uprising against Osama bin Laden, his grim ideology, and his murderous network. And the significance of this development cannot be overstated.

The terrorist movement feeds on a sense of inevitability and claims to rise on the tide of history. The accomplishments of the surge in Iraq are exposing this myth and discrediting the extremists. When Iraqi and American forces finish the job, the effects will reverberate far beyond Iraq's borders. Osama bin Laden once said: "When people see a strong horse and a weak horse, by nature they will like the strong horse." By defeating Al Qaida in Iraq, we will show the world that Al Qaida is the weak horse. We will show that men and women who love liberty can defeat the terrorists. And we will show that the future of the Middle East does not belong to terror. The future of the Middle East belongs to freedom.

The challenge in this period ahead is to consolidate the gains we have made and seal the extremists' defeat. We have learned through hard experience what happens when we pull our forces back too fast; the terrorists and extremists step in, they fill vacuums, establish safe havens, and use them to spread chaos and carnage. General Petraeus has warned that too fast a drawdown could result in such an unraveling with Al Qaida and insurgents and militia extremists regaining lost ground and increasing violence.

Men and women of the Armed Forces: Having come so far and achieved so much, we're not going to let this to happen.

Next month, General Petraeus and Ambassador Crocker will come to Washington to testify before Congress. I will await their recommendations before making decisions on our troop levels in Iraq. Any further drawdown will be based on conditions on the ground and the recommendations of our commanders. And they must not jeopardize the hard-fought gains our troops and civilians have made over the past year.

Successes we are seeing in Iraq are undeniable, yet some in Washington still call for retreat. War critics can no longer credibly argue that we're losing in Iraq, so they now argue the war costs too much. In recent months, we've heard exaggerated amounts of the costs of this war. No one are—would argue that this war has not come at a high cost in lives and treasure; but those costs are necessary when we consider the cost of a strategic victory for our enemies in Iraq.

If we were to allow our enemies to prevail in Iraq, the violence that is now declining would accelerate, and Iraq would descend into chaos. Al Qaida would regain its lost sanctuaries and establish new ones, fomenting violence and terror that could spread beyond Iraq's borders, with serious consequences for the world's economy.

Out of such chaos in Iraq, the terrorist movement could emerge emboldened, with new recruits, new resources, and an even greater determination to dominate the region and harm America. An emboldened Al Qaida with access to Iraq's oil resources could pursue its ambitions to acquire weapons of mass destruction to attack America and other free nations. Iran would be emboldened as well, with a renewed determination to develop nuclear weapons and impose its brand of hegemony across the Middle East. Our enemies would see an America—an American failure in Iraq as evidence of weakness and a lack of resolve.

To allow this to happen would be to ignore the lessons of September the 11th and make it more likely that America would suffer another attack like the one we experienced that day; a day in which 19 armed men with box cutters killed nearly 3,000 people in our—on our soil; a day after which, in the following of that attack, more than a million Americans lost work, lost their jobs. The terrorists intend even greater harm to our country. And we have no greater responsibility than to defeat our enemies across the world so that they cannot carry out such an attack.

As our coalition fights the enemy in Iraq, we've stayed on the offensive on other fronts in the war on terror. You know, just a few weeks after commencing Operation Iraqi Freedom, U.S. forces captured Khalid Sheikh Mohammed, the mastermind behind the September the 11th terrorist attacks; we got him in Pakistan. About the same time as we launched Operation Iraqi Freedom, coalition forces thousands of—hundreds of miles away launched an assault on the terrorists in the mountains of southern Afghanistan in an operation called Operation Valiant Strike.

Throughout the war on terror, we have brought the enemy—we have fought the enemy on every single battlefront. And so long as terrorist danger remains, the United States of America will continue to fight the enemy wherever it makes its stand.

We will stay on the offense. But in the long run, defeating the terrorists requires an alternative to their murderous ideology. And there we have another advantage. We've got a singular advantage with our military when it comes to finding the terrorists and bringing them to justice. And we have another advantage in our strong belief in the transformative power of liberty.

So we're helping the people of Iraq establish a democracy in the heart of the Middle East. A free Iraq will fight terrorists instead of harboring them. A free Iraq will be an example for others of the power of liberty to change the societies and to displace despair with hope. By spreading the hope of liberty in the Middle East, we will help free societies take root. And when they do, freedom will yield the peace that we all desire.

Our troops on the frontlines understand what is at stake. They know that the mission in Iraq has been difficult and has been trying for our Nation, because they're the ones who've carried most of the burdens. They're all volunteers who have stepped forward to defend America in a time of danger. Some of them have gone out of their way to return to the fight.

One of these brave Americans is a Marine Gunnery Sergeant named William "Spanky" Gibson. In May of 2006 in Ramadi, a terrorist sniper's bullet ripped through his left knee; doctors then amputated his leg. After months of difficult rehabilitation, Spanky was not only walking, he was training for triathlons.

Last year, at the Escape from Alcatraz swim near San Francisco, he met Marine General James Mattis, who asked if there's anything he could do for him. Spanky had just one request: He asked to redeploy to Iraq. Today, he's serving in Fallujah, the first full-leg amputee to return to the frontlines. Here's what he says about his decision to return: "The Iraqis where—are where we were 232 years ago as a nation. Now they're starting a new nation, and that's one of my big reasons for coming back here. I wanted to tell the people of this country that I'm back to help wherever I can."

When Americans like Spanky Gibson serve on our side, the enemy in Iraq doesn't got a chance. We're grateful to all the brave men and women of our military who have served the cause of freedom. You've done the hard work, far from home and far from your loved ones. We give thanks for all our military families who love you and have supported you in this mission.

We appreciate the fine civilians from many Departments who serve alongside you. Many of you served in Iraq and Afghanistan, and some have been on these fronts several times. You will never forget the people who fought at your side. You will always remember the comrades who served with you in combat but did not make the journey home. America remembers them as well. More than 4,400 men and women have given their lives in the war on terror. We'll pray for their families. We'll always honor their memory.

The best way we can honor them is by making sure that their sacrifice was not in vain. Five years ago tonight, I promised the American people that in the struggle ahead, "we will accept no outcome but victory." Today, standing before men and women who helped liberate a nation, I reaffirm the commitment. The battle in Iraq is noble; it is necessary; and it is just. And with your courage, the battle in Iraq will end in victory. God bless.

Questions for Research and Discussion

1. President Bush seems to be justifying the attack of Iraq as a war on terror. Were the Iraqis involved in the terrorist attack of 9/11? What were the reasons President Bush had given previously for the invasion of Iraq?

2. The Bush philosophy, in regard to perceived threats to the United States, was to conduct a preemptive first strike. What are the strengths and limitations of this approach?

3. Compare the foreign policy approaches of George W. Bush with those of George H. W. Bush. Which president had the most effective survival perspective.

End Notes

[1]Webster. Daniel. "A Union of People that is 'One and Inseparable.'" Excerpts from the Webster-Hayne Debate. *Register of Debates in Congress of the 1st Session of the 21st Congress*, Vol. VI. Washington, Gales and Seaton. January 19–27, 1830. 31–92

[2]Hayne, Robert. "A Compact between Sovereign States." Excerpts from the Webster-Hayne debate. *Register of Debates in Congress of the 1st Session of the 21st Congress*, Vol. VI. Washington. Gales and Seaton. January 19–27, 1830. 31–92.

[3]Roosevelt, Franklin D. "American Business is Moving Ahead," John T. Woolley and Gerhard Peters, *The American Presidency Project (online)*, Santa Barbara, CA. .Available from the World Wide Web: http://www.presidency.ucsb.edu/ws/?pid=15185.

[4]Eccles, Marriner S. Chairman of the Federal Reserve Board, "Government Spending is Sound: Balancing the Budget is not Essential," *Vital Speeches of the Day* (February 15, 1939), 273–274

[5]Hoover, Herbert. "A Holy Crusade for Liberty," delivered at the Republican National Convention, Cleveland, Ohio, June 10, 1936. *Vital Speeches of the Day* (June 15, 1936) 570–573.

[6]Taft, Robert A. "A Declaration of Republican Principles." delivered at the National Republican Club, New York City (March 18, 1939) Reprinted in *Congressional Record* 76th Congress, 1st Session, Appendix (1939) 1355–1357.

[7]McCarthy, Joseph R. "Communists in the State Department" McCarthy's First Speech on this topic delivered in the U. S. Senate. *Major Speeches and Debates of Senator Joe McCarthy delivered in the United States Senate, 1950–51.* Reprint from the Congressional Record. United States Government Printing Office. Washington, D.C., 5–7.

[8]Roosevelt, Franklin D. "Facing Communism: The True Conservative is Liberal," September 29 1936. John T. Woolley and Gerhard Peters. *The American Presidency Project* (online), Santa Barbara, CA. Available from World Wide Web: http://www.presidency.ucsb.edu/ws/?pid=15142

[9]Smith, Margaret Chase. "Declaration of Conscience" with Statement of Seven Senators, June 1, 1950, *Congressional Record,* 82nd Congress. 1st Session, in Arthur M. Schkesinger, Jr. and Roger Burns, *Congress Investigates: A Documented History, 1792–1974* (New York: Chelsea House, 1963) 84–88,

[10]The United Nations: An Excerpt from the Democratic Party Platform of 1960. John T. Woolley and Gerhard Peters. *The American Presidency Project* (online). Santa Barbara, CA. Available from World Wide Web: http://www.presidency.ucsb.edu/ws/?pid=29602

[11]Kennedy, John F. "One World, One Human Race, with One Common Destiny," an address before the United Nations General Assembly, September 20, 1963. Reprinted from *The Public Papers of the Presidents of the United States: John F. Kennedy. Containing the Messages, Speeches and Statements of the Presidents, January 1 to November 22, 1963,* Washington, D. C.: US Government Printing Office, 1964. 693–698.

[12]Goldwater, Barry M. "The National Interest Must be Our First Priority," An Address Before the United States Senate, March 15, 1960. Reprinted from : *Proceedings and Debates of the 86th Congress. Second Session, Volume 106, Part 5. March 15, 1960 to March 19, 1960.* Washington D. C.: US Government Printing Office, 1960. 5571–5576.

[13]Bush, George H. W. Excerpt from "The Possibility of a New World Order. . ." John T. Woolley and Gerhard Peters. *The American Presidency Project* (online). Santa Barbara, CA. Available on the World Wide Web: http://www.presidency.ucsb.edu/ws/?pid=19466

[14]Bush, George W. "Remarks on the War on Terror," delivered at the Pentagon, March 19, 2008. John T. Woolley and Gerhard Peters, *The American Presidency Project* (online) Santa Barbara, CA Available from World Wide Web: http://www.presidency.ucsb.edu/ws/?pid=76860.

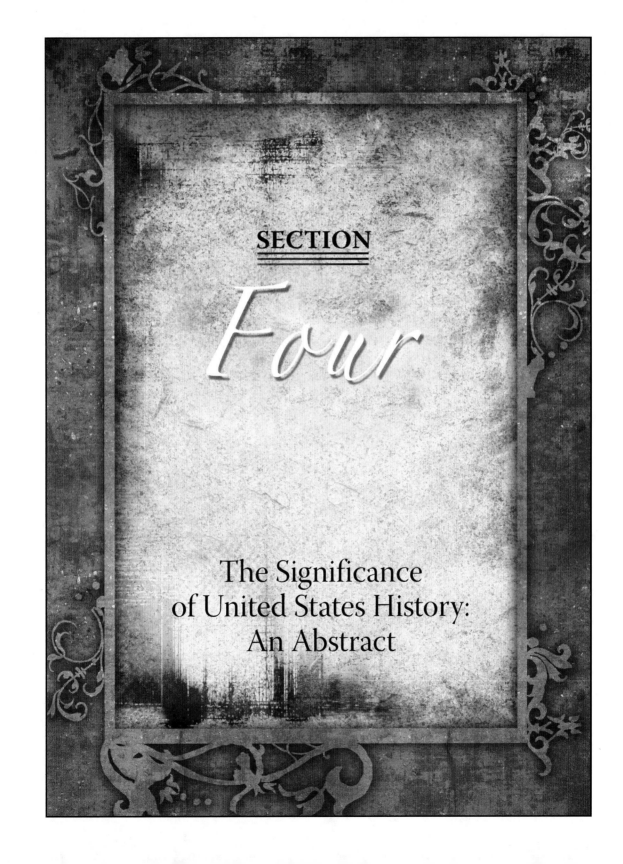

SECTION

Four

The Significance
of United States History:
An Abstract

"The dogmas of the quiet past are inadequate to the stormy present. The occasion is piled high with difficulty, and we must rise with the occasion. As our case is new we must think anew and act anew."

—Abraham Lincoln

"The only limit to our realization of tomorrow will be our doubts of today. Let us move forward with strong and active faith."

—Franklin D. Roosevelt

"A worldwide program of conservation could protect the forest and wild game preserves now in danger of extinction for all time, improve the harvest of marine food from our oceans, and prevent the contamination of air and water by industrial as well as nuclear pollution . . .

*The United Nations cannot survive as a static organization. Its obligations are increasing as well as its size. Its charter must be changed as well as its customs. The authors of that charter did not intend that it be frozen in perpetuity. The science of weapons and war have made us all, far more than eighteen years ago in San Francisco, **one world, and one human race, with one common destiny.** In such a world absolute sovereignty no longer assures us of absolute security. The conventions of peace must pull abreast and then ahead of the inventions of war. The United Nations, building on its successes and learning from its failures, must be developed into a genuine world security system."*

—John F. Kennedy

The Significance of United States History: An Abstract

United States history provides a record of human achievement under the oldest written Constitution on earth. This record of achievement is an American Testament that furnishes a compelling case for the American Constitution as a model for a world security system. Thermonuclear and environmental threats have now made the creation of a world security system a 21st Century imperative.

The Case for American Federalism

- In the tradition of American Federalism, world federalism could institutionalize freedom, harbor ideological differences and protect pluralism and diversity throughout the world. In the words of President John F. Kennedy, the world must be made "safe for diversity."

- America's federal system of separation of powers and checks and balances could be employed to curb tyranny at the international level by specifying and limiting the power of *three strengthened branches* of the United Nations—the Security Council, the General Assembly, and the International Court of Justice.

- America's federal system of division of power between the national government and the states could be adapted in a world system with a division of power between world authority and national authority.

- The American federal government has protected millions of acres of national parks and national forest reserve. World federalism could protect, for all time, the rain forests and the natural habitat that sustains life on earth.

- The American federal government has defined and advanced personal freedoms and civil liberties in a sacred Bill of Rights. Under world federalism, with vigorous enforcement of the Universal Declaration of Human Rights, the freedoms outlined in the American Bill of Rights could be advanced and maintained worldwide.

- The American federal government abolished slavery, extended citizenship and the right of the vote to former slaves, to women, and to all citizens who are eighteen years of age. A world federal system could extend freedom, extend the right of the vote, and otherwise empower world citizens.

- The American federal government provided subsidies and incentives to private companies to develop the nation's railroads and much of its infrastructure. Under world federalism, international subsidies and incentives could be granted to develop hydroelectric power sites, solar and wind energy, hydrogen power, and other alternatives to destructive fossil fuels.

- Under American federalism, massive spending held the line against complete economic collapse during the Great Depression and helped win World War II and the Cold War. Under world federalism, the United States could tap a national tax base that is currently furnishing huge sums for national defense. A peace dividend could create opportunities to re-build the cities, repair and extend the federal highways, build new schools, increase teachers' salaries, reduce class size, and subsidize a vast industry of alternative fuels. Federal money could be awarded, on a competitive basis, to private companies that were prepared to undertake various facets of new national projects.

- World federalism could provide the international structure to ban harmful environmental substances and practices, and control the use of nuclear weapons.

- World Federalism, fashioned after American federalism, could be the ultimate American triumph.

Salient Points

The United States has the oldest written Constitution on earth. It has:

- survived the transition from an agricultural to an industrial society

- survived a Civil War in which the death toll exceeded the *combined* United States death toll in all other American wars

- survived the Great Depression in which, at its lowest point, 5,000 banks had failed, one-fourth of the national labor force was idle, and one out of three families had no income

- survived two world wars and emerged from the second as one of the two great military powers in the world

- survived the challenges of a forty-year Cold War with the Soviet Union and emerged as the undisputed super power of the world

Many consider the American Constitution the greatest political document ever struck by the hand of man. It has provided:

- a national government, that is divided into legislative, executive and judicial branches, with powers delegated to each branch in a manner that has checked tyranny and provided effective executive, legislative, and judicial action

- a federal union with a division of power between the national government and the states

- a system for evolutionary change through the process of amendment

Over a period of 220 years the Constitution has been amended twenty-seven times. In the process we have promoted and guaranteed freedom of speech, freedom of religion and freedom of the press, along with other precious personal freedoms. We have slavery, extended the suffrage to former slaves, to women, and to all who are 18 years of age. We have strengthened democracy by taking the power to appoint Senators from the state legislatures and empowering the people with the right to elect them. We have abolished poll taxes and literacy tests and extended the practice of democracy in the process.

An American Testament

The theoretical foundation for the American Declaration of Independence and the United States Constitution lies in social contract theory. It was from the writings of John Locke, Thomas Hobbes and Jean Jacques Rousseau, that our founding fathers drew their rationale for equality, the institutionalization of freedom and the practice of the consent of the governed.

Thomas Hobbes identified freedom as a natural condition for mankind, but he also explained that in our natural state, mankind had a "nasty," "brutish," and "short" life experience. Our primate progenitors, it seems, were free to rape, decapitate, cannibalize, and rely on a few savage kinsmen to assist in the struggle to survive.

A social contract emerged, in this chaos, when a clan of individuals tacitly agreed to surrender the freedom to commit savagery against one another. They set rules of conduct within their society. They began to institutionalize and protect rights and positive freedoms, and they based decision making on the consent of the governed.

The clan, therefore, became the first political structure in the survival process, and the first institution to incorporate rudimentary ethical facets of modern civilization.

Clans evolved into tribes where cooperation and bonding were strengthened through rules and laws, primitive religious rituals, and perhaps a flag. In this evolutionary process, mankind institutionalized freedom, developed a rule of law, and based decision making on the consent of the governed.

As nomadic tribes became sedentary, rules for the village evolved into more sophisticated social contracts, eventually developing into city-states and thenceforth into modern nation states.

In this lengthy process, the evolutionary social contract became not only the catalyst in the development of modern civilization, but also in every progression, a survival device.

The politics of survival were operative at the Philadelphia Convention in 1787. As the delegates were fashioning the most enduring Constitution on earth, they were replacing a failed, fragmented, confederate structure that most assuredly could never have preserved the political heritage that sprung from the enlightenment. The Constitution makers were mindful that they must produce a social contract that would reflect the ideals of equality, God-given freedoms, and government based on the consent of the governed. These ideals were no longer remote concepts from social contract theorists of the past; they had become America's creed, the very reason for our new nation, embodied in our Declaration of Independence.

Problems under the Articles of Confederation (1781–1789) could not be characterized as nasty, brutish or savage, but their resolution was critical to the survival of the nation.

Foreign nations were casting suspicious eyes on our failure to create an effective executive. When a committee attempted to conduct diplomacy, British diplomats asked if we were seeking one treaty or thirteen. They also observed that American currency was not uniform, creating economic confusion at home and abroad. Disputes between states over the navigation of waterways sometimes led to armed clashes, and finally Congress could not levy and collect taxes and therefore could not finance national projects or build an effective national defense.

In this crisis the Constitution makers sought commonality in "a more perfect union." The American federal system that emerged from the Philadelphia convention brought the evolutionary social contract to new heights. The "more perfect union" has curbed tyranny through a system of checks and balances, harbored ideological differences, fostered an atmosphere of pluralism and diversity, guaranteed personal freedoms through an appended Bill of Rights, established a system of uniform justice through an effective Supreme Court, and fulfilled the goals of its makers by providing for the common defense, promoting the general welfare, and guaranteeing liberty for the founders and for their posterity.

An American Model

From 1781 to 1789, large states, small states, free states and slave states were loosely combined. They were economically, politically and culturally diverse, and fragmented to the point that the prospect of an enduring United States seemed dim. American patriots resolved the crisis with new and effective government.

Early in the 21st Century, large nations, small nations, free nations and totalitarian nations are loosely combined in a multi-lateral treaty known as the United Nations. The "United" Nations are politically and culturally diverse, and fragmented to the point that the prospect of a safe world seems dim. Who will respond in the crisis?

There is now only a brief window of opportunity to respond to "nasty" and "brutish" conditions in our world. Our rainforests are rapidly disappearing, but "the lungs of the world" have not yet been ripped out. The hole in earth's protective ozone layer is now larger than the North American continent, but there is an opportunity to minimize the damage with swift international action. Fossil fuels continue to produce oil slicks, pollute the air, and promote global warming, but the most horrible disasters from the greenhouse effect are perhaps fifty to seventy-five years away. Acid rain has destroyed vast timber acreage and tens of thousands of lakes in Europe, Northeastern United States and Canada, but rapid movement into solar, wind and hydrogen technology could help alleviate this problem as well. Dangerous stockpiles of nuclear weapons remain in the hands of various nations who could open mankind's last war, but the proposals for disarmament, and the pleas for development of world law, long sought by Presidents Eisenhower, Kennedy, and other American leaders, could still be implemented.

Has the time arrived to negotiate the ultimate social contract? Could the United Nations be developed into a genuine world security system capable of checking tyranny, promoting freedom, curbing environmental deterioration, and averting nuclear annihilation?

Should the United Nations be strengthened in order to enforce world law? **President John F. Kennedy** answered with a resounding yes to all of these questions. In 1960 he ran on a bold platform that contained the following pledge:

> "To all our fellow members of the United Nations. We shall strengthen our commitments in this, our great continuing institution for conciliation and the growth of a world community. Through the machinery of the United Nations, we shall work for disarmament, the establishment of an international police force, the strengthening of the World Court and the establishment of world law."[1]

President Kennedy was an advocate for world peace through world law in his book, *The Strategy of Peace*, in his inaugural address, in an address before the General Assembly of the United Nations on September 25, 1961, in his remarks at the signing of the bill establishing The Arms Control and Disarmament Agency, in his Third State of the Union message, In an address delivered at Commencement at American University on June 10, 1963, in a news conference of September 12, 1963, in an address before the General assembly of the United Nations on September 20, 1963, and in his 17th annual report on the United Nations, to the Congress of the United States, released two days before his death.[2] But President Kennedy was not the only advocate of a rule of law for nations.

President Eisenhower also called for a world community under law and, in a dramatic letter sent to Senator Hubert Humphrey, published in the *U. S. Department of State Bulletin* on January 25, 1960, he called for the strengthening of the International Court of Justice.[3]

President Harry S. Truman, in his First State of the Union address, January 21, 1946, called for the development "of the United Nations organization as the representative of the world as one society."[4] He also asserted the United Nations should be the cornerstone of United States foreign policy, and when Communist North Korea invaded South Korea in 1950, he organized an international police force, fighting under a U.N. flag, to contain North Korean aggression.

Albert Einstein, in an address on NBC Television, February 19, 1950, called for "a supra-national judicial and executive body (to be) empowered to decide questions of immediate concern to the security of the nations."[5] This demand is repeated numerous times in the book *Einstein on Peace*, 1960.

Dr. Edward Teller, Father of the Hydrogen Bomb, wrote in his book, *The Legacy of Hiroshima*, "We must work for the establishment of a world authority sustained by moral force and physical force—a worldwide government capable of enforcing worldwide law and worldwide disarmament."[6]

Chief Justice Earl Warren delivered an address in Geneva, Switzerland on March 12, 1966, titled, "World Peace through Law."[7]

Arnold J. Toynbee, world renowned historian and long-time advocate of world peace through world law, wrote an important article that was published in *The New York Times Magazine*, April 5, 1964. It was titled "It is One World or No World."[8]

Walter Cronkite, a legendary anchor for CBS News, wrote in his book, *A Reporter's Life* ". . . the world is unlikely to survive a third world war . . . If we are to avoid that catastrophe, a system of world order— preferably a system of world government—is mandatory."[9]

President H.W. Bush responded to Iraqi aggression against Kuwait by organizing the whole world to contain the unwarranted assault. Arabs and Jews, capitalists and communists, and every other unlikely combination, joined hands to stop Saddam Hussein. Operating under the authority of unanimous Security Council Resolutions, Operation Desert Storm was a magnificent example of use of the United Nations for swift resolution of an international crisis. Bush had a clearly defined mission with an exit strategy, and it was accomplished at minimum cost in materials and men. At Maxwell Air Force Base in Montgomery, Alabama, April 13, 1991, President Bush proudly delivered a speech titled, "The Possibility of a New World Order: Unlocking the Promise of Freedom."[10]

It is worthy of note that most advocates for development of a world security system are a generation and more removed. The wave for support for internationalism seemed to crest in the early 1970s and then recede, leaving a few bewildered voices wading in the shallow tides of conservatism. Leaders of the present day are concocting schemes of rampant nationalism and pre-emptive war. This bankrupt approach can only bring an acceleration of the rape of the earth for economic gain, a clash of new imperialisms, and perhaps mankind's last war.

Earth's alarm bells are ringing. Environmental and thermonuclear issues call for *a swift international response*. Survival lies within the realm of human possibilities, but the window of opportunity is closing and will soon be shuttered. We can ignore the world we live in and drift toward a grim, unintended fate. We can engage in crisis-to-crisis improvisation, tinkering with enormous challenges, with little chance for success. Or we can actively engage in development of a long-range global plan.

Most Americans think of survival in terms of economic gain and material comfort. Those who read books concentrate on the habits of effective people, strategies for success, fictional escapism, and books that deal with problems of our past. It is pre-eminently the time to adopt a new survival perspective—a new view that offers hope for the resolution of the major survival issues of our time.

Questions for Research and Discussion

1. If enforceable law is important for the well being of a city, a state, and a nation, why is it not important for the world?

2. What are some of the pitfalls in the pursuit of world law?

3. What are our options in dealing with worldwide environmental deterioration?

4. How can nuclear weapons be controlled for the safety of the entire world?

5. Compare President George W. Bush's foreign policy approach with that of President Kennedy.

Suggested Reading

Anthony B. Anderson, *Alternatives to Deforestation.* (1994); Joseph A. Bagnall, *The Kennedy Option: Pursuit of World Law.* (1992); *The Survival Hot List: Conquering the Seven Deadly Trends.* (2006); Bert Bolin, *A Comparative History of Social Responses to Climate Change: Ozone Depletion and Acid Rain.* (2000); Grenville Clark and Louis B. Sohn *World Peace through World Law.* (1973); Barry Commoner *et al. Alternative Technologies for Power Production.* (1975); Norman Cousins, *In Place of Folly.* (1961); Scott Douglas, The *Spread of Nuclear Weapons: A Debate.* (1998); Paul R. Ehrlich, *Extinction: The Cause and Consequences of the Disappearance of Species.* (1981); Albert Einstein, *Einstein on Peace.* (1960); Richard Elliot. *Ozone Diplomacy: New Directions in Safeguarding the Planet.* (1997); Al Gore. *Earth in the Balance: Ecology and the Human Spirit.* (1992); Peter Hoffman, *The Forever Fuel: The Story of Hydrogen.* (1981); J.T.T. Houghton, *Global Warming: The Complete Briefing.* (1997); John F. Kennedy, *the Strategy of Peace.* (1960); W. D. Nordhaus and Joseph Boyer, *Warming the World: Economic Models of Global Warming.* (2000); Jonathon Schell, The *Fate of the Earth and the Abolition.* (1999); UN Environmental Programme, *Scientific Assessment of Ozone Depletion.* (1998).

Notes

[1]John Wooley and Gerhard Peters. www.presidency.ucsb.edu/ Documents. Party Platforms. Democratic 1960. Excerpt of plank on the United Nations.

[2]Joseph A. Bagnall. *President John F. Kennedy's Grand and Global Alliance: World Order for the New Century,* University Press of America, 1992, pp. 3–82.

[3]Dwight D. Eisenhower. *U.S. Department of State Bulletin,* January 25, 1960 v. 42. pp. 128–130.

[4]*Public Papers of the Presidents of the United States, Harry S. Truman, Containing the Messages, Speeches, and Statements of the President, January 1 to December 31, 1946* Washington, D.C., U.S. Government Printing Office, 1962.

[5]Albert Einstein. "Peace in the Atomic Era," *Vital Speeches of the Day,* March 1, 1950, p. 302.

[6]Edward Teller. *The Legacy of Hiroshima.* New York: Doubleday & Company, 1962, p. 209.

[7]Earl Warren. "World Peace through Law," *Vital Speeches of the Day,* April 15, 1966, pp. 387–390.

[8]Arnold J. Toynbee. "It is One World or No World," *New York Times Magazine,* April 5, 1964, p. 28.

[9]Walter Cronkite. *A Reporter's Life.* Alfred A. Knopf, 1997, p. 128.

[10]G.H.W. Bush. "The Possibility of a New World Order," *Vital Speeches of the Day,* May 15, 1991, pp. 450–452.

Appendices

Part One
The Freedom Documents

THE AMERICAN BILL OF RIGHTS

Note: The following text is a transcription of the first ten amendments to the Constitution in their original form. These amendments were ratified December 15, 1791, and form what is known as the "Bill of Rights."

Article I

Congress shall make no law respecting an establishment of religion, or prohibiting the free exercise thereof; or abridging the freedom of speech, or of the press; or the right of the people peaceably to assemble, and to petition the Government for a redress of grievances.

Article II

A well regulated Militia, being necessary to the security of a free State, the right of the people to keep and bear Arms, shall not be infringed.

Article III

No Soldier shall, in time of peace be quartered in any house, without the consent of the Owner, nor in time of war, but in a manner to be prescribed by law.

Article IV

The right of the people to be secure in their persons, houses, papers, and effects, against unreasonable searches and seizures, shall not be violated, and no Warrants shall issue, but upon probable cause, supported by Oath or affirmation, and particularly describing the place to be searched, and the persons or things to be seized.

Article V

No person shall be held to answer for a capital, or otherwise infamous crime, unless on a presentment or indictment of a Grand Jury, except in cases arising in the land or naval forces, or in the Militia, when in actual service in time of War or public danger; nor shall any person be subject for the same offence to be twice put in jeopardy of life or limb; nor shall be compelled in any criminal case to be a witness against himself, nor be deprived of life, liberty, or property, without due process of law; nor shall private property be taken for public use, without just compensation.

Article VI

In all criminal prosecutions, the accused shall enjoy the right to a speedy and public trial, by an impartial jury of the State and district wherein the crime shall have been committed, which district shall have been previously ascertained by law, and to be informed of the nature and cause of the accusation; to be confronted with the witnesses against him; to have compulsory process for obtaining witnesses in his favor, and to have the Assistance of Counsel for his defense.

Article VII

In Suits at common law, where the value in controversy shall exceed twenty dollars, the right of trial by jury shall be preserved, and no fact tried by a jury, shall be otherwise re-examined in any Court of the United States, than according to the rules of the common law.

Article VIII

Excessive bail shall not be required, nor excessive fines imposed, nor cruel and unusual punishments inflicted.

Article IX

The enumeration in the Constitution, of certain rights, shall not be construed to deny or disparage others retained by the people.

Article X

The powers not delegated to the United States by the Constitution, nor prohibited by it to the States, are reserved to the States respectively, or to the people.

THE UNIVERSAL DECLARATION OF HUMAN RIGHTS
Preamble

Whereas recognition of the inherent dignity and of the equal and inalienable rights of all members of the human family is the foundation of freedom, justice and peace in the world,

Whereas disregard and contempt for human rights have resulted in barbarous acts which have outraged the conscience of mankind, and the advent of a world in which human beings shall enjoy freedom of speech and belief and freedom from fear and want has been proclaimed as the highest aspiration of the common people,

Eleanor Roosevelt

Figure A.1 *Eleanor Roosevelt with a copy of the Universal Declaration of Human Rights in Spanish. Mrs. Franklin D. Roosevelt was appointed U. S. Ambassador to the United Nations in the Truman administration. She served as chairman of the committee that drafted the Universal Declaration of Human Rights. President Truman recognized that she was the chief architect in the reframing of the freedoms contained in the American Bill of Rights and presenting them to the entire world. For her distinguished work, Truman called her "the First Lady of the World."*

Courtesy of the Franklin D. Roosevelt Presidential Library and Museum, Hyde Park, NY.

Whereas it is essential, if man is not to be compelled to have recourse, as a last resort, to rebellion against tyranny and oppression, that human rights should be protected by the rule of law,

Whereas it is essential to promote the development of friendly relations between nations.

Whereas the peoples of the United Nations have in the Charter reaffirmed their faith in fundamental human rights, in the dignity and worth of the human person and in the equal rights of men and women and have determined to promote social progress and better standards of life in larger freedom,

Whereas Member States have pledged themselves to achieve, in co-operation with the United Nations, the promotion of Universal respect for and observance of human rights and fundamental freedoms,

Whereas a common understanding of these rights and freedoms is of the greatest importance for the full realization of this pledge,

Now, therefore,
The General Assembly
proclaims this

From *Universal Declaration of Human Rights* by the United Nations General Assembly, © 1948 United Nations. Reprinted with the permission of the United Nations.

Universal Declaration of Human Rights as a common standard of achievement for all peoples and all nations, to the end that every individual and every organ of society, keeping this Declaration constantly in mind, shall strive by teaching and education to promote respect for these rights and freedoms and by progressive measures, national international, to secure their universal and effective recognition and observance, both among the peoples of Member States themselves and among the peoples of territories under their jurisdiction.

Article 1

All human beings are born free and equal in dignity and rights. They are endowed with reason and conscience and should act towards one another in a spirit of brotherhood.

Article 2

Everyone is entitled to all the rights and freedoms set forth in this Declaration, without distinction of any kind, such as race, colour, sex, language, religion, political or other opinion, national or social origin, property, birth or other status. Furthermore, no distinction shall be made on the basis of the political, jurisdictional or international status of the country or territory to which a person belongs, whether it be independent, trust, nonself-governing or under any other limitation of sovereignty.

Article 3

Everyone has the right to life, liberty and security of person.

Article 4

No one shall be held in slavery or servitude; slavery and the slave trade shall be prohibited in all their forms.

Article 5

No one shall be subjected to torture or to cruel, inhuman or degrading treatment or punishment.

Article 6

Everyone has the right to recognition everywhere as a person before the law.

Article 7

All are equal before the law and are entitled without any discrimination to equal protection of the law. All are entitled to equal protection against any discrimination in violation of this Declaration and against any incitement to such discrimination.

Article 8

Everyone has the right to an effective remedy by the competent national tribunals for acts violating the fundamental rights granted him by the constitution or by law.

Article 9

No one shall be subjected to arbitrary arrest, detention or exile.

Article 10

Everyone is entitled in full equality to a fair and public hearing by an independent and impartial tribunal, in the determination of his rights and obligations and of any criminal charge against him.

Article 11

1. Everyone charged with a penal offence has the right to be presumed innocent until proved guilty according to law in a public trial at which he has had all the guarantees necessary for his defence.

2. No one shall be held guilty of any penal offence on account of any act or omission which did not constitute a penal offence, under national or international law, at the time when it was committed. Nor shall a heavier penalty be imposed than the one that was applicable at the time the penal offence was committed.

Article 12

No one shall be subjected to arbitrary interference with his privacy, family, home or correspondence, nor to attacks upon his honour and reputation. Everyone has the right to the protection of the law against such interference or attacks.

Article 13

1. Everyone has the right to freedom of movement and residence within the borders of each state.

2. Everyone has the right to leave any country, including his own, and to return to his country.

Article 14

1. Everyone has the right to seek and to enjoy in other countries asylum from persecution.

2. This right may not be invoked in the case of prosecutions genuinely arising from non-political crimes or from acts contrary to the purposes and principles of the United Nations.

Article 15

1. Everyone has the right to a nationality.

2. No one shall be arbitrarily deprived of his nationality nor denied the right to change his nationality.

Article 16

1. Men and women of full age, without any limitation due to race, nationality or religion, have the right to marry and to found a family. They are entitled to equal rights as to marriage, during marriage and at its dissolution.

2. Marriage shall be entered into only with the free and full consent of the intending spouses.

3. The family is the natural and fundamental group unit of society and is entitled to protection by society and the State.

Article 17

1. Everyone has the right to own property alone as well as in association with others.

2. No one shall be arbitrarily deprived of his property.

Article 18

Everyone has the right to freedom of thought, conscience and religion; this right includes freedom to change his religion or belief, and freedom, either alone or in community with others and in public or private, to manifest his religion or belief in teaching, practice, worship and observance.

Article 19

Everyone has the right to freedom of opinion and expression; this right includes freedom to hold opinions without interference and to seek, receive and impart information and ideas through any media and regardless of frontiers.

Article 20

1. Everyone has the right to freedom of peaceful assembly and association.

2. No one may be compelled to belong to an association.

Article 21

1. Everyone has the right to take part in the government of his country, directly or through freely chosen representatives.

2. Everyone has the right of equal access to public service in his country.

3. The will of the people shall be the basis of the authority of government; this will shall be expressed in periodic and genuine elections which shall be by universal and equal suffrage and shall be held by secret vote or by equivalent free voting procedures.

Article 22

Everyone, as a member of society, has the right to a social security and is entitled to realization, through national effort and international co-operation and in accordance with the organization and resources of each State, of the economic, social and cultural rights indispensable for his dignity and the free development of his personality.

Article 23

1.   Everyone has the right to work, to free choice of employment, to just and favourable conditions of work and to protection against unemployment.

2.   Everyone, without any discrimination, has the right to equal pay for equal work.

3.   Everyone who works has the right to just and favourable remuneration ensuring for himself and his family an existence worthy of human dignity, and supplemented, if necessary, by other means of social protection.

4.   Everyone has the right to form and to join trade unions for the protection of his interests.

Article 24

Everyone has the right to rest and leisure, including reasonable limitation of working hours and periodic holidays with pay.

Article 25

1.   Everyone has the right to a standard of living adequate for the health and well-being of himself and of his family, including food, clothing, housing and medical care and necessary social services, and the right to security in the event of unemployment, sickness, disability, widowhood, old age or other lack of livelihood in circumstances beyond his control.

2.   Motherhood and childhood are entitled to special care and assistance. All children, whether born in or out of wedlock, shall enjoy the same social protection.

Article 26

1.   Everyone has the right to education. Education shall be free, at least in the elementary and fundamental stages. Elementary education shall be compulsory. Technical and professional education shall be made generally available and higher education shall be equally accessible to all on the basis of merit.

2.   Education shall be directed to the full development of the human personality and to the strengthening of respect for human rights and fundamental freedoms. It shall promote understanding, tolerance and friendship among all nations, racial

or religious groups, and shall further the activities of the United Nations for the maintenance of peace.

3. Parents have a prior right to choose the kind of education that shall be given to their children.

Article 27

1. Everyone has the right freely to participate in the cultural life of the community, to enjoy the arts and to share in scientific advancement and its benefits.

2. Everyone has the right to the protection of the moral and material interests resulting from any scientific, literary or artistic production of which he is the author.

Article 28

Everyone is entitled to a social and international order in which the rights and freedoms set forth in this Declaration can be fully realized.

Article 29

1. Everyone has duties to the community in which alone the free and full development of his personality is possible.

2. In the exercise of his rights and freedoms, everyone shall be subject only to such limitations as are determined by law solely for the purpose of securing due recognition and respect for the rights and freedoms of others and of meeting the just requirements of morality, public order and the general welfare in a democratic society.

3. These rights and freedoms may in no case be exercised contrary to the purposes and principles of the United Nations.

Article 30

Nothing in this Declaration may be interpreted as implying for any State, group or person any right to engage in any activity or to perform any act aimed at the destruction of any of the rights and freedoms set forth herein.

THE AMERICAN DECLARATION OF INDEPENDENCE

IN CONGRESS, July 4, 1776

The unanimous Declaration of the Thirteen United States of America,

When in the Course of human events, it becomes necessary for one people to dissolve the political bands which have connected them with another, and to assume among the powers of the earth, the separate and equal station to which the laws of nature and of nature's God entitle them, a decent respect to the opinions of mankind requires that they should declare the causes which impel them to the separation.

We hold these truths to be self-evident, that all men are created equal, that they are endowed by their Creator with certain unalienable Rights, that among these are life, liberty and the pursuit of happiness; that to secure these rights, governments are instituted among men, deriving their just powers from the consent of the governed; that whenever any form of government becomes destructive of these ends, it is the right of the people to alter or to abolish it, and to institute new government, laying its foundation on such principles and organizing its powers in such form, as to them shall seem most likely to effect their safety and happiness. Prudence, indeed, will dictate that Governments long established should not be changed for light and transient causes; and accordingly all experience hath shown, that mankind are more disposed to suffer, while evils are sufferable, than to right themselves by abolishing the forms to which they are accustomed. But when a long train of abuses and usurpations, pursuing invariably the same object evinces a design to reduce them under absolute despotism, it is their right, it is their duty, to throw off such government, and to provide new guards for their future security. Such has been the patient sufferance of these colonies; and such is now the necessity which constrains them to alter their former systems of government. The history of the present King of Great Britain is a history of repeated injuries and usurpations, all having in direct object the establishment of an absolute tyranny over these states. To prove this, let Facts be submitted to a candid world.

He has refused his assent to laws, the most wholesome and necessary for the public good.

He has forbidden his governors to pass laws of immediate and pressing importance, unless suspended in their operation till his assent should be obtained; and when so suspended, he has utterly neglected to attend to them.

He has refused to pass other laws for the accommodation of large districts of people, unless those people would relinquish the right of representation in the legislature, a right inestimable to them and formidable to tyrants only.

He has called together legislative bodies at places unusual, uncomfortable, and distant from the depository of their public records, for the sole purpose of fatiguing them into compliance with his measures.

He has dissolved representative houses repeatedly, for opposing with manly firmness his invasions on the rights of the people.

He has refused for a long time, after such dissolutions, to cause others to be elected; whereby the legislative powers, incapable of annihilation, have returned to the people at large for their exercise; the state remaining in the mean time exposed to all the dangers of invasion from without, and convulsions within.

He has endeavored to prevent the population of these states; for that purpose obstructing the laws for naturalization of foreigners; refusing to pass others to encourage their migrations hither, and raising the conditions of new appropriations of lands.

He has obstructed the administration of justice, by refusing his assent to laws for establishing judiciary powers.

He has made judges dependent on his will alone, for the tenure of their offices, and the amount and payment of their salaries.

He has erected a multitude of new offices, and sent hither swarms of officers to harass our people, and eat out their substance.

He has kept among us, in times of peace, standing armies without the consent of our legislatures.

He has affected to render the military independent of and superior to the civil power.

He has combined with others to subject us to a jurisdiction foreign to our constitution, and unacknowledged by our laws; giving his assent to their acts of pretended legislation:

For quartering large bodies of armed troops among us:

For protecting them, by a mock trial, from punishment for any murders which they should commit on the inhabitants of these states:

For cutting off our trade with all parts of the world:

For imposing taxes on us without our consent:

For depriving us in many cases, of the benefits of trial by jury:

For transporting us beyond seas to be tried for pretended offences

For abolishing the free system of English laws in a neighboring province, establishing therein an arbitrary government, and enlarging its boundaries so as to render it at once an example and fit instrument for introducing the same absolute rule into these colonies:

For taking away our charters, abolishing our most valuable laws, and altering fundamentally the forms of our governments:

For suspending our own Legislatures, and declaring themselves invested with power to legislate for us in all cases whatsoever.

He has abdicated Government here, by declaring us out of his protection and waging war against us.

He has plundered our seas, ravaged our coasts, burnt our towns, and destroyed the lives of our people.

He is at this time transporting large armies of foreign mercenaries to complete the works of death, desolation and tyranny, already begun with circumstances of cruelty & perfidy scarcely paralleled in the most barbarous ages, and totally unworthy the head of a civilized nation.

He has constrained our fellow citizens taken captive on the high seas to bear arms against their country, to become the executioners of their friends and brethren, or to fall themselves by their hands.

He has excited domestic insurrections amongst us, and has endeavoured to bring on the inhabitants of our frontiers, the merciless Indian savages, whose known rule of warfare, is an undistinguished destruction of all ages, sexes and conditions.

In every stage of these oppressions we have petitioned for redress in the most humble terms: Our repeated Petitions have been answered only by repeated injury. A prince whose character is thus marked by every act which may define a tyrant, is unfit to be the ruler of a free people.

Nor have we been wanting in attentions to our British brethren. We have warned them from time to time of attempts by their legislature to extend an unwarrantable jurisdiction over us. We have reminded them of the circumstances of our emigration and settlement here. We have appealed to their native justice and magnanimity, and we have conjured them by the ties of our common kindred to disavow these usurpations, which, would inevitably interrupt our connections and correspondence. They too have been deaf to the voice of justice and of consanguinity. We must, therefore, acquiesce in the necessity, which denounces our Separation, and hold them, as we hold the rest of mankind, enemies in war, in peace friends.

We, therefore, the representatives of the United States of America, in General Congress, assembled, appealing to the Supreme Judge of the world for the rectitude of our intentions, do, in the name, and by authority of the good people of these colonies, solemnly publish and declare, that these United Colonies are, and of right ought to be **Free and Independent States;** that they are absolved from all allegiance to the British crown, and that all political connection between them and the state of Great Britain, is and ought to be totally dissolved; and that as free and independent states, they have full Power to levy war, conclude peace, contract alliances, establish commerce, and to do all other acts and things which independent states may of right do. And for the support of this declaration, with a firm reliance on the protection of Divine Providence, we mutually pledge to each other our lives, our fortunes and our sacred honor.

JOHN HANCOCK [*President*] and fifty-five others

Part Two
The Constitution of The United States of America

We the people of the United States, in order to form a more perfect union, establish justice, insure domestic tranquility, provide for the common defense, promote the general welfare, and secure the blessings of liberty to ourselves and our posterity, do ordain and establish this Constitution for the United States of America.

Article I

Section 1. All legislative powers herein granted shall be vested in a Congress of the United States, which shall consist of a Senate and House of Representatives.

Section 2. The House of Representatives shall be composed of members chosen every second year by the people of the several states, and the electors in each state shall have the qualifications requisite for electors of the most numerous branch of the state legislature.

No person shall be a Representative who shall not have attained to the age of twenty five years, and been seven years a citizen of the United States, and who shall not, when elected, be an inhabitant of that state in which he shall be chosen.

Representatives and direct taxes shall be apportioned among the several states which may be included within this union, according to their respective numbers, which shall be determined by adding to the whole number of free persons, including those bound to service for a term of years, and excluding Indians not taxed, three fifths of all other Persons. The actual Enumeration shall be made within three years after the first meeting of the Congress of the United States, and within every subsequent term of ten years, in such manner as they shall by law direct. The number of Representatives shall not exceed one for every thirty thousand, but each state shall have at least one Representative; and until such enumeration shall be made, the state of New Hampshire shall be entitled to chuse three, Massachusetts eight, Rhode Island and Providence Plantations one, Connecticut five, New York six, New Jersey four, Pennsylvania eight, Delaware one, Maryland six, Virginia ten, North Carolina five, South Carolina five, and Georgia three.

When vacancies happen in the Representation from any state, the executive authority thereof shall issue writs of election to fill such vacancies.

The House of Representatives shall choose their speaker and other officers; and shall have the sole power of impeachment.

Section 3. The Senate of the United States shall be composed of two Senators from each state, chosen by the legislature thereof, for six years; and each Senator shall have one vote.

Immediately after they shall be assembled in consequence of the first election, they shall be divided as equally as may be into three classes. The seats of the Senators of the first class shall be vacated at the expiration of the second year, of the second class at the expiration of the fourth year, and the third class at the expiration of the sixth year, so that one third may be chosen every second year; and if vacancies happen by resignation, or otherwise, during the recess of the legislature of any state, the executive thereof may make temporary appointments until the next meeting of the legislature, which shall then fill such vacancies.

No person shall be a Senator who shall not have attained to the age of thirty years, and been nine years a citizen of the United States and who shall not, when elected, be an inhabitant of that state for which he shall be chosen.

The Vice President of the United States shall be President of the Senate, but shall have no vote, unless they be equally divided.

The Senate shall choose their other officers, and also a President pro tempore, in the absence of the Vice President, or when he shall exercise the office of President of the United States.

The Senate shall have the sole power to try all impeachments. When sitting for that purpose, they shall be on oath or affirmation. When the President of the United States is tried, the Chief Justice shall preside: And no person shall be convicted without the concurrence of two thirds of the members present.

Judgment in cases of impeachment shall not extend further than to removal from office, and disqualification to hold and enjoy any office of honor, trust or profit under the United States: but the party convicted shall nevertheless be liable and subject to indictment, trial, judgment and punishment, according to law.

Section 4. The times, places and manner of holding elections for Senators and Representatives, shall be prescribed in each state by the legislature thereof; but the Congress may at any time by law make or alter such regulations, except as to the places of choosing Senators.

The Congress shall assemble at least once in every year, and such meeting shall be on the first Monday in December, unless they shall by law appoint a different day.

Section 5. Each House shall be the judge of the elections, returns and qualifications of its own members, and a majority of each shall constitute a quorum to do business; but a smaller number may adjourn from day to day, and may be authorized to compel the attendance of absent members, in such manner, and under such penalties as each House may provide.

Each House may determine the rules of its proceedings, punish its members for disorderly behavior, and, with the concurrence of two thirds, expel a member.

Each House shall keep a journal of its proceedings, and from time to time publish the same, excepting such parts as may in their judgment require secrecy; and the yeas and nays of the members of either House on any question shall, at the desire of one fifth of those present, be entered on the journal.

Neither House, during the session of Congress, shall, without the consent of the other, adjourn for more than three days, nor to any other place than that in which the two Houses shall be sitting.

Section 6. The Senators and Representatives shall receive a compensation for their services, to be ascertained by law, and paid out of the treasury of the United States. They shall in all cases, except treason, felony and breach of the peace, be privileged from arrest during their attendance at the session of their respective Houses, and in going to and returning from the same; and for any speech or debate in either House, they shall not be questioned in any other place.

No Senator or Representative shall, during the time for which he was elected, be appointed to any civil office under the authority of the United States, which shall have been created, or the emoluments whereof shall have been increased during such time: and no person holding any office under the United States, shall be a member of either House during his continuance in office.

Section 7. All bills for raising revenue shall originate in the House of Representatives; but the Senate may propose or concur with amendments as on other Bills.

Every bill which shall have passed the House of Representatives and the Senate, shall, before it become a law, be presented to the President of the United States; if he approve he shall sign it, but if not he shall return it, with his objections to that House in which it shall have originated, who shall enter the objections at large on their journal, and proceed to reconsider it. If after such reconsideration two thirds of that House shall agree to pass the bill, it shall be sent, together with the objections, to the other House, by which it shall likewise be reconsidered, and if approved by two thirds of that House, it shall become a law. But in all such cases the votes of both Houses shall be determined by yeas and nays, and the names of the persons voting for and against the bill shall be entered on the journal of each House respectively. If any bill shall not be returned by the President within ten days (Sundays excepted) after it shall have been presented to him, the same shall be a law, in like manner as if he had signed it, unless the Congress by their adjournment prevent its return, in which case it shall not be a law.

Every order, resolution, or vote to which the concurrence of the Senate and House of Representatives may be necessary (except on a question of adjournment) shall be presented to the President of the United States; and before the same shall take effect, shall be approved by him, or being disapproved by him, shall be repassed by two thirds of the Senate and House of Representatives, according to the rules and limitations prescribed in the case of a bill.

Section 8. The Congress shall have power to lay and collect taxes, duties, imposts and excises, to pay the debts and provide for the common defense and general welfare of the United States; but all duties, imposts and excises shall be uniform throughout the United States;

To borrow money on the credit of the United States;

To regulate commerce with foreign nations, and among the several states, and with the Indian tribes;

To establish a uniform rule of naturalization, and uniform laws on the subject of bankruptcies throughout the United States;

To coin money, regulate the value thereof, and of foreign coin, and fix the standard of weights and measures;

To provide for the punishment of counterfeiting the securities and current coin of the United States;

To establish post offices and post roads;

To promote the progress of science and useful arts, by securing for limited times to authors and inventors the exclusive right to their respective writings and discoveries;

To constitute tribunals inferior to the Supreme Court;

To define and punish piracies and felonies committed on the high seas, and offenses against the law of nations;

To declare war, grant letters of marque and reprisal, and make rules concerning captures on land and water;

To raise and support armies, but no appropriation of money to that use shall be for a longer term than two years;

To provide and maintain a navy;

To make rules for the government and regulation of the land and naval forces;

To provide for calling forth the militia to execute the laws of the union, suppress insurrections and repel invasions;

To provide for organizing, arming, and disciplining, the militia, and for governing such part of them as may be employed in the service of the United States, reserving to the states respectively, the appointment of the officers, and the authority of training the militia according to the discipline prescribed by Congress;

To exercise exclusive legislation in all cases whatsoever, over such District (not exceeding ten miles square) as may, by cession of particular states, and the acceptance of Congress, become the seat of the government of the United States, and to exercise like authority over all places purchased by the consent of the legislature of the state in which the same shall be, for the erection of forts, magazines, arsenals, dockyards, and other needful buildings;—And

To make all laws which shall be necessary and proper for carrying into execution the foregoing powers, and all other powers vested by this Constitution in the government of the United States, or in any department or officer thereof.

Section 9. The migration or importation of such persons as any of the states now existing shall think proper to admit, shall not be prohibited by the Congress prior to the year one thousand eight hundred and eight, but a tax or duty may be imposed on such importation, not exceeding ten dollars for each person.

The privilege of the writ of habeas corpus shall not be suspended, unless when in cases of rebellion or invasion the public safety may require it.

No bill of attainder or ex post facto Law shall be passed.

No capitation, or other direct, tax shall be laid, unless in proportion to the census or enumeration herein before directed to be taken.

No tax or duty shall be laid on articles exported from any state.

No preference shall be given by any regulation of commerce or revenue to the ports of one state over those of another: nor shall vessels bound to, or from, one state, be obliged to enter, clear or pay duties in another.

No money shall be drawn from the treasury, but in consequence of appropriations made by law; and a regular statement and account of receipts and expenditures of all public money shall be published from time to time.

No title of nobility shall be granted by the United States: and no person holding any office of profit or trust under them, shall, without the consent of the Congress, accept of any present, emolument, office, or title, of any kind whatever, from any king, prince, or foreign state.

Section 10. No state shall enter into any treaty, alliance, or confederation; grant letters of marque and reprisal; coin money; emit bills of credit; make anything but gold and silver coin a tender in payment of debts; pass any bill of attainder, ex post facto law, or law impairing the obligation of contracts, or grant any title of nobility.

No state shall, without the consent of the Congress, lay any imposts or duties on imports or exports, except what may be absolutely necessary for executing it's inspection laws: and the net produce of all duties and imposts, laid by any state on imports or exports, shall be for the use of the treasury of the United States; and all such laws shall be subject to the revision and control of the Congress.

No state shall, without the consent of Congress, lay any duty of tonnage, keep troops, or ships of war in time of peace, enter into any agreement or compact with another state, or with a foreign power, or engage in war, unless actually invaded, or in such imminent danger as will not admit of delay.

Article II

Section 1. The executive power shall be vested in a President of the United States of America. He shall hold his office during the term of four years, and, together with the Vice President, chosen for the same term, be elected, as follows:

Each state shall appoint, in such manner as the Legislature thereof may direct, a number of electors, equal to the whole number of Senators and Representatives to which the State may be entitled in the Congress: but no Senator or Representative, or person holding an office of trust or profit under the United States, shall be appointed an elector.

The electors shall meet in their respective states, and vote by ballot for two persons, of whom one at least shall not be an inhabitant of the same state with themselves. And they shall make a list of all the persons voted for, and of the number of votes for each; which list they shall sign and certify, and transmit sealed to the seat of the government of the United States, directed to the President of the Senate. The President of the Senate shall, in the presence of the Senate and House of Representatives, open all the certificates, and the votes shall then be counted. The person having the greatest number of votes shall be the President, if such number be a majority of the whole number of electors appointed; and if there be more than one who have such majority, and have an equal number of votes, then the House of Representatives shall immediately choose by ballot one of them for President; and if no person have a majority, then from the five highest on the list the said House shall in like manner choose the President. But in choosing the President, the votes shall be taken by States, the representation from each state having one vote; A quorum for this purpose shall consist of a member or members from two thirds of the states, and a majority of all the states shall be necessary to a choice. In every case, after the choice of the President, the person having the greatest number of votes of the electors shall be the Vice President. But if there should remain two or more who have equal votes, the Senate shall choose from them by ballot the Vice President.

The Congress may determine the time of choosing the electors, and the day on which they shall give their votes; which day shall be the same throughout the United States.

No person except a natural born citizen, or a citizen of the United States, at the time of the adoption of this Constitution, shall be eligible to the office of President; neither shall any person be eligible to that office who shall not have attained to the age of thirty five years, and been fourteen Years a resident within the United States.

In case of the removal of the President from office, or of his death, resignation, or inability to discharge the powers and duties of the said office, the same shall devolve on the Vice President, and the Congress may by law provide for the case of removal, death, resignation or inability, both of the President and Vice President, declaring what officer shall then act as President, and such officer shall act accordingly, until the disability be removed, or a President shall be elected.

The President shall, at stated times, receive for his services, a compensation, which shall neither be increased nor diminished during the period for which he shall have been elected, and he shall not receive within that period any other emolument from the United States, or any of them.

Before he enter on the execution of his office, he shall take the following oath or affirmation:—"I do solemnly swear (or affirm) that I will faithfully execute the office of President of the United States, and will to the best of my ability, preserve, protect and defend the Constitution of the United States."

Section 2. The President shall be commander in chief of the Army and Navy of the United States, and of the militia of the several states, when called into the actual service of the United States; he may require the opinion, in writing, of the principal officer in each of the executive departments, upon any subject relating to the duties of their respective offices, and he shall have power to grant reprieves and pardons for offenses against the United States, except in cases of impeachment.

He shall have power, by and with the advice and consent of the Senate, to make treaties, provided two thirds of the Senators present concur; and he shall nominate, and by and with the advice and consent of the Senate, shall appoint ambassadors, other public ministers and consuls, judges of the Supreme Court, and all other officers of the United States, whose appointments are not herein otherwise provided for, and which shall be established by law: but the Congress may by law vest the appointment of such inferior officers, as they think proper, in the President alone, in the courts of law, or in the heads of departments.

The President shall have power to fill up all vacancies that may happen during the recess of the Senate, by granting commissions which shall expire at the end of their next session.

Section 3. He shall from time to time give to the Congress information of the state of the union, and recommend to their consideration such measures as he shall judge necessary and expedient; he may, on extraordinary occasions, convene both Houses, or either of them, and in case of disagreement between them, with respect to the time of adjournment, he may adjourn them to such time as he shall think proper; he shall receive ambassadors and other public ministers; he shall take care that the laws be faithfully executed, and shall commission all the officers of the United States.

Section 4. The President, Vice President and all civil officers of the United States, shall be removed from office on impeachment for, and conviction of, treason, bribery, or other high crimes and misdemeanors.

Article III

Section 1. The judicial power of the United States, shall be vested in one Supreme Court, and in such inferior courts as the Congress may from time to time ordain and establish. The judges, both of the supreme and inferior courts, shall hold their offices during good behaviour, and shall, at stated times, receive for their services, a compensation, which shall not be diminished during their continuance in office.

Section 2. The judicial power shall extend to all cases, in law and equity, arising under this Constitution, the laws of the United States, and treaties made, or which shall be made, under their authority;—to all cases affecting ambassadors, other public ministers and consuls;—to all cases of admiralty and maritime jurisdiction;—to controversies to which the United States shall be a party;—to controversies between two or more states;—between a state and citizens of another state;—between citizens of different states;—between citizens of the same state claiming lands under grants of different states, and between a state, or the citizens thereof, and foreign states, citizens or subjects.

In all cases affecting ambassadors, other public ministers and consuls, and those in which a state shall be party, the Supreme Court shall have original jurisdiction. In all the other cases before mentioned, the Supreme Court shall have appellate jurisdiction, both as to law and fact, with such exceptions, and under such regulations as the Congress shall make.

The trial of all crimes, except in cases of impeachment, shall be by jury; and such trial shall be held in the state where the said crimes shall have been committed; but when not committed within any state, the trial shall be at such place or places as the Congress may by law have directed.

Section 3. Treason against the United States, shall consist only in levying war against them, or in adhering to their enemies, giving them aid and comfort. No person shall be convicted of treason unless on the testimony of two witnesses to the same overt act, or on confession in open court.

The Congress shall have power to declare the punishment of treason, but no attainder of treason shall work corruption of blood, or forfeiture except during the life of the person attainted.

Article IV

Section 1. Full faith and credit shall be given in each state to the public acts, records, and judicial proceedings of every other state. And the Congress may by general laws prescribe the manner in which such acts, records, and proceedings shall be proved, and the effect thereof.

Section 2. The citizens of each state shall be entitled to all privileges and immunities of citizens in the several states.

A person charged in any state with treason, felony, or other crime, who shall flee from justice, and be found in another state, shall on demand of the executive authority of the state from which he fled, be delivered up, to be removed to the state having jurisdiction of the crime.

No person held to service or labor in one state, under the laws thereof, escaping into another, shall, in consequence of any law or regulation therein, be discharged from such service or labor, but shall be delivered up on claim of the party to whom such service or labor may be due.

Section 3. New states may be admitted by the Congress into this union; but no new states shall be formed or erected within the jurisdiction of any other state; nor any state be formed by the junction of two or more states, or parts of states, without the consent of the legislatures of the states concerned as well as of the Congress.

The Congress shall have power to dispose of and make all needful rules and regulations respecting the territory or other property belonging to the United States; and nothing in this Constitution shall be so construed as to prejudice any claims of the United States, or of any particular state.

Section 4. The United States shall guarantee to every state in this union a republican form of government, and shall protect each of them against invasion; and on application of the legislature, or of the executive (when the legislature cannot be convened) against domestic violence.

Article V

The Congress, whenever two thirds of both houses shall deem it necessary, shall propose amendments to this Constitution, or, on the application of the legislatures of two thirds of the several states, shall call a convention for proposing amendments, which, in either case, shall be valid to all intents and purposes, as part of this Constitution, when ratified by the legislatures of three fourths of the several states, or by conventions in three fourths thereof, as the one or the other mode of ratification may be proposed by the Congress; provided that no amendment which may be made prior to the year one thousand eight hundred and eight shall in any manner affect the first and fourth clauses in the ninth section of the first article; and that no state, without its consent, shall be deprived of its equal suffrage in the Senate.

Article VI

All debts contracted and engagements entered into, before the adoption of this Constitution, shall be as valid against the United States under this Constitution, as under the Confederation.

This Constitution, and the laws of the United States which shall be made in pursuance thereof; and all treaties made, or which shall be made, under the authority of the

United States, shall be the supreme law of the land; and the judges in every state shall be bound thereby, anything in the Constitution or laws of any State to the contrary notwithstanding.

The Senators and Representatives before mentioned, and the members of the several state legislatures, and all executive and judicial officers, both of the United States and of the several states, shall be bound by oath or affirmation, to support this Constitution; but no religious test shall ever be required as a qualification to any office or public trust under the United States.

Article VII

The ratification of the conventions of nine states, shall be sufficient for the establishment of this Constitution between the states so ratifying the same.

Done in convention by the unanimous consent of the states present the seventeenth day of September in the year of our Lord one thousand seven hundred and eighty seven and of the independence of the United States of America the twelfth. In witness whereof We have hereunto subscribed our Names,

G. Washington -Presidt. and deputy from Virginia

New Hampshire: *John Langdon, Nicholas Gilman*

Massachusetts: *Nathaniel Gorham, Rufus King*

Connecticut: *Wm: Saml. Johnson, Roger Sherman*

New York: *Alexander Hamilton*

New Jersey: Wil: Livingston, David Brearly, Wm. Paterson, Jona: Dayton

Pennsylvania: *B. Franklin, Thomas Mifflin, Robt. Morris, Geo. Clymer, Thos. FitzSimons, Jared Ingersoll, James Wilson, Gouv Morris*

Delaware: *Geo: Read, Gunning Bedford jun, John Dickinson, Richard Bassett, Jaco: Broom*

Maryland: *James McHenry, Dan of St Thos. Jenifer, Danl Carroll*

Virginia: *John Blair—, James Madison Jr.*

North Carolina: *Wm. Blount, Richd. Dobbs Spaight, Hu Williamson*

South Carolina: *J. Rutledge, Charles Cotesworth Pinckney, Charles Pinckney, Pierce Butler*

Georgia: *William Few, Abr Baldwin*

AMENDMENTS TO THE CONSTITUTION OF THE UNITED STATES

Amendment I (1791)

Congress shall make no law respecting an establishment of religion, or prohibiting the free exercise thereof; or abridging the freedom of speech, or of the press; or the right of the people peaceably to assemble, and to petition the government for a redress of grievances.

Amendment II (1791)

A well regulated militia, being necessary to the security of a free state, the right of the people to keep and bear arms, shall not be infringed.

Amendment III (1791)

No soldier shall, in time of peace be quartered in any house, without the consent of the owner, nor in time of war, but in a manner to be prescribed by law.

Amendment IV (1791)

The right of the people to be secure in their persons, houses, papers, and effects, against unreasonable searches and seizures, shall not be violated, and no warrants shall issue, but upon probable cause, supported by oath or affirmation, and particularly describing the place to be searched, and the persons or things to be seized.

Amendment V (1791)

No person shall be held to answer for a capital, or otherwise infamous crime, unless on a presentment or indictment of a grand jury, except in cases arising in the land or naval forces, or in the militia, when in actual service in time of war or public danger; nor shall any person be subject for the same offense to be twice put in jeopardy of life or limb; nor shall be compelled in any criminal case to be a witness against himself, nor be deprived of life, liberty, or property, without due process of law; nor shall private property be taken for public use, without just compensation.

Amendment VI (1791)

In all criminal prosecutions, the accused shall enjoy the right to a speedy and public trial, by an impartial jury of the state and district wherein the crime shall have been committed, which district shall have been previously ascertained by law, and to be informed of the nature and cause of the accusation; to be confronted with the witnesses against him; to have compulsory process for obtaining witnesses in his favor, and to have the assistance of counsel for his defense.

Amendment VII (1791)

In suits at common law, where the value in controversy shall exceed twenty dollars, the right of trial by jury shall be preserved, and no fact tried by a jury, shall be otherwise reexamined in any court of the United States, than according to the rules of the common law.

Amendment VIII (1791)

Excessive bail shall not be required, nor excessive fines imposed, nor cruel and unusual punishments inflicted.

Amendment IX (1791)

The enumeration in the Constitution, of certain rights, shall not be construed to deny or disparage others retained by the people.

Amendment X (1791)

The powers not delegated to the United States by the Constitution, nor prohibited by it to the states, are reserved to the states respectively, or to the people.

Amendment XI (1798)

The judicial power of the United States shall not be construed to extend to any suit in law or equity, commenced or prosecuted against one of the United States by citizens of another state, or by citizens or subjects of any foreign state.

Amendment XII (1804)

The electors shall meet in their respective states and vote by ballot for President and Vice-President, one of whom, at least, shall not be an inhabitant of the same state with themselves; they shall name in their ballots the person voted for as President, and in distinct ballots the person voted for as Vice-President, and they shall make distinct lists of all persons voted for as President, and of all persons voted for as Vice-President, and of the number of votes for each, which lists they shall sign and certify, and transmit sealed to the seat of the government of the United States, directed to the President of the Senate;—The President of the Senate shall, in the presence of the Senate and House of Representatives, open all the certificates and the votes shall then be counted;—the person having the greatest number of votes for President, shall be the President, if such number be a majority of the whole number of electors appointed; and if no person have such majority, then from the persons having the highest numbers not exceeding three on the list of those voted for as President, the House of Representatives shall choose immediately, by ballot, the President. But in choosing the President, the votes shall be taken by states, the representation from each state having one vote; a quorum for this purpose shall consist of a member or members from two-thirds of the states, and a majority of all the states shall be necessary to a choice. And if the House of Representatives shall not choose a President whenever the right of choice shall devolve upon them, before the fourth day of March next following, then the Vice-President shall act as President, as in the case of the death or other constitutional disability of the President. The person having the greatest number of votes as Vice-President, shall be the Vice-President, if such number be a majority of the whole number of electors appointed, and if no person have a majority, then from the two highest numbers on the list, the Senate shall choose the Vice-President; a quorum for the purpose shall consist of two-thirds of the whole number of Senators, and a majority of the whole number shall be necessary to a choice. But no person constitutionally ineligible to the office of President shall be eligible to that of Vice-President of the United States.

Amendment XIII (1865)

Section 1. Neither slavery nor involuntary servitude, except as a punishment for crime whereof the party shall have been duly convicted, shall exist within the United States, or any place subject to their jurisdiction.

Section 2. Congress shall have power to enforce this article by appropriate legislation.

Amendment XIV (1868)

Section 1. All persons born or naturalized in the United States, and subject to the jurisdiction thereof, are citizens of the United States and of the state wherein they reside. No state shall make or enforce any law which shall abridge the privileges or immunities of citizens of the United States; nor shall any state deprive any person of life, liberty, or property, without due process of law; nor deny to any person within its jurisdiction the equal protection of the laws.

Section 2. Representatives shall be apportioned among the several states according to their respective numbers, counting the whole number of persons in each state, excluding Indians not taxed. But when the right to vote at any election for the choice of electors for President and Vice President of the United States, Representatives in Congress, the executive and judicial officers of a state, or the members of the legislature thereof, is denied to any of the male inhabitants of such state, being twenty-one years of age, and citizens of the United States, or in any way abridged, except for participation in rebellion, or other crime, the basis of representation therein shall be reduced in the proportion which the number of such male citizens shall bear to the whole number of male citizens twenty-one years of age in such state.

Section 3. No person shall be a Senator or Representative in Congress, or elector of President and Vice President, or hold any office, civil or military, under the United States, or under any state, who, having previously taken an oath, as a member of Congress, or as an officer of the United States, or as a member of any state legislature, or as an executive or judicial officer of any state, to support the Constitution of the United States, shall have engaged in insurrection or rebellion against the same, or given aid or comfort to the enemies thereof. But Congress may by a vote of two-thirds of each House, remove such disability.

Section 4. The validity of the public debt of the United States, authorized by law, including debts incurred for payment of pensions and bounties for services in suppressing insurrection or rebellion, shall not be questioned. But neither the United States nor any state shall assume or pay any debt or obligation incurred in aid of insurrection or rebellion against the United States, or any claim for the loss or emancipation of any slave; but all such debts, obligations and claims shall be held illegal and void.

Section 5. The Congress shall have power to enforce, by appropriate legislation, the provisions of this article.

Amendment XV (1870)

Section 1. The right of citizens of the United States to vote shall not be denied or abridged by the United States or by any state on account of race, color, or previous condition of servitude.

Section 2. The Congress shall have power to enforce this article by appropriate legislation.

Amendment XVI (1913)

The Congress shall have power to lay and collect taxes on incomes, from whatever source derived, without apportionment among the several states, and without regard to any census of enumeration.

Amendment XVII (1913)

The Senate of the United States shall be composed of two Senators from each state, elected by the people thereof, for six years; and each Senator shall have one vote. The electors in each state shall have the qualifications requisite for electors of the most numerous branch of the state legislatures.

When vacancies happen in the representation of any state in the Senate, the executive authority of such state shall issue writs of election to fill such vacancies: Provided, that the legislature of any state may empower the executive thereof to make temporary appointments until the people fill the vacancies by election as the legislature may direct.

This amendment shall not be so construed as to affect the election or term of any Senator chosen before it becomes valid as part of the Constitution.

Amendment XVIII (1919)

Section 1. After one year from the ratification of this article the manufacture, sale, or transportation of intoxicating liquors within, the importation thereof into, or the exportation thereof from the United States and all territory subject to the jurisdiction thereof for beverage purposes is hereby prohibited.

Section 2. The Congress and the several states shall have concurrent power to enforce this article by appropriate legislation.

Section 3. This article shall be inoperative unless it shall have been ratified as an amendment to the Constitution by the legislatures of the several states, as provided in the

Constitution, within seven years from the date of the submission hereof to the states by the Congress.

Amendment XIX (1920)

The right of citizens of the United States to vote shall not be denied or abridged by the United States or by any state on account of sex.

Congress shall have power to enforce this article by appropriate legislation.

Amendment XX (1933)

Section 1. The terms of the President and Vice President shall end at noon on the 20th day of January, and the terms of Senators and Representatives at noon on the 3d day of January, of the years in which such terms would have ended if this article had not been ratified; and the terms of their successors shall then begin.

Section 2. The Congress shall assemble at least once in every year, and such meeting shall begin at noon on the 3d day of January, unless they shall by law appoint a different day.

Section 3. If, at the time fixed for the beginning of the term of the President, the President elect shall have died, the Vice President elect shall become President. If a President shall not have been chosen before the time fixed for the beginning of his term, or if the President elect shall have failed to qualify, then the Vice President elect shall act as President until a President shall have qualified; and the Congress may by law provide for the case wherein neither a President elect nor a Vice President elect shall have qualified, declaring who shall then act as President, or the manner in which one who is to act shall be selected, and such person shall act accordingly until a President or Vice President shall have qualified.

Section 4. The Congress may by law provide for the case of the death of any of the persons from whom the House of Representatives may choose a President whenever the right of choice shall have devolved upon them, and for the case of the death of any of the persons from whom the Senate may choose a Vice President whenever the right of choice shall have devolved upon them.

Section 5. Sections 1 and 2 shall take effect on the 15th day of October following the ratification of this article.

Section 6. This article shall be inoperative unless it shall have been ratified as an amendment to the Constitution by the legislatures of three-fourths of the several states within seven years from the date of its submission.

Amendment XXI (1933)

Section 1. The eighteenth article of amendment to the Constitution of the United States is hereby repealed.

Section 2. The transportation or importation into any state, territory, or possession of the United States for delivery or use therein of intoxicating liquors, in violation of the laws thereof, is hereby prohibited.

Section 3. This article shall be inoperative unless it shall have been ratified as an amendment to the Constitution by conventions in the several states, as provided in the Constitution, within seven years from the date of the submission hereof to the states by the Congress.

Amendment XXII (1951)

Section 1. No person shall be elected to the office of the President more than twice, and no person who has held the office of President, or acted as President, for more than two years of a term to which some other person was elected President shall be elected to the office of the President more than once. But this article shall not apply to any person holding the office of President when this article was proposed by the Congress, and shall not prevent any person who may be holding the office of President, or acting as President, during the term within which this article becomes operative from holding the office of President or acting as President during the remainder of such term.

Section 2. This article shall be inoperative unless it shall have been ratified as an amendment to the Constitution by the legislatures of three-fourths of the several states within seven years from the date of its submission to the states by the Congress.

Amendment XXIII (1961)

Section 1. The District constituting the seat of government of the United States shall appoint in such manner as the Congress may direct:

A number of electors of President and Vice President equal to the whole number of Senators and Representatives in Congress to which the District would be entitled if it were a state, but in no event more than t he least populous state; they shall be in addition to those appointed by the states, but they shall be considered, for the purposes of the election of President and Vice President, to be electors appointed by a state; and they shall meet in the District and perform such duties as provided by the twelfth article of amendment.

Section 2. The Congress shall have power to enforce this article by appropriate legislation.

Amendment XXIV (1964)

Section 1. The right of citizens of the United States to vote in any primary or other election for President or Vice President, for electors for President or Vice President, or for Senator or Representative in Congress, shall not be denied or abridged by the United States or any state by reason of failure to pay any poll tax or other tax.

Section 2. The Congress shall have power to enforce this article by appropriate legislation.

Amendment XXV (1967)

Section 1. In case of the removal of the President from office or of his death or resignation, the Vice President shall become President.

Section 2. Whenever there is a vacancy in the office of the Vice President, the President shall nominate a Vice President who shall take office upon confirmation by a majority vote of both Houses of Congress.

Section 3. Whenever the President transmits to the President pro tempore of the Senate and the Speaker of the House of Representatives his written declaration that he is unable to discharge the powers and duties of his office, and until he transmits to them a written declaration to the contrary, such powers and duties shall be discharged by the Vice President as Acting President.

Section 4. Whenever the Vice President and a majority of either the principal officers of the executive departments or of such other body as Congress may by law provide, transmit to the President pro tempore of the Senate and the Speaker of the House of Representatives their written declaration that the President is unable to discharge the powers and duties of his office, the Vice President shall immediately assume the powers and duties of the office as Acting President.

Thereafter, when the President transmits to the President pro tempore of the Senate and the Speaker of the House of Representatives his written declaration that no inability exists, he shall resume the powers and duties of his office unless the Vice President and a majority of either the principal officers of the executive department or of such other body as Congress may by law provide, transmit within four days to the President pro tempore of the Senate and the Speaker of the House of Representatives their written declaration that the President is unable to discharge the powers and duties of his office. Thereupon Congress shall decide the issue, assembling within forty-eight hours for that purpose if not in session. If the Congress, within twenty-one days after receipt of the latter written declaration, or, if Congress is not in session, within twenty-one days after Congress is required to assemble, determines by two-thirds vote of both Houses that the President is unable to discharge the powers and duties of his office, the Vice President shall continue to discharge the same as Acting President; otherwise, the President shall resume the powers and duties of his office.

Amendment XXVI (1971)

Section 1. The right of citizens of the United States, who are 18 years of age or older, to vote, shall not be denied or abridged by the United States or any state on account of age.

Section 2. The Congress shall have the power to enforce this article by appropriate legislation.

Amendment XXVII (1992)

No law varying the compensation for the services of the Senators and Representatives shall take effect until an election of Representatives shall have intervened.

Prepared by Gerald Murphy (Cleveland Free-Net–aa300)

Converted to HTML by Jawaid Bazyar (bazyar@hypermall.com)

Distributed by the Cybercasting Services Division of the National Public Telecomputing Network (NPTN).

Permission is hereby granted to download, reprint, and/or otherwise redistribute this file, provided appropriate point of origin credit is given to the preparer(s) and the National Public Telecomputing Network.

Charter of the United Nations and Statute of the International Court of Justice

We the peoples of the United Nations determined

> to save succeeding generations from the scourge of war which twice in our lifetime has brought untold sorrow to mankind, and

> to reaffirm faith in fundamental human rights, in the dignity and worth of the human person, in the equal rights of men and women and of nations large and small, and

> to establish conditions under which justice and respect for the obligations arising from treaties and other sources of international law can be maintained, and

> to promote social progress and better standards of life in larger freedom.

and for these ends

> to practice tolerance and live together in peace with one another as good neighbors, and

> to unite our strength to maintain international peace and security, and

> to ensure, by the acceptance of principles and the institution of methods, that armed force shall not be used, save in the common interest, and

> to employ international machinery for the promotion of the economic and social advancement of all peoples.

have resolved to combine our efforts to accomplish these aims.

Accordingly, our respective Governments, through representatives assembled in the city of San Francisco, who have exhibited their full powers found to be in good and due form, have agreed to the present Charter of the United Nations and do hereby establish an international organization to be known as the United Nations.

CHAPTER I

Purposes and Principles

Article 1

The Purposes of the United Nations are:

1. To maintain international peace and security, and to that end: to take effective collective measures for the prevention and removal of threats to the peace, and for the suppression of acts of aggression or other breaches of the peace, and to bring about by peaceful means, and in conformity with the principles of justice and international law, adjustment or settlement of international disputes or situations which might lead to a breach of the peace.

2. To develop friendly relations among nations based on respect for the principle of equal rights and self-determination of peoples, and to take other appropriate measures to strengthen universal peace;

3. To achieve international cooperation in solving international problems of an economic, social, cultural, or humanitarian character, and in promoting and encouraging respect for human rights and for fundamental freedoms for all without distinction as to race, sex, language, or religion; and

4. To be a center for harmonizing the actions of nations in the attainment of these common ends.

Article 2

The organization and its Members, in pursuit of the Purposes stated in Article 1, shall act in accordance with the following Principles.

1. The Organization is based on the principle of the sovereign equality of all its Members.

2. All Members, in order to ensure to all of them the rights and benefits resulting from membership, shall fulfil in good faith the obligations assumed by them in accordance with the present Charter.

3. All Members shall settle their international disputes by peaceful means in such a manner that international peace and security, and justice, are not endangered.

4. All Members shall refrain in their international relations from the threat or use of force against the territorial integrity or political independence of any state, or in any other manner inconsistent with the Purposes of the United Nations.

5. All Members shall give the United Nations every assistance in any action it takes in accordance with the present Charter, and shall refrain from giving assistance to any state against which the United Nations is taking preventative or enforcement action.

6. The Organization shall ensure that states which are not Members of the United Nations act in accordance with these Principles so far as may be necessary for the maintenance of international peace and security.

7. Nothing contained in the present Charter shall authorize the United Nations to intervene in matters which are essentially within the domestic jurisdiction of any state or shall require the Members to submit such matters to settlement under the present Charter; but this principle shall not prejudice the application of enforcement measures under Chapter VII.

CHAPTER II
Membership

Article 3

The original Members of the United Nations shall be the states which, having participated in the United Nations Conference on International Organization at San Francisco, or having previously signed the Declaration by United Nations of January 1, 1942, sign the present Charter and ratify it in accordance with Article 110.

Article 4

1. Membership in the United Nations is open to all other peace-loving states which accept the obligations contained in the present Charter and, in the judgment of the Organization, are able and willing to carry out these obligations.

2. The admission of any such state to membership in the United Nations will be effected by a decision of the General Assembly upon the recommendation of the Security Council.

Article 5

A Member of the United Nations against which preventive or enforcement action has been taken by the Security Council may be suspended from the exercise of the rights and privileges of membership by the General Assembly upon the recommendation of the Security Council. The exercise of these rights and privileges may be restored by the Security Council.

Article 6

A Member of the United Nations which has persistently violated the Principles contained in the present Charter may be expelled from the Organization by the General Assembly upon the recommendation of the Security Council.

CHAPTER III

Organs

Article 7

1.   There are established as the principal organs of the United Nations: A General Assembly, a Security Council, an Economic and Social Council, a Trusteeship Council, an International Court of Justice, and a Secretariat.

2.   Such subsidiary organs as may be found necessary may be established in accordance with the present Charter.

Article 8

The United Nations shall place no restrictions on the eligibility of men and women to participate in any capacity and under conditions of equality in its principal and subsidiary organs.

CHAPTER IV
The General Assembly
Composition
Article 9

1.   The General Assembly shall consist of all Members of the United Nations.

2.   Each Member shall have not more than five representatives in the General Assembly.

Functions and Powers
Article 10

The General Assembly may discuss any questions or any matters within the scope of the present Charter or relating to the powers and functions of any organs provided for in the present Charter, and except as provided in Article 12, may make recommendations to the Members of the United Nations or to the Security Council or to both on any such questions or matters.

Article 11

1.   The General Assembly may consider the general principles of cooperation in the maintenance of international peace and security, including the principles governing disarmament and the regulation of armaments, and may make recommendations with regard to such principles to the Members or to the Security Council or to both.

2.   The General Assembly may discuss any questions relating to the maintenance of international peace and security brought before it by any Member of the United Nations, or by the Security Council, or by a state which is not a Member of the United Nations in accordance with Article 35, paragraph 2, and except as provided in Article 12, may make recommendations with regard to any such questions to the state or states concerned or to the Security Council or to both. Any such question on which action is necessary shall be referred to the Security Council by the General Assembly either before or after discussion.

3.   The General Assembly may call the attention of the Security Council to situations which are likely to endanger international peace and security.

4.   The powers of the General Assembly set forth in this Article shall not limit the general scope of Article 10.

Article 12

1.   While the Security Council is exercising in respect of any dispute or situation the functions assigned to it in the present Charter, the General Assembly shall not

make any recommendation with regard to that dispute or situation unless the Security Council so requests.

2. The Secretary-General, with the consent of the Security Council, shall notify the General Assembly at each session of any matters relative to the maintenance of international peace and security which are being dealt with by the Security Council and shall similarly notify the General Assembly, or the Members of the United Nations if the General Assembly is not in session, immediately the Security Council ceases to deal with such matters.

Article 13

1. The General Assembly shall initiate studies and make recommendations for the purpose of:

    a. promoting international cooperation in the political field and encouraging the progressive development of international law and its codification;

    b. promoting international cooperation in the economic, social, cultural, educational, and health fields, and assisting in the realization of human rights and fundamental freedoms for all without distinction as to race, sex, language, or religion.

2. The further responsibilities, functions, and powers of the General Assembly with respect to matters mentioned in paragraph 1 (b) above are set forth in Chapters IX and X.

Article 14

Subject to the provisions of Article 12, the General Assembly may recommend measures for the peaceful adjustment of any situation, regardless of origin, which it deems likely to impair the general welfare or friendly relations among nations, including situations resulting from a violation of the provisions of the present Charter setting forth the Purposes and Principles of the United Nations.

Article 15

1. The General Assembly shall receive and consider annual and special reports from the Security Council; these reports shall include an account of the measures that the Security Council has decided upon or taken to maintain international peace and security.

2. The General Assembly shall receive and consider reports from the other organs of the United Nations.

Article 16

The General Assembly shall perform such functions with respect to the international trusteeship system as are assigned to it under Chapters XII and XIII, including the approval of the trusteeship agreements for areas not designated as strategic.

Article 17

1. The General Assembly shall consider and approve the budget of the Organization.

2. The expenses of the Organization shall be borne by the Members as apportioned by the General Assembly.

3. The General Assembly shall consider and approve any financial and budgetary arrangements with specialized agencies referred to in Article 57 and shall examine the administrative budgets of such specialized agencies with a view to making recommendations to the agencies concerned.

Voting

Article 18

1. Each member of the General Assembly shall have one vote.

2. Decisions of the General Assembly on important questions hall be made by a two-thirds majority of the members present and voting. These questions shall include: recommendations with respect to the maintenance of international peace and security, the election of the non-permanent members of the Security Council, the election of the members of the Economic and social Council, the election of members of the Trusteeship Council in accordance with paragraph 1 (c) of Article 86, the admission of new Members to the United Nations, the suspension of the rights and privileges of membership, the expulsion of Members, questions relating to the operation of the trusteeship system, and budgetary questions.

3. Decisions on other questions, including the determination of additional categories of questions to be decided by a two-thirds majority, shall be made by a majority of the members present and voting.

Article 19

A Member of the United Nations which is in arrears in the payment of its financial contributions to the Organization shall have no vote in the General Assembly if the amount of its arrears equals or exceeds the amount of the contributions due from it for the preceding two full years. The General Assembly may, nevertheless, permit such a Member to vote if it is satisfied that the failure to pay is due to conditions beyond the control of the Member.

Procedure

Article 20

The General Assembly shall meet in regular annual sessions and in such special sessions as occasion may require. Special sessions shall be convoked by the Secretary-General at the request of the Security Council or of a majority of the Members of the United Nations.

Procedure

Article 21

The General Assembly shall adopt its own rules of procedure. It shall elect its President for each session.

Article 22

The General Assembly may establish such subsidiary organs as it deems necessary for the performance of its functions.

CHAPTER V
The Security Council
Composition

Article 23 (as amended in 1965)

1. The Security Council shall consist of fifteen members of the United Nations. The Republic of China, France, the Union of Soviet Socialist Republics, the United Kingdom of Great Britain and Northern Ireland, and the United States of America shall be permanent members of the Security Council. The General Assembly shall elect ten other Members of the United Nations to be non-permanent members of the Security Council, due regard being specially paid, in the first instance to the contribution of Members of the United Nations to the maintenance of international peace and security and to the other purposes of the Organization, and also to equitable geographical distribution.

2. The non-permanent members of the Security Council shall be elected for a term of two years. In the first election of the non-permanent members after the increase of the membership of the Security Council from eleven to fifteen, two of the four additional members shall be chosen for a term of one year. A retiring member shall not be eligible for immediate re-election.

3. Each member of the Security Council shall have one representative.

Functions and Powers

Article 24

1. In order to ensure prompt and effective action by the United Nations, its Members confer on the Security Council primary responsibility for the maintenance of international peace and security, and agree that in carrying out its duties under this responsibility the Security Council acts on their behalf.

2. In discharging these duties the Security Council shall act in accordance with the Purposes and Principles of the United Nations. The specific powers granted to the Security Council for the discharge of these duties are laid down in Chapters VI, VII, VIII, and XII.

3. The Security Council shall submit annual and, when necessary, special reports to the General Assembly for its consideration.

Article 25

The Members of the United Nations agree to accept and carry out the decisions of the Security Council in accordance with the present Charter.

Article 26

In order to promote the establishment and maintenance of international peace and security with the least diversion for armaments of the world's human and economic resources, the Security Council shall be responsible for formulating, with the assistance of the Military Staff Committee referred to in Article 47, plans to be submitted to the Members of the United Nations for the establishment of a system for the regulation of armaments.

Voting

Article 27 (as amended in 1965)

1. Each member of the Security Council shall have one vote.

2. Decisions of the Security Council on procedural matters shall be made by an affirmative vote of nine members.

3. Decisions of the Security Council on all other matters shall be made by an affirmative vote of nine members including the concurring votes of the permanent members; provided that, in decisions under Chapter VI and under paragraph 3 of Article 52, a party to a dispute shall abstain from voting.

Procedure

Article 28

1. The Security Council shall be so organized as to be able to function continuously. Each member of the Security Council shall for this purpose be represented at all times at the seat of the Organization.

2. The Security Council shall hold periodic meetings at which each of its members may, if it so desires, be represented by a member of the government or by some other specially designated representative.

3. The Security Council may hold meetings at such places other than the seat of the Organization as in its judgment will best facilitate its work.

Article 29

The Security Council may establish such subsidiary organs as it deems necessary for the performance of its functions.

Article 30

The Security Council shall adopt its own rules of procedure, including the method of selecting its President.

Article 31

Any member of the United Nations which is not a member of the Security Council may participate, without vote, in the discussion of any question brought before the Security Council whenever the latter considers that the interests of that Member are specially affected.

Article 32

Any Member of the United Nations which is not a member of the Security Council or any state which is not a Member of the United Nations, if it is a party to a dispute under consideration by the Security Council, shall be invited to participate, without vote, in the discussion relating to the dispute. The Security council shall lay down such conditions as it deems just for the participation of a state which is not a Member of the United Nations.

CHAPTER VI
Pacific Settlement of Disputes
Article 33

1.   The Parties to any dispute, the continuance of which is likely to endanger the maintenance of international peace and security, shall, first of all, seek a solution by negotiation, enquiry, mediation, conciliation, arbitration, judicial settlement, resort to regional agencies or arrangements, or other peaceful means of their own choice.

2.   The Security Council shall, when it deems necessary, call upon the parties to settle their dispute by such means.

Article 34

The Security Council may investigate any dispute, or any situation which might lead to international friction or give arise to a dispute, in order to determine whether the continuance of the dispute or situation is likely to endanger the maintenance of international peace and security.

Article 35

1.   Any Member of the United Nations may bring any dispute, or any situation of the nature referred to in Article 34, to the attention of the Security Council or of the General Assembly.

2.   A state which is not a Member of the United Nations may bring to the attention of the Security Council or of the General Assembly any dispute to which it is a party if it accepts in advance, for the purposes of the dispute, the obligations of pacific settlement provided in the present Charter.

3.   The proceedings of the General Assembly in respect of matters brought to its attention under this Article will be subject to the provisions of Articles 11 and 12.

Article 36

1.   The Security Council may, at any stage of a dispute of the nature referred to in Article 33 or of a situation of like nature, recommend appropriate procedures or methods of adjustment.

2.   The Security Council should take into consideration any procedures for the settlement of the dispute which have already been adopted by the parties.

3.   In making recommendations under this Article the Security Council should also take into consideration that legal disputes should as a general rule be referred by the parties to the International Court of Justice in accordance with the provisions of the Statute of the Court.

Article 37

1. Should the parties to a dispute of the nature referred to in Article 33 fail to settle it by the means indicated in that Article, they shall refer it to the Security Council.

2. If the Security Council deems that the continuance of the dispute is in fact likely to endanger the maintenance of international peace and security, it shall decide whether to take action under Article 36 or to recommend such terms of settlement as it may consider appropriate.

Article 38

Without prejudice to the provisions of Article 33 to 37, the Security Council may, if all the parties to any dispute so request, make recommendations to the parties with a view to a pacific settlement of the dispute.

CHAPTER VII

Action With Respect to Threats to the Peace, Breaches of the Peace, and Acts of Aggression

Article 39

The Security Council shall determine the existence of any threat to the peace, breach of the peace, or act of aggression and shall make recommendations, or decide what measures shall be taken in accordance with Articles 41 and 42, to maintain or restore international peace and security.

Article 40

In order to prevent an aggravation of the situation, the Security council may, before making the recommendations or deciding upon the measures provided for in Article 39, call upon the parties concerned to comply with such provisional measures as it deems necessary or desirable. Such provisional measures shall be without prejudice to the rights, claims, or position of the parties concerned. The Security Council shall duly take account of failure to comply with such provisional measures.

Article 41

The Security Council may decide what measure not involving the use of armed force are to be employed to give effect to its decisions, and it may call upon the Members of the United Nations to apply such measures. These may include complete or partial interruption of economic relations and of rail, sea, air, postal, telegraphic, radio, and other means of communication, and the severance of diplomatic relations.

Article 42

Should the Security Council consider that measures provided for in Article 41 would be inadequate or have proved to be inadequate, it may take such action by air, sea, or land forces as may be necessary to maintain or restore international peace and security. Such action may include demonstrations, blockade, and other operations by air, sea, or land forces of Members of the United Nations.

Article 43

1. All Members of the United Nations, in order to contribute to the maintenance of international peace and security, undertake to make available to the Security Council, on its call and in accordance with a special agreement or agreements, armed forces, assistance, and facilities including rights of passage, necessary for the purpose of maintaining international peace and security.

2. Such agreement or agreements shall govern the numbers and types of forces, their degree of readiness and general location, and the nature of the facilities and assistance to be provided.

3.   The agreement or agreements shall be negotiated as soon as possible on the initiative of the Security Council. They shall be concluded between the Security Council and Members or between the Security Council and groups of Members and shall be subject to ratification by the signatory states in accordance with their respective constitutional processes.

Article 44

When the Security Council has decided to use force it shall, before calling upon a Member not represented on it to provide armed forces in fulfillment of the obligations assumed under Article 43, invite that Member, if the Member so desires, to participate in the decisions of the Security Council concerning the employment of contingents of that Member's armed forces.

Article 45

In order to enable the United Nations to take urgent military measure, Members shall hold immediately available national air-force contingents for combined international enforcement action. The strength and degree of readiness of these contingents and plans for their combined action shall be determined, within the limits laid down in the special agreement or agreements referred to inn Article 43, by the Security Council with the assistance of the Military Staff Committee.

Article 46

Plans for the application of armed force shall be made by the Security Council with the assistance of the Military Staff Committee.

Article 47

1.   There shall be established a Military Staff Committee to advise and assist the Security Council on all questions relating to the Security Council's military requirements for the maintenance of international peace and security, the employment and command of forces placed at its disposal, the regulation of armaments, and possible disarmament.

2.   The Military Staff Committee shall consist of the Chiefs of Staff of the permanent members of the Security Council or their representatives. Any Member of the United Nations not permanently represented on the Committee shall be invited by the Committee to be associated with it when the efficient discharge of the Committee's responsibilities requires the participation of that Member in its work.

3.   The Military Staff Committee shall be responsible under the Security Council for the strategic direction of any armed forces placed at the disposal of the Security Council. Questions relating to the command of such forces shall be worked out subsequently.

4.   The Military Staff Committee, with the authorization of the Security Council and after consultation, with appropriate regional agencies, may establish regional sub-committees.

Article 48

1.   The action required to carry out the decisions of the Security Council for the maintenance of international peace and security shall be taken by all the Members of the United Nations or by some of them, as the Security council may determine.

2.   Such decisions shall be carried out by the Members of the United Nations directly and through their action in the appropriate international agencies of which they are members.

Article 49

The Members of the United Nations shall join in affording mutual assistance in carrying out the measures decided upon by the Security Council.

Article 50

If preventive or enforcement measures against any state are taken by the Security council, any other state, whether a Member of the United Nations or not, which finds itself confronted with special economic problems arising from the carrying out of those measures shall have the right to consult the Security Council with regard to a solution of those problems.

Article 51

Nothing in the present Charter shall impair the inherent right of individual or collective self-defense if an armed attack occurs against a Member of the United Nations, until the Security Council has taken the measures necessary to maintain international peace and security. Measures taken by Members in the exercise of this right of self-defense shall be immediately reported to the Security Council and shall not in any way affect the authority and responsibility of the Security Council under the present Charter to take at any time such action as it deems necessary in order to maintain or restore international peace and security.

CHAPTER VIII
Regional Arrangements

Article 52

1. Nothing in the present Charter precludes the existence of regional arrangements or agencies for dealing with such matters relating to the maintenance of international peace and security as are appropriate for regional action, provided that such arrangements or agencies and their activities are consistent with the Purposes and Principles of the United Nations.

2. The Members of the United Nations entering into such arrangements or constituting such agencies shall make every effort to achieve pacific settlement of local disputes through such regional arrangements or by such regional agencies before referring them to the Security Council.

3. The Security Council shall encourage the development of pacific settlement of local disputes through such regional arrangements or by such regional agencies either on the initiative of the states concerned or by reference from the Security Council.

4. This Article in no way impairs the application of Articles 34 and 35.

Article 53

1. The Security Council shall, where appropriate, utilize such regional arrangements or agencies for enforcement action under its authority. But no enforcement action shall be taken under regional arrangements or by regional agencies without the authorization of the Security Council with the exception of measures against any enemy state, as defined in paragraph 2 of this Article, provided for pursuant to Article 107 or in regional arrangements directed against renewal of aggressive policy on the part of any such state, until such time as the Organization may, on request of the Governments concerned, be charged with the responsibility for preventing further aggression by such a state.

2. The term enemy state as used in paragraph 1 of this Article applies to any state which during the Second World War has been an enemy of any signatory of the present Charter.

Article 54

The Security Council shall at all times be kept fully informed of activities undertaken or in contemplation under regional arrangements or by regional agencies for the maintenance of international peace and security.

CHAPTER IX

International Economic and Social Cooperation

Article 55

With a view to the creation of conditions of stability and well-being which are necessary for peaceful and friendly relations among nations based on respect for the principle of equal rights and self-determination of peoples, the United nations shall promote:

    a. higher standards of living, full employment, and conditions of economic and social progress and development;

    b. solutions of international economic, social, health, and related problems; and international cultural and educational cooperation; and

    c. universal respect for, and observance of, human rights and fundamental freedoms for all without distinction as to race, sex, language, or religion.

Article 56

All Members pledge themselves to take joint and separate action in cooperation with the Organization for the achievement of the purposes set forth in Article 55.

Article 57

    1.   The various specialized agencies, established by intergovernmental agreement and having wide international responsibilities, as defined in their basic instruments, in economic, social, cultural, educational, health, and related fields, shall be brought into relationship with the United Nations in accordance with the provisions of Article 63.

    2.   Such agencies thus brought into relationship with the United Nations are hereinafter referred to as specialized agencies.

Article 58

The Organization shall make recommendations for the coordination of the policies and activities of the specialized agencies.

Article 59

The Organization shall, where appropriate, initiate negotiations among the states concerned for the creation of any new specialized agencies required for the accomplishment of the purposes set forth in Article 55.

Article 60

Responsibility for the discharge of the functions of the Organization set forth in this Chapter shall be vested in the General Assembly and, under the authority of the General Assembly, in the Economic and Social Council, which shall have for this purpose the powers set forth in Chapter X.

CHAPTER X

The Economic and Social Council

Composition

Article 61 (as amended in 1973)

1. The Economic and Social Council shall consist of fifty-four Members of the United Nations elected by the General Assembly.

2. Subject to the provisions of paragraph 3, eighteen members of the Economic and Social Council shall be elected each year for a term of three years. A retiring member shall be eligible for immediate re-election.

3. At the first election after the increase in the membership of the Economic and Social Council from twenty-seven to fifty-four members, in addition to the members elected in place of the nine members whose term of office expires at the end of that year, twenty-seven additional members shall be elected. Of these twenty-seven additional members, the term of office of nine members so elected shall expire at the end of one year, and of nine other members at the end of two years, in accordance with arrangements made by the General Assembly.

4. Each member of the Economic and Social Council shall have one representative.

Functions and Powers

Article 62

1. The Economic and Social council may make or initiate studies and reports with respect to international economic, social, cultural, educational, health, and related matters and may make recommendations with respect to any such matters to the General Assembly, to the Members of the United Nations, and to the specialized agencies concerned.

2. It may make recommendations for the purpose of promoting respect for, and observance of, human rights and fundamental freedoms for all.

3. It may prepare draft conventions for submission to the General Assembly, with respect to matters falling within its competence.

4. It may call, in accordance with the rules prescribed by the United Nations, international conferences on matters falling within its competence.

Article 63

1. The Economic and Social Council may enter into agreements with any of the agencies referred to in Article 57, defining the terms on which the agency concerned

shall be brought into relationship with the United Nations. Such agreements shall be subject to approval by the General Assembly.

2. It may coordinate the activities of the specialized agencies through consultation with and recommendations to such agencies and through recommendations to the General Assembly and to the Members of the United Nations.

Article 64

1. The Economic and Social Council may take appropriate steps to obtain regular reports from the specialized agencies. It may make arrangements with the Members of the United Nations and with the specialized agencies to obtain reports on the steps taken to give effect to its own recommendations to recommendations on matters falling within its competence made by the General Assembly.

2. It may communicate its observations on these reports to the General Assembly.

Article 65

The Economic and Social Council may furnish information to the Security Council and shall assist the Security Council upon its request.

Article 66

1. The Economic and Social Council shall perform such functions as fall within its competence in connection with the carrying out of the recommendations of the General Assembly.

2. It may, with the approval of the General Assembly, perform services at the request of Members of the United Nations and at the request of specialized agencies.

3. It shall perform such other functions as are specified elsewhere in the present Charter or as may be assigned to it by the General Assembly.

Voting

Article 67

1. Each member of the Economic and Social Council shall have one vote.

2. Decisions of the Economic and Social Council shall be made by a majority of the members present and voting.

Procedure

Article 68

The Economic and Social Council shall set up commissions in economic and social fields and for the promotion of human rights, and such other commissions as may be required for the performance of its functions.

Article 69

The Economic and Social Council shall invite any Member of the United Nations to participate, without vote, in its deliberations on any matter of particular concern to that Member.

Article 70

The Economic and Social Council may make arrangements for representatives of the specialized agencies to participate, without vote, in its deliberations and in those of the commissions established by it, and for its representatives to participate in the deliberations of the specialized agencies.

Article 71

The Economic and Social Council may make suitable arrangements for consultation with non-governmental organizations which are concerned with matters within its competence. Such arrangements may be made with international organizations and, where appropriate, with national organizations after consultation with the Member of the United Nations concerned.

Article 72

1. The Economic and Social Council shall adopt its own rules of procedure, including the method of selecting its President.

2. The Economic and Social Council shall meet as required in accordance with its rules, which shall include provision for the convening of meetings on the request of a majority of its members.

CHAPTER XI
Declaration Regarding Non-Self-Governing territories

Article 73

Members of the United Nations which have or assume responsibilities for the administration of territories whose people have not yet attained a full measure of self-government recognize the principle that the interests of the inhabitants of these territories are paramount, and accept as a sacred trust, the obligation to promote to the utmost, within the system of international peace and security established by the present Charter, the well-being of the inhabitants of these territories, and, to this end:

a. to ensure, with due respect for the culture of the people concerned, their political, economic, social, and educational advancement, their just treatment, and their protection against abuses;

b. to develop self-government, to take due account of the political aspirations of the people, and to assist them in the progressive development of their free political institutions, according to the particular circumstances of each territory and its peoples and their varying stages of advancement;

c. to further international peace and security;

d. to promote constructive measures of development, to encourage research, and to cooperate with one another and, when and where appropriate, with specialized international bodies with a view to the practical achievement of the social, economic, and scientific purposes set forth in this Article; and

e. to transmit regularly to the Secretary-General for information purposes, subject to such limitation as security and constitutional considerations may require, statistical and other information of a technical nature relating to economic, social, and educational conditions in the territories for which they are respectively responsible other than those territories to which Chapters XII and XIII apply.

Article 74

Members of the United Nations also agree that their policy in respect of the territories to which this Chapter applies, no less than in respect of their metropolitan areas, must be based on the general principle of good-neighborliness, due account being taken of the interests and well-being of the rest of the world, in social economic, and commercial matters.

CHAPTER XII

International Trusteeship System

Article 75

The United Nations shall establish under its authority an international trusteeship system for the administration and supervision of such territories as may be placed thereunder by subsequent individual agreements. Those territories are hereinafter referred to as trust territories.

Article 76

The basic objectives of the trusteeship system, in accordance with the Purposes of the United Nations laid down in Article 1 of the present Charter, shall be:

    a.   to further international peace and security;

    b.   to promote the political, economic, social, and educational advancement of the inhabitants of the trust territories, and their progressive development towards self-government or independence as may be appropriate to the particular circumstances of each territory and its peoples and the freely expressed wishes of the peoples concerned and as may be provided by the terms of each trusteeship agreement;

    c.   to encourage respect for human rights and for fundamental freedoms for all without distinction as to race, sex, language, or religion, and to encourage recognition of the interdependence of the peoples of the world; and

    d.   to ensure equal treatment in social, economic, and commercial matters for all Members of the United Nations and their nationals, and also equal treatment for the latter in the administration of justice, without prejudice to the attainment of the foregoing objectives and subject to the provisions of Article 80.

Article 77

1.   The trusteeship system shall apply to such territories in the following categories as may be placed thereunder by means of trusteeship agreements:

    a.   territories now held under mandate;

    b.   territories which may be detached from enemy states as a result of the Second World War; and

    c.   territories voluntarily placed under the system by states responsible for their administration.

2.   It will be a matter for subsequent agreement as to which territories in the foregoing categories will be brought under the trusteeship system and upon what terms.

Article 78

The trusteeship system shall not apply to territories which have become Members of the United Nations, relationship among which shall be based on respect for the principle of sovereign equality.

Article 79

The terms of trusteeship for each territory to be placed under the trusteeship system, including any alteration or amendment, shall be agreed upon by the states directly concerned, including the mandatory power in the case of territories held under mandate by a Member of the United Nations, and shall be approved as provided for in Articles 83 and 85.

Article 80

1. Except as may be agreed upon in individual trusteeship agreements, made under Articles 77, 79, and 81, placing each territory under the trusteeship system, and until such agreements have been concluded, nothing in this Chapter shall be construed in or of itself to alter in any manner the rights whatsoever of any states or any peoples or the terms of existing international instruments to which Members of the United Nations may respectively be parties.

2. Paragraph 1 of this Article shall not be interpreted as giving ground for delay or postponement of the negotiation and conclusion of agreements for placing mandated and other territories under the trusteeship system as provided for in Article 77.

Article 81

The trusteeship agreement shall in each case include the terms under which the trust territory will be administered and designate the authority which will exercise the administration of the trust territory. Such authority, may be one or more states or the Organization itself.

Article 82

There may be designated, in any trusteeship agreement, a strategic area or areas which may include part or all of the trust territory to which the agreement applies, without prejudice to any special agreement or agreements made under Article 43.

Article 83

1. All functions of the United Nations relating to strategic areas, including the approval of the terms of the trusteeship agreements and of their alteration or amendment, shall be exercised by the Security Council.

2. The basic objectives set forth in Article 76 shall be applicable to the people of each strategic area.

3. The Security Council shall, subject to the provisions of the trusteeship agreements and without prejudice to security considerations, avail itself of the assistance of the Trusteeship Council to perform those functions of the United Nations under the trusteeship system relating to political, economic, social, and educational matters in the strategic areas.

Article 84

It shall be the duty of the administering authority to ensure that the trust territory shall play its part in the maintenance of international peace and security. To this end the administering authority may make use of volunteer forces, facilities, and assistance from the trust territory in carrying out the obligations towards the Security Council undertaken in this regard by the administering authority, as well as for local defense and the maintenance of law and order within the trust territory.

Article 85

1. The functions of the United Nations with regard to trusteeship agreements for all areas not designated as strategic, including the approval of the terms of the trusteeship agreements and of their alteration or amendment, shall be exercised by the General Assembly.

2. The Trusteeship Council, operating under the authority of the General Assembly, shall assist the General Assembly in carrying out these functions.

CHAPTER XIII
The Trusteeship Council
Composition
Article 86

1. The Trusteeship Council shall consist of the following Members of the United Nations:

   a. those Members administering trust territories;

   b. such of those Members mentioned by name in Article 23 as are not administering trust territories; and

   c. as many other Members elected for three-year terms by the General Assembly as may be necessary to ensure that the total number of members of the Trusteeship Council is equally divided between those Members of the United Nations which administer trust territories and those which do not.

2. Each member of the Trusteeship Council shall designate one specially qualified person to represent it therein.

Functions and Powers
Article 87

The General Assembly and, under its authority, the Trusteeship Council, in carry out their functions, may:

   a. consider reports submitted by the administering authority;

   b. accept petitions and examine them in consultation with the administering authority;

   c. provide for periodic visits to the respective trust territories at times agreed upon with the administering authority; and

   d. take these and other actions in conformity with the terms of the trusteeship agreements.

Article 88

The Trusteeship Council shall formulate a questionnaire on the political, economic, social, and educational advancement of the inhabitants of each trust territory, and the administering authority for each trust territory within the competence of the General Assembly shall make an annual report to the General Assembly upon the basis of such questionnaire.

Voting

Article 89

1. Each member of the Trusteeship Council shall have one vote.

2. Decisions of the Trusteeship Council shall be made by a majority of the members present and voting.

Procedure

Article 90

1. The Trusteeship Council shall adopt its own rules of procedure, including the method of selecting its President.

2. The Trusteeship Council shall meet as required in accordance with its rules, which shall include provision for the convening of meetings on the request of a majority of its members.

Article 91

The Trusteeship Council shall, when appropriate, avail itself of the assistance of the Economic and Social Council and of the specialized agencies in regard to matters with which they are respectively concerned.

CHAPTER XIV
The International Court of Justice

Article 92

The International Court of Justice shall be the principal judicial organ of the United Nations. It shall function in accordance with the annexed Statute, which is based upon the Statute of the Permanent Court of International Justice and forms an integral part of the present Charter.

Article 93

1. All Members of the United Nations are *ipso facto* parties to the Statute of the International Court of Justice.

2. A state which is not a Member of the United Nations may become a party to the Statue of the International Court of Justice on conditions to be determined in each case by the General Assembly upon the recommendation of the Security Council.

Article 94

1. Each Member of the United Nations undertakes to comply with the decision of the International Court of Justice in any case to which it is a party.

2. If any party to a case fails to perform the obligations incumbent upon it under a judgment rendered by the Court, the other party may have recourse to the Security Council, which may, if it deems necessary, make recommendations or decide upon measures to be taken to give effect to the judgment.

Article 95

Nothing in the present Charter shall prevent Members of the United Nations from entrusting the solution of their differences to other tribunals by virtue of agreements already in existence or which may be concluded in the future.

Article 96

1. The General Assembly or the Security Council may request the International Court of Justice to give an advisory opinion on any legal question.

2. Other organs of the United Nations and specialized agencies, which may at any time be so authorized by the General Assembly, amy also request advisory opinions of the Court on legal questions arising within the scope of their activities.

CHAPTER XV
The Secretariat

Article 97

The Secretariat shall comprise a Secretary-General and such staff as the Organization may require. The Secretary-General shall be appointed by the General Assembly upon the recommendation of the Security Council. He shall be the chief administrative officer of the Organization.

Article 98

The Secretary-General shall act in that capacity in all meetings of the General Assembly, of the Security Council, of the Economic and Social Council, and of the Trusteeship Council, and shall perform such other functions as are entrusted to him by these organs. The Secretary-General shall make an annual report to the General Assembly on the work of the Organization.

Article 99

The Secretary-General may bring to the attention of the Security Council any matter which in his opinion may threaten the maintenance of international peace and security.

Article 100

1. In the performance of their duties the Secretary-General and the staff shall not seek or receive instructions from any government or from any other authority external to the Organization. They shall refrain from any action which might reflect on their position as international officials responsible only to the Organization.

2. Each Member of the United Nations undertakes to respect the exclusively international character of the responsibilities of the Secretary-General and the staff and not to seek to influence them in the discharge of their responsibilities.

Article 101

1. The staff shall be appointed by the Secretary-General under regulations established by the General Assembly.

2. Appropriate staffs shall be permanently assigned to the Economic and Social Council, the Trusteeship Council, and as required, to other organs of the United Nations. These staffs shall form a part of the Secretariat.

3. The paramount consideration in the employment of the staff and in the determination of the conditions of service shall be the necessity of securing the highest standards of efficiency, competence, and integrity. Due regard shall be paid to the importance of recruiting the staff on as wide a geographical basis as possible.

CHAPTER XVI
Miscellaneous Provisions

Article 102

1. Every treaty and every international agreement entered into by any Member of the United Nations after the present Charter comes into force shall as soon as possible be registered with the Secretariat and published by it.

2. No party to any such treaty or international agreement which has not been registered in accordance with the provisions of paragraph 1 of this Article may invoke that treaty or agreement before any organ of the United Nations.

Article 103

In the event of a conflict between the obligations of the Members of the United Nations under the present Charter and their obligations under any other international agreement, their obligations under the present Charter shall prevail.

Article 104

The Organization shall enjoy in the territory of each of its Members such legal capacity as may be necessary for the exercise of its functions and the fulfillment of its purposes.

Article 105

1. The Organization shall enjoy in the territory of each of its Members such privileges and immunities as are necessary for the fulfillment of its purposes.

2. Representatives of the Members of the United Nations and officials of the Organization shall similarly enjoy such privileges and immunities as are necessary for the independent exercise of their functions in connection with the Organization.

3. The General Assembly may make recommendations with a view to determining the details of the application of paragraphs 1 and 2 of this Article or may propose conventions to the Members of the United Nations for this purpose.

CHAPTER XVII

Transitional Security Arrangements

Article 106

Pending the coming into force of such special agreements referred to in Article 43 as in the opinion of the Security Council enable it to begin the exercise of its responsibilities under Article 42, the parties to the Four-Nation Declaration, signed at Moscow, October 30, 1943, and France, shall in accordance with the provisions of paragraph 5 of that Declaration, consult with one another and as occasion requires with other Members of the United Nations with a view to such joint action on behalf of the Organization as may be necessary for the purpose of maintaining international peace and security.

Article 107

Nothing in the present Charter shall invalidate or preclude action, in relation to any state which during the Second World War has been an enemy of any signatory to the present Charter, taken or authorized as a result of that war by the Governments having responsibility for such action.

CHAPTER XVIII

Amendments

Article 108

Amendments to the present Charter shall come into force for all Members of the United Nations when they have been adopted by a vote of two-thirds of the members of the General Assembly and ratified in accordance with their respective constitutional processes by two-thirds of the Members of the United Nations, including all the permanent members of the Security Council.

Article 109

1. A General Conference of the Members of the United Nations for the purpose of reviewing the present Charter may be held at a date and place to be fixed by a two-thirds vote of the members of the General Assembly and by a vote of any nine members of the Security Council. Each Member of the United Nations shall have one vote in the conference.

2. Any alteration of the present Charter recommended by a two-thirds vote of the conference shall take effect when ratified in accordance with their respective constitutional processes by two-thirds of the Members of the United Nations including all the permanent members of the Security Council.

3. If such a conference has not been held before the tenth annual session of the General Assembly following the coming into force of the present Charter, the proposal to call such a conference shall be placed on the agenda of that session of the General Assembly, and the conference shall be held if so decided by a majority vote of the members of the General Assembly and by a vote of any nine members of the Security Council.

CHAPTER XIX
Ratification and Signature

Article 110

1. The present Charter shall be ratified by the signatory states in accordance with their respective constitutional processes.

2. The ratifications shall be deposited with the Government of the United States of America, which shall notify all the signatory states of each deposit as well as the Secretary-General of the Organization when he has been appointed.

3. The present Charter shall come into force upon the deposit of ratifications by the Republic of China, France, The Union of Soviet Socialist Republics, the United Kingdom of Great Britain and Northern Ireland, and the United States of America, and by a majority of the other signatory states. A protocol of the ratifications deposited shall thereupon be drawn up by the Government of the United States of America which shall communicate copies thereof to all the signatory states.

4. The states signatory to the present Charter which ratify it after it has come into force will become original Members of the United Nations on the date of the deposit of their respective ratifications.

Article 111

The present Charter, of which the Chinese, French, Russian, English, and Spanish texts are equally authentic, shall remain deposited in the archives of the Government of the United States of America. Duly certified copies thereof shall be transmitted by that Government to the Governments of the other signatory states.

IN FAITH WHEREOF the representatives of the Governments of the United Nations have signed the present Charter.

DONE at the city of San Francisco the twenty-sixth day of June, one thousand nine hundred and forty-five.

STATUTE OF THE INTERNATIONAL COURT OF JUSTICE

Article 1

The International Court of Justice established by the Charter of the United Nations as the principal judicial organ of the United Nations shall be constituted and shall function in accordance with the provisions of the present Statute.

CHAPTER I
Organization of the Court

Article 2

The court shall be composed of a body of independent judges, elected regardless of their nationality from among persons of high moral character, who possess the qualifications required in their respective countries for appointment to the highest judicial offices, or are juris-consults of recognized competence in international law.

Article 3

1. The Court shall consist of fifteen members, no two of whom may be nationals of the same state.

2. A person who for the purposes of membership in the Court could be regarded as a national of more than one state shall be deemed to be a national of the one in which he ordinarily exercises civil and political rights.

Article 4

1. The members of the Court shall be elected by the General Assembly and by the Security Council from a list of persons nominated by the national groups in the Permanent Court of Arbitration, in accordance with the following provisions.

2. In the case of Members of the United Nations not represented in the Permanent Court of Arbitration, candidates shall be nominated by national groups appointed for this purpose by their governments under the same conditions as those pre-scribed for members of the Permanent Court of Arbitration by Article 44 of the Convention of the Hague of 1907 for the pacific settlement of international disputes.

3. The conditions under which a state which is a party to the present Statute but is not a Member of the United Nations may participate in electing the members of the Court shall, in the absence of a special agreement, be laid down by the General Assembly upon recommendation of the Security Council.

Article 5

1. At least three months before the date of the election, the Secretary-General of the United Nations shall address a written request to the members of the Permanent

Court of Arbitration belonging to the states which are parties to the present Statute, and to the members of the national groups appointed under Article 4, paragraph 2, inviting them to undertake, within a given time, by national groups, the nomination of persons in a position to accept the duties of a member of the Court.

2.   No group may nominate more than four persons, not more than two of whom shall be of their own nationality. In no case may the number of candidates nominated by a group be more than double the number of seats to be filled.

Article 6

Before making these nominations, each national group is recommended to consult its highest court of justice, its legal faculties and schools of law, and its national academies and national sections of international academies devoted to the study of law.

Article 7

1.   The Secretary-General shall prepare a list in alphabetical order of all the persons thus nominated. Save as provided in Article 12, paragraph 2, these shall be the only persons eligible.

2.   The Secretary-General shall submit this list to the General Assembly and to the Security Council.

Article 8

The General Assembly and the Security Council shall proceed independently of one another to elect the members of the Court.

Article 9

At every election, the electors shall bear in mind not only that the persons to be elected should individually possess the qualifications required, but also that in the body as a whole the representation of the main forms of civilization and of the principal legal systems of the world should be assured.

Article 10

1.   Those candidates who obtain an absolute majority of votes in the General Assembly and in the Security Council shall be considered as elected.

2.   Any vote of the Security Council, whether for the election of judges or for the appointment of members of the conference envisaged in Article 12, shall be taken without any distinction between permanent and non-permanent members of the Security Council.

3.   In the event of more than one national of the same state obtaining an absolute majority of the votes both of the General Assembly and of the Security Council, the eldest of these only shall be considered as elected.

Article 11

If, after the first meeting held for the purpose of the election, one or more seats remain to be filled, a second and, if necessary, a third meeting shall take place.

Article 12

1. If, after the third meeting, one or more seats still remain unfilled, a joint conference consisting of six members, three appointed by the General Assembly and three by the Security Council, may be formed at any time at the request of either the General Assembly or the Security Council, for the purpose of choosing by the vote of an absolute majority one name for each seat still vacant, to submit to the General Assembly and the Security Council for their respective acceptance.

2. If the joint conference is unanimously agreed upon any person who fulfills the required conditions, he may be included in its list, even though he was not included in the list of nominations referred to in Article 7.

3. If the joint conference is satisfied that it will not be successful in procuring an election, those members of the Court who have already been elected shall, within a period to be fixed by the Security Council, proceed to fill the vacant seats by selection from among those candidates who have obtained votes either in the General Assembly or in the Security Council.

4. In the event of an equality of votes among the judges, the eldest judge shall have a casting vote.

Article 13

1. The members of the Court shall be elected for nine years and may be re-elected; provided, however, that of the judges elected at the first election, the terms of five judges shall expire at the end of three years and the terms of five more judges shall expire at the end of six years.

2. The judges whose terms are to expire at the end of the above-mentioned initial periods of three and six years shall be chosen by lot to be drawn by the Secretary-General immediately after the first election has been completed.

3. The members of the Court shall continue to discharge their duties until their places have been filled. Though replaced, they shall finish any cases which they may have begun.

4. In the case of the resignation of a member of the Court, the resignation shall be addressed to the President of the Court for transmission to the Secretary-General. This last notification makes the place vacant.

Article 14

Vacancies shall be filled by the same method as that laid down for the first election subject to the following provision: the Secretary-General shall, within one month of the occurrence of the vacancy, proceed to issue the invitations provided for in Article 5, and the date of the election shall be fixed by the Security Council.

Article 15

A member of the Court elected to replace a member whose term of office has not expired shall hold office for the remainder of his predecessor's term.

Article 16

1. No member of the Court may exercise any political or administrative function, or engage in any other occupation of a professional nature.

2. Any doubt on this point shall be settled by the decision of the Court.

Article 17

1. No member of the Court may act as agent, counsel, or advocate in any case.

2. No member may participate in the decision of any case in which he has previously taken part as agent, counsel, or advocate for one of the parties, or as a member of a national or international court, or of a commission of enquiry, or in any other capacity.

3. Any doubt on this point shall be settled by the decision of the Court.

Article 18

1. No member of the Court can be dismissed unless, in the unanimous opinion of the other members, he has ceased to fulfil the required conditions.

2. Formal notification thereof shall be made to the Secretary-General by the Registrar.

3. This notification makes the place vacant.

Article 19

The members of the Court, when engaged on the business of the Court, shall enjoy diplomatic privileges and immunities.

Article 20

Every member of the Court shall, before taking up his duties, make a solemn declaration in open court that he will exercise his powers impartially and conscientiously.

Article 21

1. The Court shall elect its President and Vice-President for three years; they may be re-elected.

2. The Court shall appoint it Registrar and may provide for the appointment of such other officers as may be necessary.

Article 22

1. The seat of the Court shall be established at The Hague. This, however, shall not prevent the Court from sitting and exercising its functions elsewhere whenever the Court considers it desirable.

2. The President and the Registrar shall reside at the seat of the Court.

Article 23

1. The Court shall remain permanently in session, except during the judicial vacations, the dates and duration of which shall be fixed by the Court.

2. Members of the Court are entitled to periodic leave, the dates and duration of which shall be fixed by the Court, having in mind the distance between The Hague and the home of each judge.

3. Members of the Court shall be bound, unless they are on leave or prevented from attending by illness or other serious reasons duly explained to the President, to hold themselves permanently at the disposal of the Court.

Article 24

1. If, for some special reason, a member of the Court considers that he should not take part in the decision of a particular case, he shall so inform the President.

2. If the President considers that for some special reason one of the members of the Court should not sit in a particular case, he shall give him notice accordingly.

3. If in any such case the member of the Court and the President disagree, the matter shall be settled by the decision of the Court.

Article 25

1. The full Court shall sit except when it is expressly provided otherwise in the present Statute.

2. Subject to the condition that the number of judges available to constitute the Court is not thereby reduced below eleven, the Rules of the Court may provide for allowing one or more judges, according to circumstances and in rotation, to be dispensed from sitting.

3. A quorum of nine judges shall suffice to constitute the Court.

Article 26

1. The court may from time to time form one or more chambers, composed of three or more judges as the Court may determine, for dealing with particular categories of cases; for example, labor cases and cases relating to transit and communications.

2. The Court may at any time form a chamber for dealing with a particular case. The number of judges to constitute such a chamber shall be determined by the Court with the approval of the parties.

3. Cases shall be heard and determined by the chambers provided for in this Article if the parties so request.

Article 27

A judgment given by any of the chambers provided for in Articles 26 and 29 shall be considered as rendered by the Court.

Article 28

The chambers provided for in Articles 26 and 29 may, with the consent of the parties, sit and exercise their functions elsewhere than at The Hague.

Article 29

With a view to the speedy dispatch of business, the Court shall form annually a chamber composed of five judges which, at the request of the parties, may hear and determine cases by summary procedure. In addition, two judges shall be selected for the purpose of replacing judges who find it impossible to sit.

Article 30

1. The Court shall frame rules for carrying out its functions. In particular, it shall lay down rules of procedure.

2. The Rules of the Court may provide for assessors to sit with the Court or with any of its chambers, without the right to vote.

Article 31

1. Judges of the nationality of each of the parties shall retain their right to sit in the case before the Court.

2. If the Court includes upon the Bench a judge of the nationality of one of the parties, any other party may choose a person to sit as judge. Such person shall be chosen preferably from among those persons who have been nominated as candidates as provided in Articles 4 and 5.

3. If the Court includes upon the Bench no judge of the nationality of the parties, each of these parties may proceed to choose a judge as provided in paragraph 2 of this Article.

4. The provisions of this Article shall apply to the case of Articles 26 and 29. In such cases, the President shall request one or if necessary, two of the members of the Court forming the chamber to give place to the members of the Court of the nationality of the parties concerned, and failing such, or if they are unable to be present, to the judges specially chosen by the parties.

5. Should there be several parties in the same interest, they shall, for the purpose of the preceding provisions, be reckoned as one party only. Any doubt upon this point shall be settled by the decision of the Court.

6. Judges chosen as laid down in paragraphs 2, 3, and 4 of this Article shall fulfill the conditions required by Articles 2, 17 (paragraph 2), 20, and 24 of the present Statute. They shall take part in the decision on terms of complete equality with their colleagues.

Article 32

1. Each member of the Court shall receive an annual salary.

2. The President shall receive a special annual allowance.

3. The Vice-President shall receive a special allowance for every day on which he acts as President.

4. The judges chosen under Article 31, other than members of the Court, shall receive compensation for each day on which they exercise their functions.

5. These salaries, allowances, and compensation shall be fixed by the General Assembly. They may not be decreased during the term of office.

6. The salary of the Registrar shall be fixed by the General Assembly on the proposal of the Court.

7. Regulations made by the General Assembly shall fix the conditions under which retirement pensions may be given to members of the Court and to the Registrar, and the conditions under which members of the Court and the Registrar shall have their travelling expenses refunded.

8. The above salaries, allowances, and compensation shall be free of all taxation.

Article 33

The expenses of the Court shall be borne by the United Nations in such a manner as shall be decided by the General Assembly.

CHAPTER II
Competence of the Court

Article 34

1. Only states may be parties in cases before the Court.

2. The Court, subject to and in conformity with its Rules, may request of public international organizations information relevant to cases before it, and shall receive such information presented by such organizations on their own initiative.

3. Whenever the construction of the constituent instrument of a public international organization or of an international convention adopted thereunder is in question in a case before the Court, the Registrar shall so notify the public international organization concerned and shall communicate to it copies of all the written proceedings.

Article 35

1. The Court shall be open to the states parties to the present Statute.

2. The conditions under which the court shall be open to other states shall, subject to the special provisions contained in treaties in force, be laid down by the Security Council, but in no case shall such conditions place the parties in a position of inequality before the Court.

3. When a state which is not a Member of the United Nations is a party to a case, the Court shall fix the amount which that party is to contribute towards the expenses of the Court. This provision shall not apply if such state is bearing a share of the expenses of the Court.

Article 36

1. The jurisdiction of the Court comprises all cases which the parties refer to it and all matters specially provided for in the Charter of the United Nations or in treaties and conventions in force.

2. The states parties to the present Statute may at any time declare that they recognize as compulsory *ipso facto* and without special agreement, in relation to any other state accepting the same obligation, the jurisdiction of the Court in all legal disputes concerning:

    a. the interpretation of a treaty;

    b. any question of international law;

    c. the existence of any fact which, if established, would constitute a breach of an international obligation;

    d. the nature or extent of the reparation to be made for the breach of an international obligation.

3. The declarations referred to above may be made unconditionally or on condition of reciprocity on the part of several or certain states, or for a certain time.

4. Such declarations shall be deposited with the Secretary-General of the United Nations, who shall transmit copies thereof to the parties to the Statute and to the Registrar of the Court.

5. Declarations made under Article 36 of the Statute of the Permanent Court of International Justice and which are still in force shall be deemed, as between the parties to the present Statute, to be acceptances of the compulsory jurisdiction of the International Court of Justice for the period which they still have to run and in accordance with their terms.

6. In the event of a dispute as to whether the Court has jurisdiction, the matter shall be settled by the decision of the Court.

Article 37

Whenever a treaty or convention in force provides for reference of a matter to a tribunal to have been instituted by the League of Nations, or to the Permanent Court of International Justice, the matter shall, as between the parties to the present Statute, be referred to the International Court of Justice.

Article 38

1. The Court, whose function is to decide in accordance with international law such disputes as are submitted to it, shall apply:

    a. international conventions, whether general or particular, establishing rules expressly recognized by the contesting states;

    b. international custom, as evidence of a general practice accepted as law;

    c. the general principles of law recognized by civilized nations;

    d. subject to the provisions of Article 59, judicial decisions and the teachings of the most highly qualified publicists of the various nations, as subsidiary means for the determination of rules of law.

2. This provision shall not prejudice the power of the Court to decide a case *ex aequo et bono*, if the parties agree thereto.

CHAPTER III
Procedure

Article 39

1.   The official languages of the Court shall be French and English. If the parties agree that the case shall be conducted in French, the judgment shall be delivered in French. If the parties agree that the case shall be conducted in English, the judgment shall be delivered in English.

2.   In the absence of an agreement as to which language shall be employed, each party may, in the pleadings, use the language which it prefers; the decision of the Court shall be given in French and English. In this case the Court shall at the same time determine which of the two texts shall be considered as authoritative.

3.   The Court shall, at the request of any party, authorize a language other than French or English to be used by that party.

Article 40

1.   Cases are brought before the court, as the case may be, either by notification of the special agreement or by a written application addressed to the Registrar. In either case the subject of the dispute and the parties shall be indicated.

2.   The Registrar shall forthwith communicate the application to all concerned.

3.   He shall also notify the Members of the United Nations through the Secretary-General, and also any other states entitled to appear before the Court.

Article 41

1.   The Court shall have the power to indicate, if it considers that circumstances so require, any provisional measures which ought to be taken to preserve the respective rights of either party.

2.   Pending the final decision, notice of the measures suggested shall forthwith be given to the parties and to the Security Council.

Article 42

1.   The parties shall be represented by agents.

2.   They may have the assistance of counsel or advocates before the Court.

3.   The agents, counsel, and advocates of parties before the Court shall enjoy the privileges and immunities necessary to the independent exercise of their duties.

Article 43

1. The procedure shall consist of two parts: written and oral.

2. The written proceedings shall consist of the communication to the Court and to the parties of memorials, counter-memorials and, if necessary, replies; also all papers and documents in support.

3. These communications shall be made through the Registrar, in the order and within the time fixed by the Court.

4. A certified copy of every document produced by one party shall be communicated to the other party.

5. The oral proceedings shall consist of the hearing by the Court of witnesses, experts, agents, counsel, and advocates.

Article 44

1. For the service of all notices upon persons other than the agents, counsel, and advocates, the Court shall apply direct to the government of the state upon whose territory the notice has to be served.

2. The same provision shall apply whenever steps are to be taken to procure evidence on the spot.

Article 45

The hearing shall be under the control of the President or, if he is unable to preside, of the Vice-President; if neither is able to preside, the senior judge present shall preside.

Article 46

The hearing in Court shall be public, unless the court shall decide otherwise, or unless the parties demand that the public be not admitted.

Article 47

1. Minutes shall be made at each hearing and signed by the Registrar and the President.

2. These minutes alone shall be authentic.

Article 48

The Court shall make orders for the conduct of the case, shall decide the form and time in which each party must conclude its arguments, and make all arrangements connected with the taking of evidence.

Article 49

The Court may, even before the hearing begins, call upon the agents to produce any document or to supply any explanations. Formal note shall be taken of any refusal.

Article 50

The Court may, at any time, entrust any individual, body, bureau, commission, or other organization that it may select, with the task of carrying out an enquiry or giving an expert opinion.

Article 51

During the hearing any relevant questions are to be put to the witnesses and experts under the conditions laid down by the Court in the rules of procedure referred to in Article 30.

Article 52

After the Court has received the proofs and evidence within the time specified for the purpose, it may refuse to accept any further oral or written evidence that one party may desire to present unless the other side consents.

Article 53

1.   Whenever one of the parties does not appear before the Court, or fails to defend its case, the other party may call upon the Court to decide in favor of its claim.

2.   The Court must, before doing so, satisfy itself, not only that it has jurisdiction in accordance with Articles 36 and 27, but also that the claim is well founded in fact and law.

Article 54

1.   When, subject to the control of the Court, the agents, counsel, and advocates have completed their presentation of the case, the President shall declare the hearing closed.

2.   The Court shall withdraw to consider the judgment.

3.   The deliberations of the Court shall take place in private and remain secret.

Article 55

1.   All questions shall be decided by a majority of the judges present.

2.   In the event of an equality of votes, the President or the judge who acts in his place shall have a casting vote.

Article 56

1.   The judgment shall state the reasons on which it is based.

2.   It shall contain the names of the judges who have taken part in the decision.

Article 57

If the judgment does not represent in whole or in part the unanimous opinion of the judges, any judge shall be entitled to deliver a separate opinion.

Article 58

The judgment shall be signed by the President and by the Registrar. It shall be read in open court, due notice having been given to the agents.

Article 59

The decision of the Court has no binding force except between the parties and in respect of that particular case.

Article 60

The judgment is final and without appeal. In the event of dispute as to the meaning or scope of the judgment, the Court shall construe it upon the request of any party.

Article 61

1. An application for revision of a judgment may be made only when it is based upon the discovery of some fact of such a nature as to be a decisive factor, which fact was, when the judgment was given, unknown to the Court and also to the party claiming revision, always provided that such ignorance was not due to negligence.

2. The proceedings for revision shall be opened by a judgment of the Court expressly recording the existence of the new fact, recognizing that it has such a character as to lay the case open to revision, and declaring the application admissible on this ground.

3. The Court may require previous compliance with the terms of the judgment before it admits proceedings in revision.

4. The application for revision must be made at latest within six months of the discovery of the new fact.

5. No application for revision may be made after the lapse of ten years from the date of the judgment.

Article 62

1. Should a state consider that it has an interest of a legal nature which may be affected by the decision in the case, it may submit a request to the Court to be permitted to intervene.

2. It shall be for the Court to decide upon this request.

Article 63

1. Whenever the construction of a convention to which states other than those concerned in the case are parties is in question, the Registrar shall notify all such states forthwith.

2. Every state so notified has the right to intervene in the proceedings; but if it uses this right, the construction given by the judgment will be equally binding upon it.

Article 64

Unless otherwise decided by the Court, each party shall bear its own costs.

CHAPTER IV

Advisory Opinions

Article 65

1. The Court may give an advisory opinion on any legal question at the request of whatever body may be authorized by or in accordance with the Charter of the United Nations to make such a request.

2. Questions upon which the advisory opinion of the Court is asked shall be laid before the Court by means of a written request containing an exact statement of the question upon which an opinion is required, and accompanied by all documents likely to throw light upon the question.

Article 66

1. The Registrar shall forthwith give notice of the request for an advisory opinion to all states entitled to appear before the Court.

2. The Registrar shall also, by means of a special and direct communication, notify any state entitled to appear before the Court or international organization considered by the Court, or, should it not be sitting, by the President, as likely to be able to furnish information on the question that the Court will be prepared to receive, within a time limit to be fixed by the President, written statements or to hear, at a public sitting to be held for the purpose, oral statements relating to the question.

3. Should any such state entitled to appear before the Court have failed to receive the special communication referred to in paragraph 2 of this Article, such state may express a desire to submit a written statement or to be heard; and the Court will decide.

4. States and organizations having presented written or oral statements or both shall be permitted to comment on the statements made by other states or organizations in the form, to the extent, and within the time limits which the Court, or, should it not be sitting, the President, shall decide in each particular case. Accordingly, the Registrar shall in due time communicate any such written statements to states and organizations having submitted similar statements.

Article 67

The Court shall deliver its advisory opinions in open court, notice having been given to the Secretary-General and to the representatives of Members of the United Nations, of other states and of international organizations immediately concerned.

Article 68

In the exercise of its advisory functions the Court shall further be guided by the provisions of the present Statute which apply in contentious cases to the extent to which it recognizes them to be applicable.

CHAPTER V
Amendment

Article 69

Amendments to the present Statute shall be effected by the same procedure as is provided by the Charter of the United Nations for amendments to that Charter, subject however to any provisions which the General Assembly upon recommendation of the Security Council may adopt concerning the participation of states which are parties to the present Statute but are not Members of the United Nations.

Article 70

The Court shall have power to propose such amendments of the present Statute as it may deem necessary through written communications to the Secretary-General for consideration in conformity with the provisions of Article 69.

About the Author

Joseph A. Bagnall has served as an educator, teaching United State history and political science at the college level for many years.

His past publications include *Depression Dialogue: An Anthology of Representative Political Dialogue of the Depression Decade* (ed.), 1965; *United States History: The Relevant Issues* (co-author), 1973; *President John F. Kennedy's Grand and Global Alliance: World Order for the New Century,* 1992; and *The Kennedy Option: Pursuit of World Law,* 2002.

He has written and produced a television documentary titled *John F. Kennedy's Lost Pathway to Peace,* which aired on KCET Los Angeles, and a number of other PBS affiliates. It also aired on TBS on the 69th and 70th anniversaries of JFK's birth.

Dr. Bagnall was interviewed by Charles Osgood on the CBS Radio Network on the 75th anniversary of President Kennedy's birth.

Index

A

Adams, John, 15, 19, 20
Adams, John Quincy, 15, 23, 24
Adams, Sam, 11, 13
Adamson Act, 55
Adams-Onis treaty, 3
African Americans
    Civil Rights movement of 1960s
        and, 42–43, 74
    post-Civil War vengeance against,
        42–43
    Radical reconstruction and, 42
    segregation and, 41–42, 43–44
    slavery and. *See* Slavery
    as Union soldiers, 39
Agnew, Spiro, 77
Agricultural Adjustment Acts, 65
Agricultural organizations, 48
Agricultural Trade Development
    and Assistance Act, 68
Aguinaldo, Emilio, 50
Alien and Sedition Acts, 20
Alliance for Progress, 74
Allies in World War II, 72
American Tobacco Company, 52
Amendments to constitution of
    United States, 197–203
Anbar Awakening, 156
Anthracite Coal Strike, 52
Antifederalist movement, 15–16
Anti-trust policy
    under Franklin Roosevelt, 52
    under Wilson, 55

Arms Control and Disarmament
    Agency, 74
Articles of Confederation, 13–14, 165–166

B

Baker, Ray Stannard, 53
Bank of the United States
    creation of, 15, 66
    First, 15
    Second, 23
    veto of re-chartering of, 27
Barton, Bruce, 60
Baruch, Bernard M., 66
Bay of Pigs fiasco, 74
Beaumarchais, Pierre
    de, 13
Beef Trust, 52
Begin, Menachim, 78
Bell, John, 37
Bill of Rights, 175–176
"Bleeding Kansas," 35
Bonaparte, Napoleon, 21
Boston Massacre, 11
Boston Tea Party, 11
Breckenridge, John C, 37
Britain. *See* England;
    Great Britain
British East India
    Company, 11
Brooks, Preston, 35
Brown, John, 35
Brown v. *Board of Education of Topeka,*
    Kansas, 43

Bryan, William Jennings, 49
Buford, Ann, 83
"Bull Moose" party, 54
Burger, Warren, 76
Burr, Aaron, 20
Bush, George H. W., 83, 85–86
    delivered at the Maxwell Air Force
        Base, Montgomery (April 1991),
        150–153
    economic policy of, 85
    education under, 85–86
    foreign policy under, 86, 168
Bush, George W.
    delivered at the Pentagon
        (Mar. 2008), 154–159
Butler, Andrew P., 35

C

Cabot, John, 4
Calhoun, John C., 16, 22, 91
    Nullification Crisis and, 34
    as vice president, 26–27
Camp David Agreement, 78
Canadian Reciprocity Treaty, 54
Caribbean, American dominance in, 51
"The Carolina doctrine," 95
Carter, Jimmy, 78–79
Charter colonies, 6
China
    Communist rule of, 73
    Nixon's policy toward, 77–78
    Open Door Policy and, 51
    Theodore Roosevelt and, 53–54
Churchill, Winston, 71
CIA, 77
Civil Rights Act of 1866, 41–42
Civil Rights movement of 1960s, 41–42,
      43–44, 74
Civil War, 37–43
    Emancipation Proclamation and, 39
    events leading to, 34–36
    Lincoln and, 39–40
    reconstruction and, 40–43

Civilian Conservation Corps, 64
Clark, William, 21
Clay, Henry, 15, 22, 23–24, 27, 28, 34
Clayton Anti-Trust Act, 55
Cleveland, Grover, 48, 52
Clinton, Bill, 86
Coercive Act of 1774, 11
Cold War
    emergence of, 73
    Kennedy and, 75
    Reagan and, 83–84
Columbus, Christopher, 3
Command of the Army Act, 41–42
Committees of Correspondence, 11
Common Sense (Paine), 12
Compact theory of union, 20
Company colonies, 6
Compromise of 1850, 34
Compromise Tariff of 1833, 26, 34
Confederacy, 33, 38. *See also*
      Civil War
Congress of Racial Equality
      (CORE), 43
Conservation, 166
    under George H. W. Bush, 85
    under Kennedy, 75
    under Reagan, 84
    under Theodore Roosevelt, 53
Constitution of the United States,
      164–165, 166, 167, 187–203
    amendments to, 197–203
    Bill of Rights and, 175–176
    12th Amendment to, 20
    14th Amendment to, 69
    16th, 17th, 18th, and 19th
      Amendments to, 55
Constitutional Unionist party, 37
Continental Army, 12
Continental Congress
    First, 11
    Second, 11–12, 13
"Contract with America," 86
Coolidge, Calvin, 61–62

Cornwallis, Charles, 13
Corporate colonies, 6
Council of National Defense, 66
Crawford, William, 23
"The Crime Against Kansas," 35
Cronkite, Walter, 168
Cuba
      Bay of Pigs fiasco and, 74
      Spanish-American War and, 50–51
Currency Act of 1764, 10

D
Daugherty, Harry M., 61
Davis, Jefferson, 36
de Grasse, Francois, 13
de la Salle, Robert Cavelier, 4
de Lome letter, 50
Dean, James, III, 77
Declaration of Independence, 12, 183–185
Defenders of the status quo, 110–121
Democratic party, 16, 37, 49
      platform of 1960, 138
      states' rights, 16
Democratic-Republicans, 16, 23
"Desert Storm," 86, 168, 137, 151
Doheny, Edward, 61
Douglas, Stephen A., 16, 35, 37
Dred Scott case, 35
Dukakis, Michael, 85

E
Eaton, John, 26
Eaton, Peggy, 26
Eccles, Marriner S.
      address on National Broadcasting
        Network (Jan. 1939), 104–109
Economic collapse crisis, 98–121
Ehrlichman, John, 77
Einstein, Albert, 167
Einstein on Peace, 167
Eisenhower, Dwight D., 68–69
      foreign policy under, 74
      in Korean War, 73–74

as president, 43, 56
on world peace, 167
Elections
      of 1796, 19
      of 1800, 20–21
      of 1824, 23–24
      of 1840, 27
      of 1860, 35, 37, 40
      of 1892, 48
      of 1896, 49
      of 1900, 49
      of 1968, 76
      of 1988, 83, 85
      of 1992, 86
Elkins Act, 52
Emancipation Proclamation, 39
Embargo Acts, 21
Emergency Banking Act, 63
England. *See also* Great Britain
      conflict with France, 4–5
      events leading to American
        Revolution and, 10–11
      Grenville administration in, 10
      mercantilism before 1763 and, 9
      middle colonies of, 5–6
      New England colonies of, 5
      Seven Years War and, 4–5
      southern colonies of, 6
      Townshend government in, 10–11
      in War of 1812, 21–23
Era of Good Feelings, 23
Expansion, American, roots of, 29–30

F
Fair Deal, 68
Fair Labor Standards Act of 1938, 65
      amendment to, 69
Fall, Albert, 61
Farm Credit Administration, 64
Farmers, Populist revolt and, 48–49
Farmers Home Administration, 68
Faubus, Orval, 43
FBI, 77

Federal Aid Highway Act, 69

Federal Deposit Insurance Corporation, 63–64

Federal Reserve Banking System, 55

Federal Trade Commission, 55

Federalism, case for, 163–164

Federalist party, 15, 20, 23, 25

Food Administrator, 67

Forbes, Charles R., 61

Force Act of 1833, 26

Ford, Gerald, 77, 78

Ford, Henry, 60

"Fourteen Points," 56

Fowler, Mark, 83

France

    assistance to American Revolution, 13

    colonies of, 4–5

    commissioners sent to, by Adams, 19

    conflict with England, 4–5

    in World War II, 71

Franklin, Benjamin, 5, 12

Free Soil party, 35

Freedmen's Bureau, 41–42

"Freedom rides," 43

G

Garfield, Harry A., 67

Germany

    terrorist attack on U.S. servicemen in, 84

    in World War I, 55

    in World War II, 71, 72

Ghent, Treaty of, 23

Gipson, Lawrence Henry, 5

Glasnost, 85

Goldwater, Barry M.

    address delivered on Floor of the United States Senate (Mar. 1960), 146–149

Gorbachev, Mikhail, 84–85

Government Spending, 104–109

Granada invasion, 85

Grand Coulee Dam, 64

Grant, Ulysses S., 39, 41–42

Great Britain. *See also* England

    in World War II, 72

Great Depression

    causes of, 62–63

    New Deal and, 63–65, 67, 97

Grundy, Felix, 22

Guadalupe-Hidalgo, Treaty of, 4, 30

Guffey Coal Act, 116

H

Hamilton, Alexander, 14–15, 20, 66, 91

    financial plan of, 15, 23

Hanna, "Uncle" Mark, 49

Harding, Warren G., 60–61

Harrison, William Henry, 22, 23, 27–28

Hartford Convention, 23

Hay, John, 51, 53–54

Hayes, Rutherford B., 48

Haymarket Riot, 48

Hayne, Robert, 95–96

Helper, Hinton R., 34

Henry, Patrick, 10, 11, 13

Hepburn Act, 53

Herrera, Torrijos, 78

Hiss, Alger, 124

Hitler, Adolph, 71

Hobbes, Thomas, 165

Home Owners Loan Corporation, 64

Homestead Strike, 48

Hoover, Herbert, 62, 67

    address at Republican National Convention, Cleveland (June 1936), 110–114

Hoover, J. Edgar, 77

House of Representatives, conflict over representation in, 33

House Un-American Activities Committee, 124

Housing and Urban Development
agency
under Reagan, 83
Hughes, Charles Evans, 61
Humphrey, Hubert, 76
Hussein, Saddam, 168

I

Immigration before 1800, 19–20
Impending Crisis of the South (Helper), 34
Independence, American, winning of,
12–13
Indian Removal Act of 1830, 26
Intermediate Nuclear Forces (INF)
Treaty, 85
International Court of Justice, statute of,
253–271
Iran hostage situation, 78–79
Iran-Contra scandal, 84
Iraqi invasion of Kuwait, 86, 168

J

Jackson, Andrew, 16, 23, 128
election of 1824, 23–24
as president, 25–27
Jamestown, Virginia, 5
Japan in World War II, 72
Jefferson, Thomas, 13, 14, 34, 91, 95,
101, 128
Committees of Correspondence
and, 11
Declaration of Independence and, 12
letter to Mr. Giles, 95
as president, 16, 19, 20–21
"Jim Crow" laws, 42
John Brown's raid, 35
Johnson, Andrew, 41, 42
impeachment of, 42
Johnson, Lyndon, 76
civil rights under, 44
Jones Act of 1916, 50
The Jungle (Sinclair), 53

K

Kellogg-Briand Pact, 61
Kennedy Commission on Equal
Employment, 74
Kennedy Commission on Registration and
Voter Participation, 74
Kennedy, John F., 69, 74–76, 137, 162
address before General Assembly
of the United Nations (Sep. 1963),
139–145
assassination of, 76
foreign policy under, 74–75
on peace, 167
on United Nations, 167
Key, Francis Scott, 23
King, Martin Luther, Jr., 43, 44, 74
Kissinger, Henry, 77
Knights of Labor, 48
Knox, Philander, 52
Korean War, 73–74
Ku Klux Klan, 42, 59–60
Kuwait, Iraqi invasion of, 86, 168

L

Labor unions, 47–48, 52, 55
Lantos, Tom, 83
League of Nations, 56
Lease, Mary Ellen, 48–49
Lebanon, terrorist attack in, 84
Lee, Robert E. *See* Civil War
The Legacy of Hiroshima (Teller), 167
Lend-Lease, 72
Lewis, Drew, 83
Lewis, Meriwether, 21
Liberty party, 35
Libya, 84
Lincoln, Abraham, 15, 30, 35, 162
assassination of, 41
election as president, 35, 37
first inaugural address of, 37–38
as president, 36, 37–40
second inaugural address of, 40

Lincoln-Douglas debates, 35
Literacy tests, 42
Lodge, Henry Cabot, Jr., 56
Louisiana Purchase, 21
Loyalists, 12
Lyons, Eugene, 148

M
Madison, James, 16, 22, 91
"Malefactors of great wealth," 99
Malone, Dumas, 66
The Man Nobody Knows (Barton), 60
Manifest Destiny, 29
Marcy, William L., 25
Marshall, John, 15, 25–26
Marshall, Thurgood, 43
Marshall Plan, 73
McCarthy, Joseph R., 123
        delivered his first speech in the
            Senate on Communists in the
            State Department (Jan. 1950),
            124–127
McCarthyism crisis
        views on defeating communism,
            123–136
McClellan, George B., 40
McKinley, William, 49
        assassination of, 51
        as president, 50
Medicare, 74
Mellon, Andrew, 62
Merriam, Charles E., 66
Mexican cession, 4, 34
Mexican War, 4
Mexico, 3–4
Middle colonies, 5–6
Middle East
        Camp David Agreement and, 78
        Iran hostage situation, 78–79
        Iran-Contra scandal, 84
        Iraqi invasion of Kuwait, 86, 168
        Reagan's policy on, 84
        terrorist attack in Lebanon and, 84

"Midnight Appointees," 20
Military, 51
        under Theodore Roosevelt, 53
Miller, Thomas W., 60–61
Missouri Compromise, 34
Mitchell, Broadus, 66
Mondale, Walter, 82
Monopolies, 47, 52
Monroe, James, 16, 23
Monroe Doctrine, 54
"Muckrakers," 53

N
National Labor Relations Act, 118
National Republicans, 15, 25, 27
Nationalism, Hamiltonian, 23
Native Americans, Jackson's policy on,
            25–26
Naturalization Act, 20
Navigation Acts, 9
New Deal, 63–66, 69, 98–109
        vs. defenders of the status quo,
            110–121
        under Eisenhower, 68
        objectives of, 67
        under Truman, 68
New England colonies, 5
"New Era," 61
New Frontier, 74–76
New Mexico Territory, 30
New Nationalism, 54
New Orleans, Battle of, 23
Nicaragua, Iran-Contra scandal
            and, 84
Nixon, Richard M., 76–77
        foreign policy of, 77–78
        resignation of, 77
Norris, Frank, 53
North, Oliver, 84
North Atlantic Treaty
            Organization, 73
North Korea, 73–74
Northern Securities Company, 52

North-South confrontations
    during 1787–1850, 33–34
    Civil War, 34–36
Nuclear Test Ban Treaty of 1963, 74
Nullification Crisis
    of 1832, 26, 34
    Webster-Hayne debate and, 91–96

O

Omaha Platform, 48
Open Door Policy, 51
Operation Desert Storm, 86, 168
Oregon Territory, 29
O'Sullivan, John, 29

P

Packenham, Edward, 23
Paine, Thomas, 12
Palmer, A. Mitchell, 60
Panama Canal, 51, 53, 78
Panic of 1837, 27
Parkes, Harry Bamford, 66
Parks, Rosa, 43
Paula Jones case, 86
Payne-Aldrich tariff, 54
Peace Corps, 74
Pearl Harbor attack, 72
Perestroika, 85
Perry, Oliver Hazard, 22
"Pet Banks," 27
Philadelphia Convention, 165
Philippines, 50, 51
Phillips, David Graham, 53
Pinchot, Gifford, 53, 54
Platt Amendment, 50
Poindexter, John, 84
Polk, James K., 4, 29–30
Poll taxes, 42
Populist Party, 48
Populist revolt, 48–49
Progressive Era, 52, 61–62, 66
Proprietary colonies, 6

Public works, under
    Eisenhower, 68–69
Public Works Administration, 64
Pullman Strike, 48

Q

Quartering Act of 1765, 10
Quebec Act of 1774, 11

R

Radical reconstruction, 41–42
Railroad strike of 1877, 47–48
Railroads
    laws against corrupt practices
      on, 52–53
    Railroad strike of 1877 and, 47–48
    United States Railroad
      Administration and, 67
Reagan, Ronald Wilson, 81–82, 84–85
    conservatism of, 81
    economic policy of, 81, 82
    foreign policy of, 83–85
    inauguration day of, 78
Reaganomics, 82, 84
Reconstruction Act of 1867, 41–42
"Remember the Maine," 50
A Reporter's Life (Cronkite), 168
Representation in House of
    Representatives, conflict
    over, 33
Republican party, 15, 23, 35, 37
Resolution of Independence, 12
Revolution, American, 12–13
    events leading to, 10–11
Riis, Jacob, 53
Rochambeau, Jean Baptiste,
    Count de, 13
"Roosevelt Corollary," 54
Roosevelt, Franklin Delano, 162
    address at the New York State
      Democratic Convention at
      Syracuse (Sep. 1936), 128–132

Delano (*Continued*)
    delivered in
    1936), 98–103
    ., 63–66, 67
    I and, 71–72
    .dore, 51–54
    .ation of 1764, 10
    .opment Program, 68
    .ctrification Association, 68
    .agot Agreement of 1817, 23
    .-Japanese War, 54

Sadat, Anwar, 78
Saratoga, Battle of, 13
Savings and loan policy, under Reagan, 83
Schlesinger, Arthur, Jr., 66
Schultz, John, 84
Scott, Dred, 35
Secession, 36
Securities Act of 1933, 64
Securities and Exchange Commission, 64
Segregation
    Civil Rights movement of 1960s
      and, 41–42, 43–44
    legalization of, 43
Selective Service, 69
Self-judging reservation, 138
Seven Years War, 4–5
Sherman, William T., 39
Sherman Anti-Trust Act, 52
Simpson, "Sockless" jerry, 48
Sinclair, Harry, 61
Sinclair, Upton, 53
Slavery
    abolition of, 41
    Civil War and, 35. *See* Civil War
    conflict over, 33–34
    Emancipation Proclamation and, 39
Slidell, John, 4, 30
Smith, Jess, 61
Smith-Hughes Act, 55
Smith-Lever Act, 55

Smith, Margaret Chase
    statement delivered on Floor of the
      United States Senate (June 1950),
      133–136
Smoot-Hawley tariff, 63
Social contract, 165
Social Security Act, 65, 69
Sons of Liberty, 10
South Carolina Exposition and Protest
    (Calhoun), 26
South Korea, 73–74
Southern colonies, 6
Soviet Union
    Carter's policy toward, 78
    Cold War and, 73, 75, 83–84
    "hot line" and, 74
    Reagan's policy on, 83–84
    Truman Doctrine and, 72–73
    in World War II, 72
Spain
    colonies of, 3–4
    Ten Years' War with Cuba, 50
Spanish-American War, 50–51
Spot Resolutions, 30
"Square Deal," 52
Stamp Act Congress, 10
Stamp Act of 1765, 10
Standard Oil Company of New Jersey, 52
Stanton, Edwin, 41–42
Star Spangled Banner, 23
Star Wars, 84
States' rights Democrats, 16
Steffens, Lincoln, 53
Stephens, Alexander H., 36
Stevens, Thadeus, 41
Stockman, David, 82
Stowe, Harriet Beecher, 34
Strategic Defense Initiative, 83–84
The Strategy of Peace (Kennedy), 75, 167
Strikes, 47–48, 52
Student Non-violent Coordinating
    Committee (SNCC), 43
Subversive Activities Board, 77

Sugar Act of 1764, 10
Sumner, Charles, 35, 41
Supreme Court
    Brown v. Board of Education of
        Topeka, Kansas and, 43
    Nixon's appointments to, 76
    Worcester v. Georgia and, 25–26

T
Taft, Robert A.
    address at National Republican Club
        (Mar. 1939), 115–121
Taft, William Howard, 54
Tarbell, Ida M., 53
Tariff Commission, 62
Tariffs
    of 1828 and 1832, 34
    Compromise Tariff of 1833,
        26, 34
    Payne-Aldrich tariff, 54
    Smoot-Hawley tariff, 63
    Underwood-Simmons tariff, 54–55
    under Wilson, 54–55
    Wilson-Gorman Tariff, 50
Taxes
    American Revolution and, 10–11
    under Reagan, 82
    under Wilson, 67
    World War I and, 67
Taylor, Zachary, 30
Teapot Dome scandal, 61
Teller, Edward, 137
Tennessee Valley Authority, 65
Tenure of Office Act, 41–42
Texas Republic, 4, 30
Thermonuclear and environmental
        threats crises, 137–159
Three-Fifths Compromise, 33
Townshend Duties of 1767, 11
Toynbee, Arnold J., 167
Trail of Tears, 26
Treaty of Ghent, 23
Treaty of Guadalupe-Hidalgo, 4, 30

Treaty of Versailles, 56
The Triumph of Politics: Why the
        Reagan Revolution Failed
        (Stockman), 82
Truman Doctrine, 72–73
Truman, Harry S., 68, 72, 124
    as president, 72–73
    on United Nations, 167
Tugwell, Rexford D., 66
Twelfth Amendment, 20
Tydings-McDuffie Act of 1934, 50
Tyler, John, 16, 28, 30

U
Uncle Tom's Cabin (Stowe), 34
Underwood-Simmons tariff, 54–55
Unions, 47–48, 52, 55
United Nations, 72, 138, 167–168
    charter of, 204–251
    Kennedy and, 74
United States of America
    amendments to, 197–203
    constitution of, 187–203
United States Railroad
        Administration, 67
Universal Declaration of Human
        Rights, 177–182

V
Van Buren, Martin, 27
Vance, Cyrus, 78
Versailles, Treaty of, 56
Vietnam War, 74, 76, 77
Virginia and Kentucky Resolutions
        of 1798, 20

W
Wade, Benjamin, 41
Wade-Davis Bill, 41
Wage-Hour Law, 116
Wage-price freeze under Nixon, 77
War Hawks, 22
War Industries Board, 66

1–23

, 76, 167

n Naval Conference, 61

gton, George, 5

n American Revolution, 12–13

as Commander of Continental
Army, 12

as president, 14

Watergate break-in, 77

Watt, James, 83

Weaver, James B., 48

Webster, Daniel, 15, 28, 92–94

Webster-Hayne debate (1830),
92–96

Weyler, Valeriano "Butcher," 50

Whig party, 15, 25, 27, 28, 30, 35

Whiskey Rebellion, 19–20

"White House Plumbers," 77

Whitewater Land Corporation, 86

Wilson, Woodrow, 66, 138

legislation under, 55

policy and appointments under,
66–67

tariffs under, 54–55

World War I and, 55–56

Wilson-Gorman Tariff, 50

Wiltse, Charles M., 66

Wire taps, 77

Worcester v. *Georgia* (1832), 25–26

Works Progress Administration, 64

World War I, 55–56, 67

World War II, 69

Writ of Habeas Corpus, Lincoln's
suspension of, 39–40

Y

Yalta Agreement, 72

"Yellow dog" contracts, 47